1981

Administration
of Justice

Principles
and Procedures

West's
Criminal Justice Series

WEST PUBLISHING COMPANY

St. Paul, Minnesota 55102

February 1980

CONSTITUTIONAL LAW

Cases and Comments on Constitutional Law 2nd Edition by James L. Maddex, Professor of Criminal Justice, Georgia State University, 486 pages, 1979.

CORRECTIONS

Corrections—Organization and Administration by Henry Burns, Jr., Professor of Criminal Justice, University of Missouri–St. Louis, 578 pages, 1975.

Legal Rights of the Convicted by Hazel B. Kerper, Late Professor of Sociology and Criminal Law, Sam Houston State University and Janeen Kerper, Attorney, San Diego, Calif., 677 pages, 1974.

Selected Readings on Corrections in the Community 2nd Edition by George G. Killinger, Member, Board of Pardons and Paroles, Texas and Paul F. Cromwell, Jr., Director of Juvenile Services, Tarrant County, Texas, 357 pages, 1978.

Readings on Penology—The Evolution of Corrections in America 2nd Edition by George G. Killinger, Paul F. Cromwell, Jr., and Jerry M. Wood, 350 pages, 1979.

Selected Readings on Introduction to Corrections by George G. Killinger and Paul F. Cromwell, Jr., 417 pages, 1978.

Selected Readings on Issues in Corrections and Administration by George G. Killinger, Paul F. Cromwell, Jr., and Bonnie J. Cromwell, San Antonio College, 644 pages, 1976.

Probation and Parole in the Criminal Justice System by George G. Killinger, Hazel B. Kerper and Paul F. Cromwell, Jr., 374 pages, 1976.

Introduction to Probation and Parole 2nd Edition by Alexander B. Smith, Professor of Sociology, John Jay College of Criminal Justice and Louis Berlin, Formerly Chief of Training Branch, New York City Dept. of Probation, 270 pages, 1979.

CRIMINAL JUSTICE SYSTEM

Fundamentals of Law Enforcement by V. A. Leonard, 350 pages, 1980.

Administration of Justice: Principles and Procedures by Garrith D. Perrine, Professor of Administration of Justice, Shasta College, Redding, California, 300 pages, 1980.

Introduction to the Criminal Justice System 2nd Edition by Hazel B. Kerper as revised by Jerold H. Israel, 520 pages, 1979.

Introduction to Criminal Justice by Joseph J. Senna and Larry J. Siegel, both Professors of Criminal Justice, Northeastern University, 540 pages, 1978.

iii

CRIMINAL JUSTICE SYSTEM—Continued

Study Guide to accompany Senna and Siegel's Introduction to Criminal Justice by Roy R. Roberg, Professor of Criminal Justice, University of Nebraska–Lincoln, 187 pages, 1978.

Introduction to Law Enforcement and Criminal Justice by Henry M. Wrobleski and Karen M. Hess, both Professors at Normandale Community College, Bloomington, Minnesota, 525 pages, 1979.

CRIMINAL LAW

California Law Manual for the Administration of Justice by Joel Greenfield, Sacramento City College and Rodney Blonien, Executive Director, California State Peace Officers' Association, 800 pages, 1979.

Basic Criminal Law: Cases and Materials 2nd Edition by George E. Dix, Professor of Law, University of Texas, and M. Michael Sharlot, Professor of Law, University of Texas, 600 pages, 1980.

Readings, on Concepts of Criminal Law by Robert W. Ferguson, Administration of Justice Dept. Director, Saddleback College, 560 pages, 1975.

Criminal Law 2nd Edition by Thomas J. Gardner, Professor of Criminal Justice, Milwaukee Area Technical College and Victor Manian, Milwaukee County Judge, about 600 pages, 1980.

Principles of Criminal Law by Wayne R. LaFave, Professor of Law, University of Illinois, 650 pages, 1978.

CRIMINAL PROCEDURE

Teaching Materials on Criminal Procedure by Jerry L. Dowling, Professor of Criminal Justice, Sam Houston State University, 544 pages, 1976.

Criminal Procedure for the Law Enforcement Officer 2nd Edition by John N. Ferdico, Assistant Attorney General, State of Maine, 409 pages, 1979.

Cases, Materials and Text on the Elements of Criminal Due Process by Phillip E. Johnson, Professor of Law, University of California, Berkeley, 324 pages, 1975.

Cases, Comments and Questions on Basic Criminal Procedure 4th Edition by Yale Kamisar, Professor of Law, University of Michigan, Wayne R. LaFave, Professor of Law, University of Illinois and Jerold H. Israel, Professor of Law, University of Michigan, 790 pages, 1974. Supplement Annually.

EVIDENCE

Criminal Evidence by Thomas J. Gardner, Professor of Criminal Justice, Milwaukee Area Technical College, 694 pages, 1978.

Criminal Evidence by Edward J. Imwinkelried, Professor of Law, University of San Diego; Paul C. Giannelli, Associate Professor, Case Western Reserve University; Francis A. Gilligan, Adjunct Professor, Jacksonville State University; Fredric I. Lederer, Associate Professor, Judge Advocate General's School, U.S. Army, 425 pages, 1979.

Law of Evidence for Police 2nd Edition by Irving J. Klein, Professor of Law and Police Science, John Jay College of Criminal Justice, 632 pages, 1978.

Criminal Investigation and Presentation of Evidence by Arnold Markle, The State's Attorney, New Haven County, Connecticut, 344 pages, 1976.

INTRODUCTION TO LAW ENFORCEMENT

The American Police—Text and Readings by Harry W. More, Jr., Professor of Administration of Justice, California State University of San Jose, 278 pages, 1976.

INTRODUCTION TO LAW ENFORCEMENT—Continued

Police Tactics in Hazardous Situations by the San Diego, California Police Department, 228 pages, 1976.

Law Enforcement Handbook for Police by Louis B. Schwartz, Professor of Law, University of Pennsylvania and Stephen R. Goldstein, Professor of Law, University of Pennsylvania, 333 pages, 1970.

Police Operations—Tactical Approaches to Crimes in Progress by Inspector Andrew Sutor, Philadelphia, Pennsylvania Police Department, 329 pages, 1976.

Introduction to Law Enforcement and Criminal Justice by Henry Wrobleski and Karen M. Hess, both Professors at Normandale Community College, Bloomington, Minnesota, 525 pages, 1979.

JUVENILE JUSTICE

Text and Selected Readings on Introduction to Juvenile Delinquency by Paul F. Cromwell, Jr., George G. Killinger, Rosemary C. Sarri, Professor, School of Social Work, The University of Michigan and H. N. Solomon, Professor of Criminal Justice, Nova University, 502 pages, 1978.

Juvenile Justice Philosophy: Readings, Cases and Comments 2nd Edition by Frederic L. Faust, Professor of Criminology, Florida State University and Paul J. Brantingham, Department of Criminology, Simon Fraser University, 467 pages, 1979.

Introduction to the Juvenile Justice System by Thomas A. Johnson, Professor of Criminal Justice, Washington State University, 492 pages, 1975.

Cases and Comments on Juvenile Law by Joseph J. Senna, Professor of Criminal Justice, Northeastern, University and Larry J. Siegel, Professor of Criminal Justice, Northeastern University, 543 pages, 1976.

MANAGEMENT AND SUPERVISION

Selected Readings on Managing the Police Organization by Larry K. Gaines and Truett A. Ricks, both Professors of Criminal Justice, Eastern Kentucky University, 527 pages, 1978.

Criminal Justice Management: Text and Readings by Harry W. More, Jr., 377 pages, 1977.

Effective Police Administration: A Behavioral Approach 2nd Edition by Harry W. More, Jr., Professor, San Jose State University, 360 pages, 1979.

Police Management and Organizational Behavior: A Contingency Approach by Roy R. Roberg, Professor of Criminal Justice, University of Nebraska at Omaha, 350 pages, 1979.

Police Administration and Management by Sam S. Souryal, Professor of Criminal Justice, Sam Houston State University, 462 pages, 1977.

Law Enforcement Supervision—A Case Study Approach by Robert C. Wadman, Rio Hondo Community College, Monroe J. Paxman, Brigham Young University and Marion T. Bentley, Utah State University, 224 pages, 1975.

POLICE—COMMUNITY RELATIONS

Readings on Police—Community Relations 2nd Edition by Paul F. Cromwell, Jr., and George Keefer, Professor of Criminal Justice, Southwest Texas State University, 506 pages, 1978.

PSYCHOLOGY

Interpersonal Psychology for Law Enforcement and Corrections by L. Craig Parker, Jr., Criminal Justice Dept. Director, University of New Haven and Robert D. Meier, Professor of Criminal Justice, University of New Haven, 290 pages, 1975.

VICE CONTROL

The Nature of Vice Control in the Administration of Justice by Robert W. Ferguson, 509 pages, 1974.

Cases, Text and Materials on Drug Abuse Law by Gerald F. Uelman, Professor of Law, Loyola University, Los Angeles and Victor G. Haddox, Professor of Criminology, California State University at Long Beach and Clinical Professor of Psychiatry, Law and Behavioral Sciences, University of Southern California School of Medicine, 564 pages, 1974.

Administration of Justice

Principles and Procedures

Garrith D. Perrine

A.A., B.S., M.P.A.
Director, Applied Science Division
Shasta College
Redding, California

Past President,
California Assn. of Administration of Justice Educators

West Publishing Company
St. Paul   New York   Los Angeles   San Francisco

CONTRIBUTING AUTHORS
Judith Hail Kaci, Long Beach University — Chapters 10, 12
Joel Greenfield, Sacramento City College — Chapter 11
Gary Miller, Gavilan College — Chapter 13
Henry J. Prager, San Jose State University — Chapter 6
Doug Oliver, Skyline College — Chapter 7

PHOTO CREDITS

pp. 34,184, Wide World Photos; pp. 54,85,254, EKM Nepenthe; p. 118, Dartmouth College; pp. 128,257, UPI; pp. 172,235, H. Armstrong Roberts; p. 281, Stock Boston, Steve Hansen, Photographer.

COPYRIGHT (c) 1980 By WEST PUBLISHING CO.
          50 West Kellogg Boulevard
          P.O. Box 3526
          St. Paul, Minnesota 55165

Printed in the United States of America

Library of Congress Cataloging in Publication Data

Perrine, Garrith D
    Administration of justice.

    (Criminal justice series)
    Bibliography: p.
    Includes index
    1. Criminal justice, Administration of—United States. 2. Criminal procedure—
United States.
I. Title. II. Series
KF9223.P47   345.73'05   79-28738
ISBN 0-8299-0345-3

To Criminal Justice Education
and its professionals
and to my wife and best friend
Linnea

Preface

The purpose of this book is to bring together the entire subject matter included in the principles and procedures of justice course for the state of California. This text takes into account the curriculum which was developed by educators in criminal justice throughout California. This is not a law book, but a text designed for administration of justice majors in both community and four-year colleges.

In a complex legal system such as in the United States and California, no one text can deal sufficiently with the necessary subject matter outlined in the justice system. The many functions of the varied criminal justice systems throughout the United States differ to the extent that special attention must be given to a specific jurisdiction in order to adequately address the most important functions. For this reason, the authors present subject details that are consistent with laws and procedures of California, incorporating United States procedures where applicable.

Due to the varied subjects covered in this text, no one author can have the necessary background and expertise to discuss the details necessary for a successful text. Hence, contributing authors (from both community and four-year institutions) were utilized, to research and write material dealing with their areas of expertise and training.

The first two chapters of this book deal with the legal foundation applicable to all criminal justice concepts. The formation of our laws and legal structure, the Constitution of the United States, and the California legal system are discussed in detail. The "actors" in the California system are described, along with their duties, responsibilities, and functions.   This text includes specific cases decided on the federal and state levels.

To further assist the student's learning experience, this book possesses the following distinctive features:

1. Each chapter is broken into subject matter in a logical order, allowing the student to follow the legal system from beginning to end.
2. Each chapter possesses an introduction and a summary.
3. Discussion questions are provided at the end of each chapter.
4. Footnoting provides reference for further discussion and study.
5. Historical, as well as the most recent court decisions, are utilized for supportive subject content.
6. Selected chapter illustrations, charts, and tables help to clarify important concepts.

The authors believe that the student aspiring to a career in any one of the many criminal justice components will find this text satisfying in providing a thorough, well-rounded foundation necessary to building a knowledge of the principles and procedures of the justice system in California.

G. D. Perrine

Contents

Preface   xi

Chapter 1
Legal Authority for the System   1

Chapter Objectives   1
Constitution of the United States   3
Bill of Rights   6
The California Constitution   18
Summary   21
Discussion Questions   21
References   21

Chapter 2
Constitutional Protections: Rights of the Accused   23

Chapter Objectives   23
Speedy and Public Trial   24
Public Trial   26
Right to Counsel   29
Summary   41
Discussion Questions   41
References   41

Chapter 3
Police Function and Process   43

Chapter Objectives   43
Police Role in the System   44

Police Powers Defined   46
Authority to Stop and Question   49
Process of Arrest   52
Responsibility of Arrestee   71
The Uniform Fresh Pursuit Act   73
Extradition   75
Arraignment on Warrant   76
Summary   77
Discussion Questions   78
References   78

Chapter 4
The Coroner   81

Chapter Objectives   81
History of the Coroner   82
Legal Considerations   83
Duties of Coroner   83
Medical Duties   88
Deaths Reportable to the Coroner   90
Combined Responsibilities of the Coroner
     and Other County Officers   92
Summary   94
Discussion Questions   95
References   95

Chapter 5
Related State Agencies and Regulatory Commissions   97

Chapter Objectives   97
Related State Agencies   98
Federal Regulatory Agencies   106
Summary   111
Discussion Questions   112
References   113

Chapter 6
The Legal Profession   115

Chapter Objectives   115
History of the Legal Profession   116
Training and Education of the Legal Profession   120
Roles and Responsibilities of the Legal Profession   123
Summary   131
Topics for Discussion   132
References   133

Chapter 7
The Court and Its Officers   **135**

Chapter Objectives   135
Court Organization and Structure   136
Judges, Magistrates and Referees   142
Court Support Personnel   146
Court Enforcement Officers   150
Summary   153
Discussion Questions   154
References   155

Chapter 8
Grand Juries/Trial Jurors   **157**

Chapter Objectives   157
The Grand Jury   158
Trial Jurors   171
Summary   182
Discussion Questions   182
References   183

Chapter 9
Initial Confinement   **185**

Chapter Objectives   185
Incarceration   186
Plea Bargaining   200
Summary   203
Discussion Questions   204
References   204

Chapter 10
Accusatory Pleadings   **205**

Chapter Objectives   205
Accusatory Pleadings   206
Complaint   207
Information   211
Indictment   212
Principles of Pleading   214
Amendment   219
Attacks on Pleadings   220
Summary   222
Discussion Questions   223
References   224

Chapter 11
Arraignments, Pleas and Preliminary Hearings   **225**

Chapter Objectives   225
The Arraignment   226
Pleas   230
Demurrer   240
Preliminary Hearings   242
Summary   248
Discussion Questions   249
References   249

Chapter 12
Trial Procedure   **251**

Chapter Objectives   251
Procedures at Trial   252
Post Conviction Motions   264
Entry of Judgment Probation and Sentencing Hearing   265
Sentencing Process   266
Summary   268
Discussion Questions   269

Chapter 13
Correctional Concepts   **271**

Chapter Objectives   271
The Adult Correctional Process   272
Community Release Board   277
Corrections and Correctional Institutions   278
The Juvenile Correctional Process   286
The History of the California Department of Corrections   290
Summary   299
Discussion Questions   300
References   301

Annotated Bibliography   303
Index   307

We the People

of the United States, in Order to form a more perfect Union, establish Justice, insure domestic Tranquility, provide for the common defence, promote the general Welfare, and secure the Blessings of Liberty to ourselves and our Posterity, do ordain and establish this Constitution for the United States of America.

Article. I.

Section. 1. All legislative Powers herein granted shall be vested in a Congress of the United States, which shall consist of a Senate and House of Representatives.

Section. 2. The House of Representatives shall be composed of Members chosen every second Year by the People of the several States, and the Electors in each State shall have the Qualifications requisite for Electors of the most numerous Branch of the State Legislature.

No Person shall be a Representative who shall not have attained to the Age of twenty five Years, and been seven Years a Citizen of the United States, and who shall not, when elected, be an Inhabitant of that State in which he shall be chosen.

Representatives and direct Taxes shall be apportioned among the several States which may be included within this Union, according to their respective Numbers, which shall be determined by adding to the whole Number of free Persons, including those bound to Service for a Term of Years, and excluding Indians not taxed, three fifths of all other Persons. The actual Enumeration shall be made within three Years after the first Meeting of the Congress of the United States, and within every subsequent Term of ten Years, in such Manner as they shall by Law direct. The Number of Representatives shall not exceed one for every thirty Thousand, but each State shall have at Least one Representative; and until such enumeration shall be made, the State of New Hampshire shall be entitled to chuse three, Massachusetts eight, Rhode Island and Providence Plantations one, Connecticut five, New York six, New Jersey four, Pennsylvania eight, Delaware one, Maryland six, Virginia ten, North Carolina five, South Carolina five, and Georgia three.

When vacancies happen in the Representation from any State, the Executive Authority thereof shall issue Writs of Election to fill such Vacancies.

The House of Representatives shall chuse their Speaker and other Officers; and shall have the sole Power of Impeachment.

Section. 3. The Senate of the United States shall be composed of two Senators from each State, chosen by the Legislature thereof, for six Years; and each Senator shall have one Vote.

Immediately after they shall be assembled in Consequence of the first Election, they shall be divided as equally as may be into three Classes. The Seats of the Senators of the first Class shall be vacated at the Expiration of the second Year, of the second Class at the Expiration of the fourth Year, and of the third Class at the Expiration of the sixth Year, so that one third may be chosen every second Year; and if Vacancies happen by Resignation, or otherwise, during the Recess of the Legislature of any State, the Executive thereof may make temporary Appointments until the next Meeting of the Legislature, which shall then fill such Vacancies.

No Person shall be a Senator who shall not have attained to the Age of thirty Years, and been nine Years a Citizen of the United States, and who shall not, when elected, be an Inhabitant of that State for which he shall be chosen.

The Vice President of the United States shall be President of the Senate, but shall have no Vote, unless they be equally divided.

The Senate shall chuse their other Officers, and also a President pro tempore, in the Absence of the Vice President, or when he shall exercise the Office of President of the United States.

The Senate shall have the sole Power to try all Impeachments. When sitting for that Purpose, they shall be on Oath or Affirmation. When the President of the United States is tried, the Chief Justice shall preside: And no Person shall be convicted without the Concurrence of two thirds of the Members present.

Judgment in Cases of Impeachment shall not extend further than to removal from Office, and disqualification to hold and enjoy any Office of honor, Trust or Profit under the United States: but the Party convicted shall nevertheless be liable and subject to Indictment, Trial, Judgment and Punishment, according to Law.

Section. 4. The Times, Places and Manner of holding Elections for Senators and Representatives, shall be prescribed in each State by the Legislature thereof; but the Congress may at any time by Law make or alter such Regulations, except as to the Places of chusing Senators.

The Congress shall assemble at least once in every Year, and such Meeting shall be on the first Monday in December, unless they shall by Law appoint a different Day.

Section. 5. Each House shall be the Judge of the Elections, Returns and Qualifications of its own Members, and a Majority of each shall constitute a Quorum to do Business; but a smaller Number may adjourn from day to day, and may be authorized to compel the Attendance of absent Members, in such Manner, and under such Penalties as each House may provide.

Each House may determine the Rules of its Proceedings, punish its Members for disorderly Behaviour, and, with the Concurrence of two thirds, expel a Member.

Each House shall keep a Journal of its Proceedings, and from time to time publish the same, excepting such Parts as may in their Judgment require Secrecy; and the Yeas and Nays of the Members of either House on any question shall, at the Desire of one fifth of those Present, be entered on the Journal.

Neither House, during the Session of Congress, shall, without the Consent of the other, adjourn for more than three days, nor to any other Place than that in which the two Houses shall be sitting.

Section. 6. The Senators and Representatives shall receive a Compensation for their Services, to be ascertained by Law, and paid out of the Treasury of the United States. They shall in all Cases, except Treason, Felony and Breach of the Peace, be privileged from Arrest during their Attendance at the Session of their respective Houses, and in going to and returning from the same; and for any Speech or Debate in either House, they shall not be questioned in any other Place.

No Senator or Representative shall, during the Time for which he was elected, be appointed to any civil Office under the Authority of the United States, which shall have been created, or the Emoluments whereof shall have been increased during such time; and no Person holding any Office under the United States, shall be a Member of either House during his Continuance in Office.

Section 7. All Bills for raising Revenue shall originate in the House of Representatives; but the Senate may propose or concur with Amendments as on other Bills.

Every Bill which shall have passed the House of Representatives and the Senate, shall, before it become a Law, be presented to the President

1

Legal Authority
for the System

CHAPTER OBJECTIVES

Upon reading the chapter the student will be able to:

1. Describe the major reasons for establishment of the Declaration of Independence, and its importance to the justice system.

2. Define and list the separation of powers and their significance to the legal process.

3. Identify the specific guarantees under the Constitution and the effects of the guarantees on the justice system.

4. Compare the U.S. Constitution with the California Constitution, and list the similarities and differences.

The administration of justice is founded on the Constitution of the United States and those of individual states, as well as on statutory provisions authorized by these constitutions. We cannot comprehend the workings and proceedings of the justice system without a thorough understanding of the constitutions of both the United States and of California. In this chapter we have emphasized the development of constitutional law on the federal and state levels. It is essential that the reader thoroughly understand the provisions contained in the Bill of Rights, both from the federal level and from the state level. The following chapters will explicitly discuss the constitutional amendments, as well as other statutory provisions, in the overall workings of the justice system in California.

Declaration of Rights

Our great legal system did not develop in a test tube. It grew out of the hard experiences of our forefathers that ultimately led to their decision to break away from England to set up a new form of government. The first declaration of rights proclaimed by the Stamp Act Congress of 1765 enumerated the problems between the American colonists and the English Crown. It stated that "trial by jury is the inherent and invaluable right of every British subject in the Colonies." The colonists complained that this right was being denied them and that the King was guilty of "extending the jurisdiction of the courts of admiralty beyond its ancient limits."[1]

The second declaration of rights of 1774 sounded another warning.[2] Several rights were agreed upon and resolved by the "inhabitants of the English Colonies in North America," such as that: "All people are entitled to life, liberty and property . . ."; to " . . . the great and inestimable privilege of being tried by the peers of the vicinage (neighborhood) according to the course of the law"; and to "the right peaceably to assemble, consideration of their grievances and to petition the king; and that all prosecutions, prohibiting proclamations, and commitments for the same are illegal."

Declaration of Independence

Finally, in 1776 the Declaration of Independence reiterated for the final time the injustices imposed by the crown. Specifically, the colonists contended that the king of Great Britain was violating their inalienable rights. For example, they contended that he refused to assent to laws; he forbade his Governors to pass laws of immediate and impressing importance. He obstructed the administration of justice by refusing assent to laws for establishing judicial powers. He made judges dependent on his will alone for the tenure of their offices and for the amount of their salaries. He allowed the armed troops to commit grave crimes and protected them from punishment by mock trials. He deprived the colonists in many cases of the benefits of a trial by jury. He transported the colonists beyond the seas to be tried for pretended offenses. These are just a few of the violations that oppressed the colonies as they formed our new government. This was the final warning which the colonists would deliver to the Crown complaining of the injustices that were in operation in the new country.

Articles of Confederation

Up to this point the colonists were concerned with separating from the control of the British Crown. In 1778 the Articles of Confederation were written; they designated some of the individual states rights and freedoms as envisioned by the original colonies. Of primary importance was the philosophy that the states should retain their sovereignty of freedom and independence from any outside governmental rule. This was the first time that the United States of America was used as our country's name. Article Four stated the inherent right of the citizens to be free, and to be allowed to ingress and regress to and from any other state. It also stated that they should have the privileges established for the citizens of any state of the nation. The early procedure for extradition was also contained in the Articles of Confederation, and allowed for return of any persons committing high crimes in one state to the original state where the crime had occurred.

Thus the citizens of the United States began to formulate the early laws of our country. Nine years later, in September, the Constitution of the United States was introduced.

CONSTITUTION OF THE UNITED STATES

The Preamble to the Constitution called for a "more perfect union to establish justice to provide for common defense and promote the general welfare of the citizens of the United States." The various articles and sections contained in the Constitution were established for a new government to exist and survive in a world where "liberty" and "justice" were only words. Of primary importance was a recognition that in order for a free government to survive there must be a separation of powers. Article 1, Section 1 invested the Congress with the powers to legislate all laws of this country. It further provided for the rules in establishing laws, stating that every bill having been passed by the House of Representatives and the Senate shall, before it becomes law, be presented to the President of the United States, who has responsibility to approve or disapprove. If approved, the law is effected—if disapproved, then approval by two-thirds of the house could cause the law to go into effect over the objections of the President.

Congressional Powers Defined

In following the philosophy of the Articles of Confederation and its concern for the 'states' sovereignty, Section 8 of the Constitution delineates the powers granted to the Congress. For example, the Congress has power: to provide for the punishment of counterfeiting; to control the securities, currency and coin of the United States; to constitute tribunals inferior to the Supreme Court; and to make all laws which shall be necessary and proper for carrying into execution the foregoing powers. Some of the provisions indicated are that no bill of attainder or expost facto laws shall be passed. This, of course, prevents the government from establishing a law after the fact. An example of an expost facto law would be if a citizen conducted an act which is distasteful in the eyes of the government; the government then would enact a law to prohibit that act and then arrest the citizen for committing the act prior to a time when it was in fact a violation of the law.

Judicial Powers Defined

Article Three describes the judicial branch of government and the powers of that branch. Section 2 of Article Three specifies the jurisdiction of the United States' courts. It states in part that the judicial power shall extend to all cases in law and equity arising under the Constitution and the laws of the United States. It also gives power to rule in cases where there were controversies between two or more states, between the state and a citizen of another state, and between citizens of different states. The provisions go on to state that the Supreme Court shall have apellate jurisdiction both as to law and fact with such exceptions and under such regulations as Congress shall make. This gives the Supreme Court the authority to review the decisions of the lower courts.

Article Six of the Constitution provides for the general provisions of importance. Of significance is the statement that the Constitution of the United States shall be the supreme law of the land and that the judges in every state shall be bound by provisions contained in the Constitution.

The Constitution . . . A framework for a Legal System

In reviewing the very limited provisions established in the Constitution, it can be seen that the system which our government established is now much more complex than the simple words stated in the Constitution.

We must remember that the Constitution was designed to provide only a framework for the complex necessities that society would develop over the period of years. At the time the new government began, it operated under a document that asked more questions than gave answers. When we analyze the specific provisions contained in the Bill of Rights, we can see why a tremendous turmoil developed in interpreting the meanings of words and phrases. As will be discussed later, such things as due process, unreasonable searches and seizures, the right to counsel, and many, many other issues took a period of many years to develop. In order for these fundamental issues to have developed, it was necessary that a government structure be extremely workable, and flexible enough to accommodate the needs of a changing society.

Our Constitution today is the basic authority for federal and state laws which regulate air transportation, television stations, space explorations, heart transplants, abortions, and other aspects of our everyday lives which the founding fathers would have considered miracles beyond belief. This capacity to grow with social conditions and technology while preserving the structure of the Government has been the Constitution's most important characteristic, proving that our Constitution is in fact a living document.

The Constitution: A Breathing Document

The Constitution has been amended relatively few times since its formation in 1778, as seen by the mere twenty-one amendments. The reason for this is that most of the changes required by our government have been processed through the passage of ordinary laws or by new interpretations. The significance of this is the ability to interpret the provisions of the Constitution as our society dictates.

Influence of the Constitution

Each of the branches of government has had a significant effect on the interpretation of the Constitution. The executive branch has had enormous influence on expanding the Constitution. Presidents Tyler, Jefferson, and Theodore Roosevelt, to name a few, had a great deal to do with changing or interpreting the meaning of the Constitution during their administrations.

Congress has also expanded the Constitution by interpretation. One of the issues of importance to us as citizens is the issue of taxation. If we read Article One of the Constitution, it allows Congress the power to lay and collect taxes. However, from a specific point of view, just what those taxes are and how they are to be collected were not enumerated; therefore, the Congress had that responsibility.

As we will see in subsequent chapters, the judiciary branch of the United States, specifically the Supreme Court, has interpreted the meaning of the Constitution throughout our history. That interpretation has had a profound effect on the citizens and government of the United States. By far, the majority of interpretations have centered on the Bill of Rights.

BILL OF RIGHTS

Because of the extreme importance of the Bill of Rights, we will now turn to the meaning of the provisions of the amendments which relate to the administration of justice.

First Ten Amendments

The Bill of Rights consists of the first ten amendments to the Constitution. These first ten amendments developed from a long series of problems. Before we get into the specifics of the Bill of Rights, it would be helpful to reminisce for a few minutes so that we can better understand the problems that our forefathers faced.

English Bill of Rights

The first ten amendments to the Constitution concern the rights of persons against arbitrary government action. Many of these rights derived from the English Bill of Rights of 1689. However, these rights also arose from the American colonial experience. Each amendment was a colonial answer to governmental violations of rights—rights which were widely accepted by self-governing men in the eighteenth century. Let us consider the experience that shaped them.

Amendment one. Freedom of Religion, Speech, Press and Assembly. The English Crown tampered with religious freedom, often suppressed free speech and the press, and forbade peaceable assembly and petition for redress of grievances.

Amendment Two. Right to Bear Arms. The Crown disarmed at will by mere decree without lawful process.

Amendment Three. No Quartering of Soldiers. The Crown billetted soldiers in private houses in peace time—often without recompense.

Amendment Four. Unreasonable Searches and Seizures. The Crown denied it needed a warrant issued by a court for searches and seizures of houses or persons. If they used warrants, the warrant could be based on hearsay, rather than testimony under oath or sworn affidavit. Consequently, soldiers of the Crown would conduct mass searches of houses or of persons who were felt to be enemies of the Crown, with the intent of harrassing them and obtaining all possible evidence that could be used against them.

Amendment Five. Due Process, Double Jeopardy, Self Incrimination. The Crown asserted the right to seize a person for high crimes on hearsay; it reserved the power to try him more than once for the same offense. He could be deprived of life, liberty, and property in kangaroo courts and could be seized or deprived of property without compensation. The Crown did not care whether information was factual and was oblivious to the fact that convictions were obtained for crimes for which there was no evidence.

Amendment Six. Public Trial, Right to Counsel, Confrontation of Witnesses, Compulsory Process. Trials did not need to be public or before an impartial jury. One who had incurred the wrath of the Crown could be held for years without trial, and without being informed of the charges or witnesses against him. There was also no process for obtaining witnesses on one's own behalf. One could eventually face trial without having any guarantee that one's own side of the story would be told or that there would be a legitimate verdict based on all the evidence available.

Amendment Seven. Jury Trial. Failure by a jury to find a defendant guilty could be nullified by the Crown. Also, in Henry VIII's time, juries were quasi-religious bodies imbued with some degree of religious jurisdiction, and therefore a person could be denounced by a member of the clergy and consequently fined or imprisoned.

Amendment Eight. Excessive Bail, Cruel and Unusual Punishment. Exorbitant sums could be set for bail, and defendants could also be required to pay confiscatory fines. Before 1689 one could be tortured while in custody to exact confessions. Therefore, a person who had been arrested could be held without any hope for a trial, and furthermore be tortured to any extent desired by the Crown.

Amendment Ten. Powers Not Delegated Reserved to the States and People. This article delineates a confederated form of government in which certain powers are lodged in the states, and which therefore may not be exercised by the Federal government unless delegated by the Constitution. Here again the concern of our forefathers is evident in providing states with sovereignty and the right to govern themselves without hindrance from the federal government.

Thus the Bill of Rights was written in response to the colonists' bitter experience with tyranny in the Old World. It is ultimately the shield of common man against despotic individuals in public office.

Constitution For the People

Some of the fundamental concepts contained in the Bill of Rights are very elemental definitions of human dignity and human rights. For example, a person charged with a crime is presumed to be innocent until convicted by jury. It is not a defendant's responsibility to prove his innocence but rather the government's responsibility to prove that he committed the crime. If we were to compare a democracy with a totalitarian state, we would see the fundamental difference between the two. The individuals in a democracy are free to disagree with the wishes and demands of government. Because we are free to speak, to write and to vote as we feel, the changes in our government arise from an orderly election process rather than through revolution. Obviously. it was deemed of primary importance that the citizens in our government be allowed to dissent. If we do not agree with the conduct of our government officials, we need to be allowed to express those concerns.

Because of the extreme legal importance of many of the articles in the Bill of Rights, we will evaluate several of them in further detail and explain their significance as they relate to the administration of justice.

AMENDMENT I. Congress shall make no law respecting an establishment of religion or prohibiting the free exercise thereof; or abridging the freedom of speech, or of the press, or the right of the people peaceably to assemble, to petition the government for a redress of grievances.

Religion

The significance of the first portion of this amendment relating to religion is that the government supports the exercise of religion in any number of perfectly constitutional ways. There are numerous religious persons employed in our government in that capacity. An ordinary citizen is free to go to church or stay at home as he chooses. The government, however, does not allow those who worship in a particular fashion to interfere with the freedoms or the rights of other citizens. There have been numerous claims that people who are simply practicing their religious rights are also violating the laws of our country, such as utilizing certain drugs in the performance of religious sacraments. However, the California Supreme Court, in its *Woody* decision, decided that the use of peyote, for example, was entitled to First Amendment protection as part of a tribal religious ritual.[3]

Freedom of Speech

The freedom of speech portion of the First Amendment means that we have the right to express our thoughts and ideas. Freedom of speech, as well as freedom of the press, permits us to share our ideas and express our points of view regarding political and social changes and permits us to keep fully informed about the conduct of public officials. Ideas and thoughts must be protected even though they may be extremely unpopular. The constitutional guarantees of free speech and free press do not permit a state to forbid the advocacy of force or of law violation, except where such advocacy incites lawless action, or is likely to incite or produce such action.[4]

As is true of the right to freedom of religion, however, the right to freedom of speech is not an absolute right. The amendment does not give anyone the right to speak in a way which injures any person or his property, which corrupts public morals, which incites criminal activities, or which advocates specific action for overthrowing the government by force.

California Freedom of Speech

However, in order for speech to be restricted, there must be a clear and present danger to someone or someone's property, and it is the responsibility of the person claiming that danger to establish such facts beyond any reasonable doubt. The right to freedom of speech does not protect obscene material. Article One, Section 9 of the California Constitution contains an "abuse" clause which is not present in the federal amendment.[5] The U. S. Supreme Court stated that the, "Sum of the experience, including that of the past two decades, affords an ample basis for legislatures to conclude that a sensitive, key relationship of human existence, central to family life, community welfare, and the development of human personality, cannot be debased and distorted by crass, commercial exploitation of sex."

The First Amendment right to expression is not absolute; there may be regulations as to time, place, and manner when reasonably related to a valid public interest.[6]

In 1974, California prisons had rules which restricted personal correspondence of prison inmates. Among other matters they authorized censorship of statements that unduly magnify grievances, and inflammatory, political, racial, or religious views, or other views and matters deemed defamatory or otherwise inappropriate. The issue before the California Supreme Court was the appropriate standard of review for prison regulations restricting freedom of speech. The immediate case depended not upon the prisoner's rights but on the outsider to whom correspondence is directed. The Supreme Court stated that censorship of prisoner mail places a consequential restriction on the constitutional rights of those who are not prisoners. Justifiable censorship would be the refusal to send or deliver letters concerning escape plans, letters regarding proposed criminal activity, or letters with encoded messages. The court further ruled that prison officials may not censor mail simply to eliminate unflattering, unwelcome, or factually inaccurate statements. "They must show that a regulation authorizing mail censorship requires one of the substantial governmental interest of the security, order and rehabilitation of the prison. Limitation of First Amendment freedoms must be no greater than is necessary."[7]

Freedom of the Press

Freedom of the press involves the same basic restrictions as freedom of speech. The First Amendment also applies to books, newspapers, television, and radio. Obscene speech or writing is not protected by the First Amendment any more than any other violation of the law. In the United States Supreme Court decision, Miller v. California, the court attempted to establish the basic guidelines for determining what constitutes obscene material. The court stated that the rule shall be whether the average person, applying contemporary community standards, would find that the work taken as a whole appeals to one's prurient interest. The key is whether or not the work, taken as a whole, lacks serious literary, artistic, political or scientific value. The court also stated that sex and nudity in films or pictures exhibited or sold in public places may not be exploited without limit any more than live sex or nudity can be exhibited or sold without limit in such public places.

Peaceable Assembly

The clause of the First Amendment pertaining to peaceable assembly protects the right to picket, a right which has been exercised quite often in labor relations and civil rights disputes.

Antigovernment demonstrators are also protected as long as their conduct is orderly and does not violate other statutory provisions.

At such times when the assembly can be defined as other than peaceable, then the right is relinquished. Contemporary standards establish values by enacting laws prohibiting specific conduct. As society's values change, so do its laws.

The Right to Petition

The right of petition is exemplified by the Declaration of Independence, which was a statement to the world explaining our rebellion, and declaring that repeated petitions to King George III had been to no avail. Any citizen who wishes to petition the government, either local, state or federal, has the right to do so under this protection.

AMENDMENT IV. The right of the people to be secure in their persons, houses, papers and effects against unreasonable searches and seizures shall not be violated and no warrants shall issue, but upon probable cause supported by oath or affirmation and particularly describing the place to be searched, and the persons or things to be seized.

The Fourth Amendment is the primary authority relating to the rules and regulations that govern the arrest, search, and seizure of persons or property in the United States. We must recognize that although there are state rules and regulations established through constitutions and statutory provisions, all searches and seizures, as well as arrests, must fall within the framework established in the Fourth Amendment of the United States Constitution.

The Fourth Amendment has generally been divided into two clauses: the search and seizure clause, and the warrant clause.

Search and Seizure

The search and seizure clause deals primarily with the issue of what is considered to be a reasonable search and seizure. The Supreme Court of the United States has had a profound effect on determining this issue. The word "unreasonable" is the key issue to the search and seizure clause of the Fourth Amendment. In Harris vs. United States,[8] the court pointed out that it is only the unreasonable searches and seizures which are scrutinized in order to determine if they fall within the Constitutional guidelines; what is "reasonable" cannot be stated in rigid and absolute terms. The court went on to state that each situation must be decided individually.

In People vs. Fourshey, the court again stated that there is no exact formula for determining the reasonability of a search. Each case must be decided upon its own facts.[9]

Warrant

The warrant clause of the Fourth Amendment relates to search warrants as well as arrest warrants. It specifically requires the documentation of facts surrounding the issue of a warrant to the satisfaction of the court. The amendment requires that warrants only be issued upon probable cause. This requires the government to justify making the arrest, or the search of one's person or property. The justification must be written in the form of a statement that establishes the facts behind the officer's request. The government is also required to specifically describe the place to be searched, and must list the things to be seized. This prohibits the government from obtaining blank warrants and utilizing them at their discretion. A warrant must apply to a specific person or place, or to specific property.

We cannot ignore the judicial interpretation of the amendment which relates to the right of privacy. The Supreme Court has interpreted the language of the Fourth Amendment to include a person's home and privacy. Supreme Court decisions have stated that there are certain areas in which a citizen can expect a certain degree of privacy. In People vs. Krivda,[10] the California Supreme Court went so far as to state that a man's garbage, placed in front of his home, affords the same Fourth Amendment protection as does his residence.

AMENDMENT V. No person shall be held to answer for a capital, or otherwise infamous crime, unless on a presentment or indictment of a Grand Jury, except in cases arising in the land or naval forces, or in the Militia, when in actual service in time of War or public danger; nor shall any person be subject for the same offense to be twice put in jeopardy of life or limb; nor shall be compelled in any criminal case to be a witness against himself; nor be deprived of life, liberty, or property, without due process of law; nor shall private property be taken for public use, without just compensation.

Indictment by Grand Jury

On the federal level, the Fifth Amendment guarantees citizens the right to indictment by a grand jury. This, however, does not apply to individual states. In California, the indictment process through the grand jury is one of two ways in which an accused is brought to trial; for a felony offense, the other way is by information which is initiated and processed by the district attorney's office.

Double Jeopardy

The double jeopardy provision in the Fifth Amendment prevents either the state or the federal government from trying a person twice for the same crime. It is designed to prevent government from harassing citizens, and to prevent continual prosecution designed to achieve a desired verdict.

Jones vs. Breed involved a juvenile who was tried in a juvenile court hearing and consequently transferred to superior court. The Supreme Court ruled that the juvenile was put in jeopardy at the juvenile court adjudicative hearing, the object of which was to determine whether he had committed any acts that violated a criminal law. The consequences included both the stigma inherent in that determination, and the deprivation of liberty for many years. Jeopardy began when the juvenile court began to hear evidence. The juvenile's subsequent superior court trial as an adult for the same offense violated the double jeopardy clause. The juvenile was subjected to the burden of two trials for the same offense. He was twice put to the task of pitting his resources against those of the state, and was twice subjected to the heavy personal strain that such an experience represents.[11]

There are exceptions to the rule, which state that if a defendant appeals a case to the higher courts, and errors are discovered by the higher courts, the defendant can be returned to trial. This does not constitute double jeopardy.

Self Incrimination

Probably the most well known clause contained in the Fifth Amendment is the self incrimination clause. This prevents the government from requiring testimony by defendants charged with criminal offenses. This right is designed to protect citizens against the powers of government, both from the police and from the court. The criminal justice system should establish guilt of criminal acts by independent evidence, rather than base their case on statements made by a defendant alone. As we will discuss in subsequent chapters, the Fifth Amendment has developed a set of stringent rules applying to defendants accused of crimes, and to where statements relating to their guilt are solicited. The Fifth Amendment provides that no person shall be compelled in any criminal case to be a witness against himself. The right has been given broad scope; it has been applicable to grand jury proceedings, to civil proceedings, to congressional investigations, to juvenile proceedings, and to other statutory inquiries. It has also been applied to state judicial systems by virtue of the Fourteenth Amendment. In recent years it has been extended to cases involving state police investigation. Where state actions offend standards of fundamental fairness under the Due Process Clause, prosecutors have been deprived of the right to use resulting confessions in court.[12]

During the Watergate trials, the president of the United States was compelled to turn over the material to the district court judge for his incamera determination of whether it should be released to the special prosecutor. The Court ruled that neither the doctrine of separation of powers, nor the generalized need for confidentiality of high level communications, can sustain an absolute, unqualified presidential privilege of immunity to judicial processes under all circumstances. Excepting a claim of need to protect military, diplomatic, or sensitive national security secrets, the confidentiality of presidential communications is not significantly diminished by producing material for a criminal trial, under protected conditions of an incamera inspection. An absolute executive privilege under the United States Constitution would plainly conflict with the function of the courts under the constitution. The president's generalized assertion of privilege must yield to the demonstrated specific need for evidence in pending criminal trials, and to the fundamental demands of due process of law in a fair administration of justice.[13]

It must be remembered that the self-incrimination clause of the Fifth Amendment applies only to oral or written testimony, including books and records. Any physical evidence that is not communicated in some way would not come under the protections of the Fifth Amendment. For example: compelling a defendant to provide a sample of hand-writing does not violate his Fifth Amendment Protection; identification through a line up is not self incriminating; being asked to produce identification which ultimately can be incriminating in itself is not a violation of the Fifth Amendment. This is considered a nontestimonial act. [14]

For all intents and purposes, the Fifth Amendment relates to admissions or confessions obtained from suspects involved in criminal activities. The due process clause of the Fifth Amendment applies only to the federal government. The due process clause applying to the states, although parallel with the Fifth Amendment, is actually the Fourteenth Amendment, which will be discussed in a later section. Fundamentally, the due process definition simply means that there must be fair play regarding the law. It requires compliance not only with the specific forms of the law, but with all that is meant by, "liberty and justice for all."

AMENDMENT SIX. In all criminal prosecutions, the accused shall enjoy the right of a speedy and public trial, by an impartial jury of the State and district wherein the crime shall have been committed, which district shall have been previously ascertained by law, and to be informed of the nature and cause of the accusation; to be confronted with the witnesses against him, to have compulsory process for obtaining witnesses in his favor, and to have the Assistance of Counsel for his defense.

Of the Bill of Rights amendments, the Fifth and Sixth amendments relate significantly to the principals and procedures of the justice system.   There are several very important clauses in the Sixth Amendment, which is the foundation for court procedures, and it sets the limits by which government intrusion is justified.

Speedy and Public Trial

The first clause of the Sixth Amendment states that all persons in criminal actions shall enjoy the right to a speedy and a public trial. The first section indicates that a defendant cannot be kept in jail or in custody for any lengthy period of time without his "day in court." If not for this restriction, the government could incarcerate a subject in jail for an indefinite period of time under the pretense of awaiting trial. This particular provision applies to both the state and federal government.

There has been considerable interpretation of what is actually a speedy trial. The court seems to have the opinion that as long as the defendant is tried in his turn, mere delay in reaching trial, due to over-crowded court conditions, etcetera, does not violate his constitutional rights. In effect, a deliberate and purposeful detention for a lengthy period of time is what the court has objected to. In determining whether the defendant receives a speedy trial, the Supreme Court has developed a "balancing test" to be used, in which four factors are to be weighed; the length of the delay; reason for delay; defendant's ability to assert his rights; and the prejudice shown against him.

The public trial segment is present to prevent any branch of government from trying a person without public knowledge. This allows the citizens to maintain a careful eye on the activities of the government. Although the right applies to the defendant, the citizens of the community also have a sharing right, inasmuch as it is the duty of the government to sufficiently punish those people who have committed criminal wrongs, regardless of their status or position in a community.

Jury Trial, District and Location of Crime

There would appear to be a requirement that all defendants be tried by jury. This, however, has been interpreted to apply only to federal crimes. In California, a defendant has the opportunity to request that his right to jury trial be waived, and that the court be his trier of fact. The clause also requires that a person charged with a criminal offense be tried in the district and location where the crime was committed. In returning to the original intent of the Constitution, we should remember that one of the primary objections stated in the declarations of rights was that persons charged with a crime could be returned to England for trial. Jurors were often loyal to the Crown, and at times had absolutely no knowledge or understanding of the offense, or of the defendant, thereby making a fair and impartial trial impossible. The local citizens have the exclusive interests in carrying out justice in that community. Therefore, they have a right to be involved in the decision of guilt or innocence.

The only exception to this rule would be if the defendant is unable to obtain a fair and impartial trial. In this case, a change of venue would allow for the defendant to be taken to another jurisdiction, to be tried where the prospective jurors and citizens do not have a personal vendetta against the accused.

Informed of the Nature and Cause of Accusation

The clause of the Sixth Amendment which states that a defendant is to be informed of the nature and cause of the accusation is so fundamental a right that it would appear unnecessary to discuss it in much detail. However, it must be remembered that it was not too long ago when the government would charge citizens with crimes, and would not then inform them whatsoever of what crime they might have comitted. This clause prevents imprisonment for non-criminal acts, as well as preventing the government from conducting a trial against the accused where the accused has had no opportunity to defend himself properly, let alone know what he is being tried for. The defendant must have time to prepare his case so that he may intelligently question witnesses and obtain witnesses on his behalf.

Confrontation and Cross-examination

The right to confrontation and cross-examination of witness clause in the Sixth Amendment is also a fundamental right of the accused. This clause gives the defendant the right to examine witnesses who have been called against him. This also requires that the defendant be present in the court room so that he may observe and listen to the testimony of all witnesses against him in court.

Compulsory Process

The compulsory process clause requires that the defendant be allowed to introduce evidence on his behalf through testimony. This means that the defendant must be allowed to have a process by which he can require a witness to take the stand and testify on his behalf. This compulsory process is normally completed through the process of a subpoena; at criminal trials the defendant need only request the presence of certain material witnesses, and the government is then required to make contact if at all possible, with the witnesses, serving them with a subpoena. If at the onset a witness refuses to acknowledge the subpoena, then he himself can be held accountable on a contempt of court charge and fined and/or imprisoned for failure to obey.

Right to Attorney

The last clause of the Sixth Amendment relates to the right to have council for the defense. Some very significant changes have occurred in interpreting the meaning of this section. In later chapters we will discuss in detail the right to council issue and its history, describing the various cases which have been decided by the Supreme Court.

AMENDMENT EIGHT. Excessive bail shall not be required, nor excessive fines imposed nor cruel and unusual punishments inflicted.

Bail, Fines, and Punishment

The obvious intent of this amendment is to prevent the government from detaining a person in confinement until his trial, as well as from imposing extreme fines or punishments based on the whimsical or personal judgments of government officials. We must realize the intent of bail is not to penalize a person charged with an offense, but to ensure that he will meet his obligations in determining the issue of his guilt or innocence. Therefore, only that amount necessary to ensure his attendance at trial is allowed.

Cruel and unusual punishments are those which are shocking to the conscience of the civilized world. They include inhumane, barbaric or degrading acts of punishment, as well as any punishments that would be out of proportion accordingly with the offense that had been comitted. For example, we can readily understand that fifty years of imprisonment for a petty theft would be considered cruel, unusual, and shocking to the conscience of the civilized world. The issue of the indeterminate sentence has been under attack for several years. Morrissey vs. Brewer[15] began the decline of the indeterminate sentence in California. The California Supreme Court, in Re Lynch[16], and in Re Foss[17], attempted to limit the terms of the indeterminate sentence. The result of the above decisions, plus several more, resulted in SB 42 being drafted and finally signed into law on September 21, 1976, abolishing the indeterminate sentencing laws which had been in effect in California since 1917. In later chapters detailed discussion will be devoted to the new determinate sentence laws of California.

Due Process

AMENDMENT FOURTEEN Section I . . . nor shall any state deprive any person of life, liberty, or property, without due process of law; nor deny any person within its jurisdiction the protection of the law.

This amendment was proposed in 1866 and ratified in 1868. The Fourteenth Amendment for all intents and purposes is considered the due process clause. The Supreme Court of the United States, through a series of decisions, extended the provisions of the Bill of Rights to the states, thereby requiring that these rights apply to all citizens of the United States, whether on the federal or state level.

Because of this interpretation the U.S. Constitution finally became an instrument for all citizens of our country and the protections cont-tained in the Bill of Rights pertain to all.

This particular clause has been a subject of more Supreme Court cases than any other. The Supreme Court during its recent history has greatly expanded the meaning of this clause.

THE CALIFORNIA CONSTITUTION

History

Beginning with the first Spanish settlement in California in 1769, the government was divided between the *padres*, who exercised control of the missions, and the *commandantes*, who exercised military control of the soldiers, administrative procedures, and generally over the crime. Along with new settlements (*pueblos*) a short time later, a simple government was established which consisted merely of a governor, but for a long period of time he was not of any practical importance.

The independence of Mexico was secured from Spain in 1821. In 1837 a new constitution was drawn up by which the government of the providences was substantially altered and the missions were confiscated.

At the time of the occupation of California by the Americans, the providence was governed by the laws of March 20 and May 23, 1837, which provided for a government divided into executive, legislative, and judicial departments. The division was not as carefully followed as in our present state and national governments, but was closer to most county governments. The government was also more centralized than our own. When the Americans took control of the providence of California, many of them were unfamiliar with the Mexican system. As more and more Americans occupied California, the American form of government became more and more prevalent. In our early history there were many unofficial forms of government in existence. For example, during the gold rush days, when serious offenses occurred and there were no judges available, the miners frequently tried cases by jury without a judge. These "miner's courts" had the advantage of quickly and finally disposing of the cases. These examples of the administration of justice are considered to be extremely primitive, and are similar to the early justice exercised by the Saxons.

Bill of Rights

On September 1, 1849, a constitutional convention was held for the purpose of developing a constitution for California. A Bill of Rights was drawn up by the convention members and submitted to the convention for approval, along with thirteen additional sections and twelve articles, Article One being the Bill of Rights. The Bill of Rights provided that all men were free and independent: that political powers were inherent with the people; that the people have guaranteed trial by a jury, and freedom of religion; that the writ of habeas corpus should not be suspended; that excessive bail should not be required; that the people have guaranteed free speech and the right of free assembly; and that the laws of a general nature should have a uniform operation. It also provided that the military powers should be subordinate to civil power, and that soldiers should not be quartered in private houses in times of peace. It required that representation should be apportioned according to population. No person should be imprisoned for a debt, and no bill of indenture, ex post facto laws or law impairing the operation of contracts should be passed. Slavery was prohibited. Unreasonable searches were forbidden. Treason against the state was defined. It also stipulated that the enumeration of rights should not be so constructed as to deny others retained by the people.

If we analyze the specific Bill of Rights article enumerated in the California Constitution, we will find that, by far, the majority of those rights are exactly the same as those in the U.S. Bill of Rights.

Powers of Government

Also of interest for the purposes of the administration of justice system is Article Three of the California Constitution, which contains the distribution of powers of government. These powers are broken into three separate branches: the legislative, the executive and the judicial. Very explicitly stated in Article Three is the separation between these branches; no person charged with the exercise of powers in one branch could exercise any function in any of the others.

Legislative Powers

Article Four detailed the authority of powers in the legislative department. The legislative power of the state was vested in the senate and the assembly. The article required that the sessions were to be public except, when in the opinion of the house, secrecy was required.

The article states that after a bill had been passed by both houses it was to be submitted to the governor for his approval or disapproval. It also outlines the procedures for overruling the governor's objection. Every law is required to have one subject, which should be stated in the title, and if any section is omitted, it is required that it be reenacted and published at length. This prevents the government from enacting extremely complicated laws which the citizens might not clearly understand.

Executive Powers

Article Five defined the duties and responsibilities of the executive department. The governor of the State of California had the supreme executive power of the state. It requires that he be elected in the same manner as the members of the assembly, and to hold office for four years. The governor has the authorization to grant reprieves and pardons.

Judicial Powers

Article Six stated the powers and duties of the judicial department. The judicial power of the State of California was broken down to the Supreme Court, district court, county court, and justice court levels. The composition of the state supreme court was also defined. The legislature was given the responsibility to divide the state into judicial districts, and to provide elections for district attorneys, sheriffs, and other necessary officers. There must be a county court in each county, and its judge must be elected. This article notes that all the processes are to be in the name of the "People of California."

Penal Code Provisions

The penal code is another extremely important source of legal authority in the administration of justice. The penal code is normally broken into two sections; one is crimes and punishments, and the other, criminal procedures. Criminal procedure here relates basically to the specific laws that are necessary in order to process an accused throughout the criminal justice system.

Each state has its own procedures, as deemed necessary by the citizens of that state. However, it must be remembered that the states have a requirement to stay within the framework of the United States Constitution. As our forefathers mandated, the states were to have sovereign rule except in matters where there was a federal question involved. Because of this, the numerous detailed procedures such as process for public offenses, the mode of prosecution, the proceedings of the grand jury, types of pleadings, judgments, and execution appeals, etcetera, are all found in the state codes.

As we discuss the specific procedures required in the administration of justice system, we will make reference to the specific Penal Code provisions stipulating the proper conduct of government, keeping in mind that California requires written law to enable government officials to act against the citizens of the state.

The Penal Code provisions are a followup of the federal and state constitutions. Both constitutions provide the necessary framework for the legal system, and the statutory codes fill in the details for the accomplishments of the goals established.

SUMMARY

In this chapter we have discussed the formation of the constitutional authority as it relates to the federal government in the state of California. We began with the establishment of the Declaration of Independence, and made specific reference to the Constitution of the United States, emphasizing the Bill of Rights. The major amendments to the Bill of Rights and their significance to the principles and procedures of the justice system were discussed.

We saw that the California constitution has basically the same provisions as the federal constitution. Finally, the specific statutes contained in the Penal Code were discussed. The majority of all laws as they relate to the justice system are contained in the Penal Code, as well as other statutory codes in California. The Constitutions on the state and federal levels act as the foundation of all of the laws that govern the citizens of the state of California on a daily basis.

DISCUSSION QUESTIONS

1. Identify the specific amendments dealing with the criminal justice system. What protection against governmental intrusion were intended by our forefathers?

2. Discuss the major protections written into the U. S. Constitution. What protections have been strengthened or weakened by the judicial branch of government?

3. The California Constitution differs slightly from the U. S. Constitution. How can these differences be explained? List them.

REFERENCES

1.   Journal of the Stamp Act Congress, New York 1765, as printed in the re-publication of *The Principles and Acts of the Revolution in America* by Hezekiah Niles (1876).

2.   Journals of the Continental Congress 1774-1789. Edited from the original records in the Library of Congress by Worthington Chauncey Ford, Chief, Division of Manuscripts. Washington: Government Printing Office.

3.   People v. Woody 61 Cal. 2d 716, 40 Cal.Rptr.69, 394 P.2d 813 (1964).

4.   Communist Party of Indians v. Whitcomb, 414 U.S. 441, 94 S.Ct. 656, 38 L. Ed. 2d 635 (1974).

5.   Bloom v. Municipal Court, 36 Cal. App. 3d 117, 111 Cal. Rptr. 253 (1974).

6.   Phillips v. Adult Probation Department of San Francisco, 494 F. 2d 951 (1974).

7.   Procunier v. Martinez, 416 U.S. 396, 94 S. Ct. 1800, 40 L.Ed. 2d 224 (1974).

8.   Harris v. United States, 331 U.S. 145, 67 S.Ct. 1098, 91 L.Ed. 1399 (1947).

9.   People v. Fourshey, 38 Cal. App. 3d 426, 113 Cal. Rptr. 275 (1974).

10.   Cal. 3d 357, 96 Cal. Rptr. 62, 486 P. 2d 1262 (1971).

11.   Jones V. Breed, 519 F. 2d 1314 (9th Cir. 1975).

12.   Michigan v. Tucker, 417 U.S. 433, 94 S.Ct. 2357, 41 L. Ed. 2d 182, (1974).

13.   United States v. Nixon, 418 U.S. 683, 94 S.Ct. 3090, 41 L.Ed. 2d 1039 (1974).

14.   United States v. Camacho, 506 F. 2d 594 (9th Cir. 1974).

15.   Morrissey v. Brewer, 408 U.S. 471, 92 S.Ct. 2593, 33 L.Ed. 2d 484 (1972).

16.   In re Lunch, 8 Cal. 3d 410, 105 Cal. Rptr. 217, 503 P. 2d 921 (1972).

17.   In re Foss, 10 Cal. 3d 910, 112 Cal. Rptr. 649, 519 P. 2d 1073 (1974).

2

Constitutional Protections: Rights of the Accused

CHAPTER OBJECTIVES

Upon reading this chapter, the student will be able to:

1. List five major constitutional protections for an accused and their significance.

2. Develop the right to counsel in the U. S. and California, making specific reference to case decisions.

3. Distinguish the right to counsel at the trial stage and investigative stage.

4. List the Miranda requirements and the obligations of police officers when interrogating suspects.

In Chapter 1 we discussed in general terms the constitutional protections of all citizens of the United States and of California. We discussed the specific legal authority for the system, including the Declaration of Independence, and the specific constitutional provisions contained in the Bill of Rights. Some of the rights discussed in Chapter 1 will have more importance than others as they relate to the principles and procedures of the justice system. The intent of this chapter is to identify those protections which are crucial to any accused in a criminal prosecution. The right to a speedy trial, the right to counsel, the production and confrontation of witnesses, and legal convictions in a criminal prosecution are of paramount importance to the legal system as a whole. Each of these major areas will be discussed separately, with particular case decisions given as primary references. In the second segment of this chapter, under Right to Counsel, the development and history of the right to counsel will be discussed. Major case decisions and their significance to the development of the right to counsel, as the concept grew both in the United States and in California, will be discussed.

SPEEDY AND PUBLIC TRIAL

"In all criminal prosecutions, the accused shall enjoy the right of a speedy and public trial . . . " (Amendment 6 of the United States Constitution). The California constitution basically contains the same provisions, with a slight difference in wording. "In criminal prosecutions, in any court whatsoever, the party accused shall have the right to a speedy and public trial . . . ." The California Penal Code also contains provisions, in statutory form, which address the issue of the defendant's right to a speedy and public trial. Penal Code Section 1050 states that, "The welfare of the people in the state of California requires that all proceedings in criminal cases shall be set for trial and heard and determined at the earliest possible time." This is an example of the wording in most statutes dealing with the right to a speedy trial in California. In most cases, no specific reference is made to time guidelines, but rather a philosophical statement is made in terms of the right of the defendant to have a speedy trial. The Penal Code has several provisions for eliminating delays that might occur during the adjudication process. For example, the law provides a schedule for when the accusatory pleading must be filed in the criminal court, and states when the defendant has a right to go to trial once the information has been filed, etcetera. The purpose of these provisions is to require the prosecutor to initiate the proceedings as quickly as possible. In the case of delays that exceed the statutory schedule, in most cases the matter will be dismissed; to do otherwise would only cause a delay in the overall proceedings, as the charges may be refiled and the proceedings, initated all over again. For misdemeanors, the delay would be grounds for a permanent dismissal and a bar to further prosecution.

Dismissal of Criminal Action by the Court

"The court, unless good cause to the contrary is shown, must order the action to be dismissed in the following case: 1. When a person has been held to answer for a public offense and an information is not filed against him within 15 days thereafter.[1] As we will discuss in chapter 9, the defendant in a criminal prosecution has certain legal plateaus that are reached during the judicial process. Each one of those plateaus deals with the protection of his constitutional rights, and with ways to avoid unnecessary violations of his rights to freedom, etcetera, as stated in the constitutions and statutes. Since there are several steps that must be followed, the statutory provisions contained in this section prevent unnecessary delay in bringing the case to trial. In felony cases, one of the normal processes for bringing a case to trial is through filing an information. Prior to this, there must be a preliminary hearing. Once the preliminary hearing has been held, the prosecutor would have fifteen days to file the information.

2. "When a defendant is not brought to trial in Superior Court within 60 days after the finding of an indictment or the filing of an information . . . ." This provision follows the previous one inasmuch that once the information has been filed, then the defendant has the right to go to trial within sixty days from that time. This also includes indictments, stating that once the indictment has been filed with the court, then the sixty day statutory limitation would be in effect.[2]

Subpart 3 of 1382 of the Penal Code discusses misdemeanors: "Regardless of when the complaint is filed, when a defendant in a misdemeanor case in an inferior court is not brought to trial within 30 days after he is arraigned if he is in custody at the time of arraignment, or in all other cases, within 45 days after his arraignment . . .." The time limit specified for misdemeanors is much shorter than for felonies in proportion to the seriousness of the offense. It should be noted that in a misdemeanor case the defendant will be arraigned in inferior court, and then have the right to be tried from that original arraignment within thirty days if he is in custody, or forty-five days if he is not. Several steps have been eliminated for misdemeanors compared to felony offenses. In chapter 9, 10, and 11 we will discuss the specifics as they relate to felonies and misdemeanors.

Constitutional and statutory provisions allow more time for bringing a person to trial when that individual is not in custody. The logical explanation for this is apparent; since the accused has not been convicted of any wrongdoings until he has had his "day in court," the government can use only that amount of restriction necessary to protect the citizens of the state.   If the defendant is released, then his freedoms are minimumly restricted and the schedule is extended.

PUBLIC TRIAL

As we found in the previous section, the Constitution and Penal Code guarantee the right of the defendant to have a public trial.[3]   Just exactly what a public trial entails has been subject to much controversy over the years.   At first glance, this would ordinarily mean a trial open to the public, with newspapers and media broadcasters free to report the proceedings.   In other words, the public trial issue is of concern not only to the defendant but also to the public.   The two concepts dealing with the issue of public trial are the issue's relationship to the rights of the defendant and to the rights of the public.

Rights of the Defendant

In order to receive a fair and impartial trial, it is extremely important that the public be involved and be available to observe the method and technique of prosecuting the accused.   In other words, if the public were not able to observe the proceedings, it is conceivable that the state could conduct a kangaroo court affair, whereby the court would go through the motions of giving the defendant a fair and impartial trial when actually the sentence had been predetermined. With the presence of the public, particularly the news media, an accused can be more sure of his ability to receive a fair and impartial trial. With the news media present, pressure placed on those who are involved in the judicial system, could be tremendous if there were improprieties which violated constitutional and statutory provisions. In other words, the public acts as a check and balance to ensure a fair and impartial trial in a criminal prosecution.

Right of the Public to a Public Trial

The public, on the other hand, has a genuine interest in the criminal prosecution of a accused person in the community for obvious reasons. The California Constitution and the California Penal Code advise that in criminal prosecution, all of the people in the state of California are in effect the victims of a criminal wrongdoing.   Even though a specific person is in fact the victim, as in the case of a murder, it is the State of California that prosecutes and is responsible for ensuring that an accused is justly brought to trial.   For example, suppose a prominent citizen with a great deal of power runs into problems with the law.   He is arrested for vehicular manslaughter while under the influence of alcohol.

With his power, it is conceivable that enough pressure could be placed on a local prosecutor, and perhaps the magistrate, to afford him special attention. If the public did not have the right to be present and to witness the proceedings, the prosecutor could give special attention, such as finding the defendant guilty but waiving all sentencing and placing the individual on informal probation. The public should be aware of this kind of activity. The public's presence, through the news media or other interested individuals, should prevent this kind of activity from occurring.

The defendant's right to a public trial, on the other hand, is not absolute. The magistrate has limited authority, for good cause, to eliminate the public's presence during certain aspects of the trial. This authority is only used during those parts of a trial in which certain testimony is needed to fully understand the involvement of the defendant, victims, or witnesses. For example, in child molestation case, a young female who was molested would be hesitant to discuss the details of the incident in front of the public. In this situation, the magistrate could order the court cleared for the limited testimony of the female victim so that the jury could hear in detail what took place.

The defendant may waive his right to a public trial for reasons similar to those discussed in the previous paragraph. He may be willing to take the stand and testify regarding his involvement in the criminal activity, but may desire that the public be removed from the courtroom in order to assure privacy on certain matters to which he would testify. When the defendant waives his right to a public trial, what he is doing in effect is actually waiving a subsequent challenge of a non-public trial. In other words, he has the right to a public trial, but not necessarily to a private trial.

The magistrate, as previously stated, has the power to exclude segments of the public, or on rare occasions, the entire public, for certain segments of the trial. The magistrate also has the right to control the number of persons allowed into the courtroom due to space limitations and for proper control. The magistrate will normally allow representation of various segments of the news media, such as the press, radio, or television, so that they may report the proceedings. He could make a valid order stating that only one representative of each of the segments would be allowed into the trial. Any time it is necessary to maintain order in a courtroom, the magistrate may exclude portions of the public. Any observer in the courtroom who is acting unruly or causing a disturbance can be removed without problem. Magistrates, on occasion, advise the public that there will be specific testimony which could be extremely vulgar or indecent, so that members of the audience may remove themselves during this testimony.

Simply put, the defendant comes first in a criminal prosecution in respect to his right to a public trial, and the public right comes second.

News Coverage

Over the years the news media has taken an extremely active role in representing the public in criminal trials. Specific problems concerning this involvement do develop and have in the past, particularly the problem of improper publicity. Without some restrictions or control over the news media, the selection of an impartial jury could become extremely difficult, if not impossible, and extreme prejudices could develop toward the defendant. The California appeals courts have given numerous opinions on improper publicity, and have placed restrictions on the freedom of the news media in criminal prosecutions.

The ultimate in abuse by the news media in a criminal prosecution occurred in the Estes v. Texas case in 1965. Because of the public interest in the Estes case, the local news station thought it would be worthy to televise the entire trial. The court allowed the television station to set up its television equipment, lighting sources, microphones, etcetera, throughout the courtroom. There were several cameramen and other individuals in the courtroom throughout the trial, recording testimony and the presentation of evidence. The jurors were televised, as were the spectators and everyone else in the courtroom. The performance was rebroadcast in the evening in place of the late movie. The Supreme Court of the United States reversed the conviction, stating that Estes had not received a fair trial, and that he had been denied his due process. The presence of the news media made participants pay more attention to the goings on of the television production rather than to the testimony and its merits, according to the provisions of law. As a result of the Supreme Court decision, several states, including California, adopted some very restrictive rules preventing such activities in a criminal prosecution. California Rules of Court 980 prohibits photographing, recording, and broadcasting in a courtroom during any session. The only exception to this rule is in a ceremonial proceeding, and this only with the consent of the court. Consequently, in California, the only recording devices of any kind that are allowed are those that are required by the court clerk to preserve the testimony and the proceedings of the trial.

The right to a speedy and public trial is a constitutional protection that is not taken lightly in our legal system. The courts have a legal obligation to ensure that the defendant does receive a speedy trial. He is innocent until proven guilty, and therefore his freedom should be limited only to the extent absolutely necessary for the protection of citizens and the community. He will not be found guilty or innocent until such time as he has a trial, and, therefore, that trial should be held as quickly as is reasonable.

The court's interpretation of the right to a speedy trial has not resulted in absolute schedules being placed on the various stages of the criminal proceedings. In most cases it is a matter of common sense as to what would be violation of a right to a speedy trial. The right to a public trial as defined by the courts and statutory provisions provides for a two-fold right: the first deals with the defendant's protection, and states that he must have a right to a public trial; the second deals with the right of the public to have its representation during a criminal process to ensure that a defendant is properly accused and ajudicated according to our laws. Again, the court has a certain amount of discretion in protecting the public's defendant's rights to a public trial, and on some occasions will exclude the public when in the fairness to justice it is necessary. The primary protection however, is for the defendant, who has the right to a public trial; this right cannot be violated.

RIGHT TO COUNSEL

The right to counsel in the United States has evolved over the years from a complete lack of protection, to modern day requirements for legal representation in all phases of the criminal procedure. The right to counsel does not, however, go so far back into history as one might assume. If we first look at the protections provided by English Common Law, we see a completely different philosophy then we ended up with in the United States today. The Common Law of England did not allow a man accused of treason or felonies to be represented by counsel, except that a lawyer could argue legal points if so requested by the accused. Oddly enough, the English Common Law allowed for full representation in misdemeanor cases. As is easily recognized, this is in direct proportion to today's attitudes and philosophies—that the more serious the offense, the more protections that a defendant should have. The theory at that time was apparently that the greater the charge the less chance that the accused should have the opportunity to "beat the rap." It must be remembered that up through the 17th century, defendants who committed serious offense were treated, in most respects, with what seems today to be complete unfairness, and their rights were not acknowledged. They were not allowed to testify, and they could not, in most situations, have witnesses sworn in so that they could testify in behalf of the accused. Most of the other constitutional protections that were made a part of the Bill of Rights were omitted in English Common Law. When the Bill of Rights was enacted in 1776, it was very clear that the intent of our forefathers was to ensure the right to counsel for all defendants charged with criminal offenses in this country. The Sixth Amendment provided, amoung other things, that,

"In all criminal prosecutions, the accused shall enjoy the right . . . to have the assistance of counsel for his defense." This provision was not strictly adhered to for some time; in fact, it was not until the 1900s that the right to counsel finally applied to all, regardless of ability to pay. The Sixth Amendment was designed to assure that the right to all individuals who might be charged with crimes in the United States be represented by legal counsel to aid in providing for all adequate defense.

Historically speaking, when our forefathers wrote the Sixth Amendment, there were many factors which they did not take into consideration. One was the inability of certain individuals to buy "their protection." In other words, services rendered require adequate compensation. Therefore, those who could not afford to hire a lawyer would not have one provided for them. This strict interpretation of the Sixth Amendment was that the defendant had the right to counsel, but only in the cases where he could afford it. Over the years this became a real problem in the American criminal justice system. If we observe today's statistics on who can afford an attorney, we get a pretty good idea of the problem that developed in establishing right to counsel rules in the United States. It has been estimated that between 30 and 60 percent of all those accused of a criminal offense today cannot afford to hire a lawyer at their own expense.

Let us examine how the right to counsel developed in the United States with respect to the provision that all individuals should have legal counsel, and that legal counsel should be available at all stages of the criminal prosecution. This is a rather fascinating example of how constitutional doctrine develops slowly and deliberately, case by case. It also shows how the Supreme Court of the United States has influenced the constitutional doctrine of the right to counsel for all individuals.

Powell v. Alabama[4]

The first time our Supreme Court significantly discussed the issue of the right to counsel in the United States was in 1932, in the Powell vs. Alabama case, or Scottsborough Case. The major issue was actually not effective counsel, but whether or not the defendants received a fair and impartial trial, and whether their due process rights had been protected. The case history began in a freight train moving slowly across the countryside in northern Alabama. At the time there was extreme economic distress and social unrest throughout the United States. In one of the cars there were two groups of youths; one consisted of several negroes and the other of several whites. Among the white youths were a couple of white girls. A dispute broke out between the negroes and the whites and there was a fight. All but one of the white boys was thrown off the train. Word was sent ahead, and when the train approached the town of Scottsborough, the Negroes were met by a sheriff and posse who charged them with raping the white girls. A few days later the defendants were tried in three separate proceedings. Each trial was completed in the space of a single day, and all the defendants were convicted of rape. The juries imposed the death sentence on each defendant.

The case was appealed to the Supreme Court with the question of whether or not the Scottsborough boys had received effective assistance of counsel. They had been tried only six days after their indictment. At the time they were tried the judge appointed all members of the bar in Scottsborough to defend them. There was no preparation on the part of the counsel. The defendants were young and ignorant; they were also illiterate. There was an extreme amount of hostility around the town; in other words, the conditions were such that it was more than just a simple problem of lack of counsel. The questions that arose out of the Supreme Court review were: whether or not the defendants' due process had been violated; and whether or not the defendants had received effective counsel.

The Supreme Court decided to sidestep the issue of the right to counsel, but decided that in this case the 14th Amendment had been violated. The defendants had not received due process because of the "special circumstances"; that is there were several serious problems such as mob action, a quick trial, no lawyer, etc. There was a denial of due process as provided by the 14th Amendment.

As the right to counsel rule developed in the United States then, there were two theories developing; the defendant who did not have counsel could not adequately defend himself, and therefore there should be protection for all; and a due process violation would constitute several factors (illiteracy or ignorance on the part of the defendant, racial tension, public outrage) to indicate to the justices that the defendant could not receive a fair and impartial trial, as was found in this case. The Supreme Court found that the defendants had not had effective counsel, but that only their constitutional right of due process had been violated.

Johnson v. Zerbst[5]

The second major case dealing with the right to counsel occurred in 1938. This was a federal case dealing with two soldiers who were charged with counterfeit. They were found guilty of the crime as charged. They did not have the right to counsel, and it was noted that they could not afford one. However they had not actually requested counsel due to the fact that they were not aware that they had any such rights. In the first major decision, written by Justice Black, the issue was of whether or not the defendants should have been allowed the right to counsel. Justice Black wrote that in all federal prosecutions, the defendant should have the right to counsel. In deciding the case, denial of the right to counsel was found to be a constitutional violation, which caused the reversal decision. The leading question was whether the defendant could waive his right; however, before he could do so he had to be advised that he did have the right to counsel. Beginning in 1938, in all federal prosecutions the defendants could enjoy the right to counsel regardless of their ability to pay. Justice Black was careful to word his opinion to include only federal prosecutions, indicating that the states had the right to develop constitutional rights as they deemed fit.

Betts v. Brady[6]

In 1942, a Maryland defendant was accused of robbery, a state violation. During the trial the defendant was not represented by counsel, even though he had asked that the court appoint him a lawyer. He stated that he was unable to pay for one and felt that it was the obligation of the state to provide counsel for him. The court denied his request, stating that it was only their responsibility to appoint attorneys in very serious offenses where the defendant could receive the death penalty. There were no special circumstances involved in this case other than the fact that the defendant was being charged with a felony. After his conviction, Betts appealed his case to the Supreme Court which denied his appeal because there were no "special circumstances" involved in his case. The court decided to use the "special circumstances theory," rather than the Sixth Amendment right to counsel, which had been used in the Zerbst case. Since there had been no obvious due process violation, the court upheld the philosophy that it was the responsibility of the states to decide whether or not all the defendants in criminal prosecutions should be allowed the right to counsel, regardless of ability to pay. Again the "special circumstances" rule was being further refined; that is, the only time the defendants would be allowed counsel would have to do with the complexity of the offenses or the offense charged (the severity of the penalty; circumstances surrounding the trial; confusing issues; the inability of the defendant to understand; the educational background of the accused; and other such factors). Only when several of these circumstances were apparent would the courts rule in favor of the right to counsel in state cases.

Gideon v. Wainwright[7]

It was not until 1963 that the next major decision regarding the right to counsel was decided. From the time of the Betts v. Brady case until the Gideon case, the Supreme Court reviewed cases dealing with the right to counsel.   The only time they would decide in favor of the defendant was when there appeared to be enough "special circumstances" to warrant finding in favor of the defendant under the due process clause of the U.S. Constitution.   When Gideon v. Wainwright was decided in 1963, the timing was right; the case was almost identical to the Betts v. Brady case.   Gideon was an individual who had been exposed to the criminal justice process many times.   His adjudicatory history began in 1928, when he was convicted of burglary in Missouri.   In 1934 he was convicted of federal charges of possession of government property, and spent several years in prison.   In 1940 he was convicted of burglary in Missouri, and spent some ten years in prison before he escaped in 1944. He was recaptured a year later and was released in 1950.   In 1951 there was a burglary in Texas and he spent two years in prison.   After that there was nothing serious until 1961, when he was charged with breaking and entering a poolroom.   At the beginning of the trial Gideon had asked for counsel, stating that he could not afford a lawyer and wished the court to appoint one for him.   As was the policy in Florida, the judge refused, stating that the only time counsel was appointed was in capital offenses.   Gideon tried to act as his own counsel, attempting to cross-examine witnesses and to call witnesses on his behalf.   A court transcript shows that he did a rather inadequate job; also, there were questions as to whether or not there was bias on the judge's part.   After being convicted and sent to prison, Gideon learned that he could appeal his case to the Supreme Court.   He handwrote a writ of certiorari, requesting that the Supreme Court review his case.   Normally requests in this form would be ignored, but by chance the Supreme Court decided to review the case.

The Supreme Court appointed a very prominent attorney named Abe Fortus to represent Gideon; he presented the case to the Court, arguing as to why counsel should be provided in all criminal prosecutions.   The case was timely; at this point thirty-seven states provided counsel as a matter of right in all felony cases.   This left only thirteen states that did not require a provision of counsel, except in the case of capital offenses. Florida was one of those five states.   Even in Florida, however, there were local public defenders who provided legal assistance for those charged with serious offenses.   Nearly half of the states at this time went beyond this practice to provide counsel for misdemeanor defendants.

The Supreme Court of the United States, in ruling in favor of Gideon, stated that it was time for the states to fall in line with the Sixth Amendment protection.   For the first time the Supreme Court of the United States established a uniform rule with regard to the right to counsel, stating that in all criminal prosecutions the defendant would have the right to counsel regardless of his ability to pay during the trial stage. In looking at the two theories that had developed in 1932, the Supreme Court utilized the Sixth Amendment right-to-counsel theory. They threw out the "special circumstances," rule, and simplified the issues which had been cumbersome and awkward. The decision required that in all criminal prosecutions the defendant would have the right to counsel regardless of his ability to pay during the trial stage.

Escobedo v. Illinois [8]

To this point the right to counsel issue has been limited to discussion involving the defendant's rights during the trial process. The right to counsel rule, however, did not extend to questioning by police prior to the trial stages. In 1964, Escobedo v. Illinois was decided by the Supreme Court. In this particular case, Escobedo had been charged with the murder of his brother-in-law. Police arrested Escobedo and interrogated him for some two and a half hours. Escobedo made no statement, and was finally released on a writ of habeas corpus filed by his attorney. Some eleven days later, an informer, who was also involved in the crime, indicated that Escobedo was responsible for the killing. He was then arrested again and interrogated by police. His attorney was aware of the interrogation, and traveled to the police station in an

Daniel Escobedo with his attorney in court in Chicago. Courtesy Wide World Photos.

attempt to assist his client. He requested to see Escobedo, and was denied this request on several occasions. After a lengthy interrogation, and over the objections of his attorney, Escobedo confessed to his involvement and admitted his guilt. The evidence that resulted from the interrogation was entered at the trial and he was consequently convicted. Upon appeal to the Supreme Court, the Court reversed the decision, stating that the right to counsel must be extended to the accusatory stage. The Court stated: "When the crime has focused on a particular suspect, the suspect has been taken into police custody, the police carry out a process of interrogation which results in incriminating statements by the accused, the suspect has been denied an opportunity to consult with his lawyer and not effectively warned of his absolute right to remain silent, then the accused has been denied the assistance of counsel as provided by the Sixth Amendment." As a result of this decision, the right to counsel was extended to the accusatory stage. It was clearly stated that police, before interrogating suspects who had been accused of criminal activity, must be careful to protect the defendants' right to counsel. They must effectively warn any defendant of his right to remain silent; if he requests to see his attorney, then that request must be granted prior to any interrogation.

People v. Dorado[9]

The People v. Dorado case was a California case dealing with a defendant who had been sentenced to life in San Quentin for murder. While in prison, Dorado was charged with killing a fellow inmate. Specific evidence (his abandoned blood-soaked clothing was found, along with other evidence) connected Dorado to the crime. He was brought to the warden's office, where he was interrogated. He was not informed of his right to counsel or given the opportunity to seek the services of counsel. Despite the defendant's claim of coercion, the trial judge found that he had freely and voluntarily admitted to the killing. Dorado appealed his case to the Supreme Court of California, where the case was reversed. The court extended the Escobedo rule to the following areas: 1. The defendant has the right to counsel at all stages of the criminal procedures where he is an accused. 2. His right to counsel should not depend upon a request. 3. There can be no waiver of the right to counsel unless the defendant is informed of it, and the same is true of his absolute right to remain silent. The court made it very clear that at the accusatory stage, the defendant has to be informed of his right to remain silent and of his right to effective counsel.

Miranda v. Arizona[10]

The ultimate decision on the right to counsel in the United States occurred in 1966 in Miranda v. Arizona. This was a rather complex issue of dealing with more than the Sixth Amendment right to counsel; it also included the Fifth Amendment right against self-incrimination. In the Miranda case, the police arrested the defendant at his home and transported him to the Phoenix police station. He was there identified by the complaining witness, and the police then took him to an interrogation room. There he was questioned by two police officers. (The officers admitted at the trial that Miranda was not advised that he had a right to have an attorney present). Two hours later, the officers emerged from the interrogation room with a written confession signed by Miranda. At the top of the statement was a typed paragraph stating that the confession was made voluntarily, without threats or promises of immunity and "with full knowledge of my legal rights, understanding any statement I make may be used against me." One of the officers testified that he read the paragraph to Miranda. Apparently, however, he did not do so until after Miranda had made a spoken confession. At the trial, the written confession was admitted as evidence over the objection of the defense counsel, and the officer testified to the prior oral confession made by Miranda during the interrogation. Miranda was found guilty of kidnapping and rape. On appeal, the Supreme Court of the United States reversed the decision, stating that both the Fifth and Sixth amendments of the United States Constitution had been violated. As a result of the opinion of the court, the now established Miranda rule became a requirment for police, who must now advise accused persons whom they wish to interview regarding their involvement in criminal activities. The specific warning is as follows: 1. You have the right to remain silent. 2. Anything you say can and will be used against you in a court of law. 3. You have the right to a lawyer and have him present while you are being questioned. 4. If you cannot afford to hire a lawyer one will be appointed to represent you before any questioning, if you wish one.

The above warnings, now required by the Supreme Court of the United States, are very explicit, and the method by which the admonishment must be given is clearly defined. As seen, Miranda was given the opportunity to know his rights by reading a statement on a standard confession form. The problem was that he was not informed of his constitutional rights prior to being interrogated. The Supreme Court challenged this procedure, stating that prior to asking an accused incriminating statements, police must give the Miranda warning. The court went beyond the point of simply requiring that the warning be given; they also stated that after this is done, and prior to securing the waiver on the part of the defendant, the defendant has to understand the specific rights that had been explained to him. In other words, it was more than just a requirement that he be informed of his rights; prior to him waiving his rights and then freely talking to police, he must thoroughly understand each of the rights that has been explained to him.

Specific Rules Established

Let's examine the specific rules that were established in the Miranda decision, and what the effects of those rules were on police conducting interrogations of accused individuals.

1. *Informing the suspect of his right to remain silent.* Prior to actual questioning of an accused regarding his involvement in a criminal activitity, he must be informed that he has the right to remain silent. It cannot be assumed that he already possesses this knowledge; therefore the statement is required of all individuals regardless of their background.

2. *Explanation that what is said can be used against him.* In the words of the court, "The warning of the right to remain silent must be accompanied by the explanation that anything said can and will be used against an individual in court." The purpose of this admonition is to fully inform the accused that if he does elect to remain silent, the police will try to obtain statements or any other bits of information which can be used as evidence against him in a court of law.

3. *Informing him of his right to presence of counsel.* Again, quoting the court, "Accordingly we hold that an individual held for interrogation must be clearly informed that he has the right to consult with a lawyer and to have a lawyer with him during the interrogation under the system for protecting the privleged." The court felt very strongly that a person could not effectively be aware of his constitutional rights unless he had counsel present with him during any interrogation or interview. The Sixth Amendment held that the accusatory stage of the preceedings is as important as any other stage, due to the effects of a confession and the evidential effects of such a confession at a subsequent trial. The court was concerned that the majority of accused individuals would not fully understand the effects of a confession, and in some cases may not know that they are actually confessing to a crime. By having an attorney present during this particular stage of the proceedings, they would be more informed of the legal involvement with respect to the confession. The court also extended the warning to include the defendant's right to be represented by counsel even though he cannot afford it. The court would be required to appoint counsel and the interrogation could not commence until such time as the counsel had been appointed for the defendant in those cases where he was unable to financially afford hiring his own legal advisor.

4. The last issue that the Supreme Court discussed was the right of the accused to stop interrogation at any point that he so desired; "once the warnings have been given a subsequent procedure is clear if the individual indicates in any manner, at any time prior to or during a questioning that he wishes to remain silent, the interrogation must cease." Very clearly, the defendant may stop an interrogation at any time he desires. Once he has advised the police or has indicated in any way that he wishes the questioning to cease, any subsequent information given to the police inadmissable in a court of law.

MIRANDA WARNING
1. YOU HAVE THE RIGHT TO REMAIN SILENT.
2. IF YOU GIVE UP THE RIGHT TO REMAIN SILENT, ANYTHING YOU SAY CAN AND WILL BE USED AGAINST YOU IN A COURT OF LAW.
3. YOU HAVE THE RIGHT TO SPEAK WITH AN ATTORNEY AND TO HAVE THE ATTORNEY PRESENT DURING QUESTIONING.
4. IF YOU SO DESIRE AND CANNOT AFFORD ONE, AN AT-TORNEY WILL BE APPOINTED FOR YOU WITHOUT CHARGE BEFORE QUESTIONING.

WAIVER
1. DO YOU UNDERSTAND EACH OF THESE RIGHTS I HAVE READ TO YOU?
2. HAVING THESE RIGHTS IN MIND, DO YOU WISH TO GIVE UP YOUR RIGHTS AS I HAVE EXPLAINED TO YOU AND TALK TO ME NOW?

When a Miranda Warning is Required

We have been discussing the specific Miranda warning and what is required by police in effectively informing a defendant of his constitutional rights. Little discussion has been given as to what particular time the police must inform a defendant of those rights. The Miranda warning is given when the accused has been placed in police custody, or when there is enough evidence to indicate to a reasonable person that the defendant has committed a particular offense. Court decisions have stated that at the time a suspect becomes an accused, before questioning, the police must have informed him of his constitutional rights. We must at this point distinguish between the accusatory stage and the investigatory stage. During the investigatory stage, police would not be required to advise individuals who they are interviewing of their Miranda rights. At this stage, it is no more than an inquiry into a person's general involvement or lack of involvement in a criminal prosecution. The police do not have a specific individual in mind who they think is responsible for an offense; they are merely attempting to eliminate suspects, as well as focus in on the most likely individuals. When a suspect is taken into custody for the purpose of being charged with a crime, this becomes the critical element which triggers the necessity for warning against self-incrimination.

Effects of Miranda Violations by Police

Before we leave discussion of the Miranda decision, we must emphasize the importance of fully satisfying the requirements stipulated by the court. The simple rule is that if a person had not adequately been informed of his Miranda rights, or if the accused elects to assert his constitutional protections provided by the Miranda decision, then any subsequent statement or confessions given to police would be held inadmissable. This requirement was clearly stated in the Warden v. Williams Case in 1977. This case dealt with an individual who was charged with murdering a 10-year-old girl in Des Moines, Iowa. The suspect turned himself in to police in a city some 160 miles away from Des Moines. He was given the Miranda warning at the time of arrest, and again shortly thereafter upon arraignment. He had attorneys both in the city where he was arrested and in Des Moines. It was agreed that the defendant would not be questioned by police, who were to drive him back to Des Moines. Nonetheless, during the trip the police indicated to Williams that the girl's body, which had not been found, was entitled to a Christian burial, and that they should stop and locate it on the way, rather than waiting until morning and trying to come back after a snow storm to search for it. This information was presented during the trial, over the objections of the defense counsel. Williams was convicted, and the case was appealed to the Supreme Court of the United States. The Court reversed the conviction, stating that the defendant had not waived his right to counsel during the journey back to Des Moines, and that evidence regarding any statements leading to the discovery of the girl's body should have been suppressed. The Supreme Court unequivocally stated that it does not consider how guilty a person might be; the fact is that his constitutional protections are far more important, and that the police must be discouraged from soliciting incriminating statements when an accused has asserted his constitutional rights.

As can be seen from reviewing the decisions from Powell to Miranda, the protections against unreasonable questioning by police must be safeguarded at the expense of allowing an accused person to go free because of these violations. From the extension of the right to counsel at the trial stage to the accusatory stage, the courts have established a very clear interpretation of the meaning of the Fifth and Sixth amendments. The interrogation of an accused individual with the presence of counsel, if it is desired, and the assertion of the right to remain silent are protections that cannot be violated.

Production and Confrontation of Witnesses

"In all Criminal Prosecution, the accused shall enjoy the right . . . to be confronted with the witnesses against him; to have compulsory process for obtaining witnesses in his favor . . . ." This protection, found in the Sixth Amendment, is extremely fundamental to the defendant in receiving a fair and impartial trial. If the accused were not able to call witnesses in his behalf, then the criminal prosecution would be one-sided in favor of the prosecutor. Penal Code Section 686 also provides for the defendant's rights; the statute reads that in a criminal action, the defendant is entitled to produce witnesses on his behalf, and to be confronted with the witnesses against him, in the presence of the court. This right is so fundamental that there has been little problem in securing the defendant's protection. Our legal system has established an unquestionable procedure in providing for the confrontation of witnesses, as well as for providing a method for obtaining witnesses, at the request of the defendant, to testify in his behalf during a criminal prosecution.

Subpoena

The subpoena is the instrument that is used to compel the attendance of a witness at a criminal prosecution. The defendant need only inform the court of the names and addresses of those persons who he feels are material to his case. The court will then compel the constable, marshal, or other court officer to serve the subpoena at no charge to the defendant. Once a person has been served with a subpoena then he is required under the law, subject to a fine and/or imprisonment, to attend and testify as required by the defendant. This provision then ensures that the defendant will have accessible all pertinent information to aid in establishing his innocence. The only exception to the subpoena requirement is provided in statutory form; Penal Code Section 686, paragraph 3, provides for exceptions to the witness confrontation in three situations: 1. When a witness has previously been examined with an opportunity for cross-examination. 2. When the witness has died. 3. When the witness cannot, with due deligence, be found within the state.

Unless these exceptions apply to the witness confrontation requirement, then it can be assumed that the witnesses will be required to attend and testify in behalf of the defendant. In addition, the defendant will be allowed to confront those witnesses against him, and can request their testimony for the purpose of examination and cross-examination.

SUMMARY

In this chapter we have discussed the fundamental rights of the defendant in a criminal prosecution. We paid particular attention to the defendant's right to a speedy and public trial, and discussed in detail the requirements for ensuring that the defendant receive those rights. The defendant, as well as the public, have individual rights to a public trial; not only does the defendant have this right, but the public has a right to know the outcome of a criminal prosecution.

The interpretation of right to counsel in the United States has been a slow and methodical process. Even though the Sixth Amendment to Bill of Rights specifically authorizes the defendant's right to be represented by counsel, the full interpretation of that right did not come into focus until 1966 with Miranda v. Arizona. The major cases which brought about the specific right to counsel policy in the United States, as well as in California were discussed. A distinction was made between the right to counsel at the trial stage and the right to counsel at the accusatory stage. The specific requirements under Miranda v. Arizona were listed, along with an indication of when police are required to inform a defendant of his constitutional rights.

DISCUSSION QUESTIONS

1. Identify the five major constitutional protections of an accused and discuss their significance.

2. Develop the right to counsel in the U.S. and California, making specific reference to case decisions.

3. When must a police officer deliver the Miranda warning? What are the specific warnings?

REFERENCES

1. California Penal Code, Section 1382.

2. California Penal Code, Section 1382 has additional provisions for cases being brought to trial in Superior Court. For further information the student should refer to this section for exact wordage.

3. U.S. Constitution, Amendment 6; California Constitution, Article 1, 13; California Penal Code, Section 686.

4. 287 U.S. 45, 53 S.Ct. 55, 77 L.Ed. 158 (1932).

5.   304 U.S. 458, 58 S. Ct. 1019, 82 L. Ed. 1461 (1938).

6.   316 U.S. 455, 62 S. Ct. 1252, 86 L. Ed. 1595 (1942).

7.   372 U.S. 335, 83 S. Ct. 792, 9 L. Ed. 799 (1963).

8.   378 U.S. 478, 84 S. Ct. 1758, 12 L. Ed. 2d 977 (1964).

9.   62 Cal. 2d 338, 42 Cal. Rptr. 169, 398 P. 2d 361 (1965).

10.   384 U.S. 436, 86 S. Ct. 1602, 16 L. Ed. 2d 694 (1966).

3

Police Function
and Process

CHAPTER OBJECTIVES

Upon reading this chapter, the student will be able to:

1. List and discuss the five major roles of the police.
2. Define general police powers and compare them with citizens' powers.
3. Define authority to stop and question citizens.
4. Define probable cause as it relates to infringing on the constitutional rights of a citizen.
5. List and compare the specific laws of arrest for private citizens and police officers.
6. List when an arrest may be made.
7. Define and discuss search and arrest warrants and the specific procedure for their issuance.
8. Define and discuss the laws relating to fresh pursuit and identify the procedure for pursuing across a state line.
9. Describe extradition procedures from the time the person leaves the state until he is returned for trial.

In this chapter we will be discussing the major responsibilities of the police as they relate to the administration of justice in California. We will introduce their role in the system and discuss their major responsibilities.   We will analyze in detail police powers of identification, apprehension and incarceration of suspects involved in criminal activity in the state of California.   Also included in this chapter will be the discretionary powers of police officers, the responsibility of arrestees, the Uniform Fresh Pursuit Act, and extradition procedures for both international and interstate situations.

POLICE ROLE IN THE SYSTEM

Traditionally there have been several major roles that police agencies, both nationally and in the state of California, have identified as priorities in job functions.   The more common roles will be identified and briefly discussed:

1. *Prevention of Crime.*   The saying, "An ounce of prevention is worth a pound of cure," is certainly true in relation to police responsibility in the administration of justice.   Through their visibility, (operating in plainly marked patrol vehicles, wearing distinguishable uniforms) police have been an unquestionable deterrent in the prevention of crime.   Through a familiarity with his beat and its hotspots, and through an awareness of any unrest occurring in his area, an officer can effectively help to prevent crime.   These are a few of the techniques utilized by modern day law enforcement people in preventing crime in their districts.

2. *Protection of Lives and Property.*   On the sides of many patrol cars driving on the streets of California today, the motto, "To Protect and To Serve," can be seen very often.   One of the main functions of the police in the criminal justice system today is to protect the lives and property of the citizens which they serve.   It has been said that law enforcement serves as a barrier between the law-abiding citizens of the community and those who wish to be destructive.   The citizens of the community expect the police to protect them from criminals and their illegal activity.

3. *Discovery of Criminal Activity.*   The police are responsible for discovering criminal activity as soon as possible after its occurrence in order to deter continued criminal conduct.   Prompt discovery of criminal behavior aids in the successful suppression, identification, apprehension, and incarceration of those responsible for the commission of crimes.   Modern-day techniques such as electronics, alarm systems, communication systems, and specialized patrol techniques aid in the discovery of criminal activity much faster than in days past.

4. *Suppression of Crime.* Once the crime has been discovered, law enforcement's role is not over. Suppression of crime is becoming more and more important to the police role as it is defined today. Understanding deviant behavior of criminals and involvement in rehabilitation programs in the community all aid in the suppression of crime in the community. Being aware of problem spots in the community, recommending changes to increase security, and discouraging further

Law Enforcement Code of Ethics. International Assn. of Police Chiefs.

Law Enforcement Code of Ethics

As a Law Enforcement Officer, my fundamental duty is to serve mankind; to safeguard lives and property; to protect the innocent against deception, the weak against oppression or intimidation, and the peaceful against violence or disorder; and to respect the Constitutional rights of all men to liberty, equality and justice.

I will keep my private life unsullied as an example to all; maintain courageous calm in the face of danger, scorn, or ridicule; develop self-restraint; and be constantly mindful of the welfare of others. Honest in thought and deed in both my personal and official life, I will be exemplary in obeying the laws of the land and the regulations of my department. Whatever I see or hear of a confidential nature or that is confided to me in my official capacity will be kept ever secret unless revelation is necessary in the performance of my duty.

I will never act officiously or permit personal feelings, prejudices, animosities or friendships to influence my decisions. With no compromise for crime and with relentless prosecution of criminals, I will enforce the law courteously and appropriately without fear or favor, malice or ill will, never employing unnecessary force or violence and never accepting gratuities.

I recognize the badge of my office as a symbol of public faith, and I accept it as a public trust to be held so long as I am true to the ethics of the police service. I will constantly strive to achieve these objectives and ideals, dedicating myself before God to my chosen profession . . . law enforcement.

criminal behavior also are important functions of law enforcement in the suppression of crime.

5. *Identification, Apprehension and Incarceration of Suspects.* The law enforcement officer in the state of California spends a great deal of time learning the methodolgy of identifying, apprehending, and incarcerating suspects who are involved in criminal activity. Through a commitment to professionalism and advanced training, police officers are learning new techniques in the apprehension and conviction of those individuals responsible for criminal activity. A great deal of specialization has occurred in law enforcement over the years because of the complicated process of identifying and apprehending suspects. Knowing methods of operation, the specific laws relating to crimes, and techniques for apprehending are but a few of the requirements that are necessary for law enforcement to be effective in a community.

POLICE POWERS DEFINED

In the Anglo-Saxon culture in England a thousand years ago, every able-bodied freeman was a policeman. From that era until today, the police have historically developed clear definitions of what the powers of police officers should be. In California the local law enforcement agencies receive their authority from the state constitution, state statutes, and specific county and city ordinances. Since the state and local governments authorize the police to perform specific functions within their jurisdictions, law enforcement officers are able to perform only those functions that have been granted to them. In other words, unless there is a specific authorization to perform certain duties and to use certain powers, police officers have no more authority and no more power than any other citizen in the community in which he serves. The actual powers which are granted to police officers are basically covered in the Penal Code, commencing with chapters four and five, which state the primary powers which police are granted to arrest citizens for alledged criminal offenses. Also in the Penal Code are statutes which deal with the jurisdiction of police officers in the performance of their duties and the types of responsibilities with which they are inpowered. The most significant authority granted to police officers allows limited interference with constitutional protections such as rights to freedom and other civil liberties. Because of the flexibility contained in the penal provisions, the judicial branch of government has helped to determine the specific powers which police officers possess today. An example of this interpretation is explicitly demonstrated in the area of search and seizure; the courts have authorized police officers to conduct searches and seizures of persons and their property only in specific, clearly articulated circumstances.

In this section we will discuss the powers of the police with respect to the initial detention of a citizen through to an actual arrest. Also discussed will be the responsibilities of private citizens, their duties, and their powers in regulating the conduct of their fellow citizens.

Police Officer Defined

Penal Code Section 830 defines the police officer in general terms. In effect, Section 830 states that any person who comes within the provisions of several sections, beginning with 830.1 of the Penal Code, is defined as a peace officer in the state of California. We will see that there are police officers who have what is considered to be general police officer powers, and who perform functions dealing with the total process of the administration of justice; there are also those who have very restricted responsibilities, and their functions deal primarily with the specific charge that they have been given by the various statutes within the state of California.

Because of the importance of 830.1 of the Penal Code, it is reprinted in its entirety below so that the reader can understand the general classification of the police officer in the state of California, and the authority of that police officer as it extends to any place in the state:

> Any sheriff, undersheriff, or deputy sheriff, regularly employed and paid as such, of a county, and policeman of a city, any policeman of a district authorized by a statute to maintain a police department, any marshal or deputy marshal of any municipal court, . . . any constable or deputy constable, regularly employed and paid as such of a judicial district, or an inspector or investigator who is regularly employed and paid as such in the office of the district attorney is a police officer . . . ."

The group of peace officers contained in the above section are categorized as the peace officers having general powers in the jurisdiction for which they are employed. The duties and powers of police officers in this category include the enforcement of all laws within the jurisdiction for which the officer is employed, be it whether a citizen is committing a traffic violation, a penal code violation, or a specific subject area violation, (such as Alcholic Beverage Control Laws, Department of Motor Vehicle Laws, or Health and Safety Laws). The Police Officer has the duty and responsibility to take what appropriate action is necessary to enforce the law. Police Officers in other categories have what is termed "limited jurisdiction," and are concerned with enforcing certain subject area laws with respect to the codes and statutes which they have been hired to enforce. There are in excess of forty-one specific categories of peace officers having limited powers and acting within specific jurisdictions. For a detailed examination of the categories, the reader should turn to the Penal Code, beginning with

Section 830.2 and ending with 830.12. Some of the categories of police officers are familiar to most citizens of the state of California, whereas there are other categories for which there is very little familiarity. Some of the better known categories of special interest law enforcement personnel are as follows: 1. the California Highway Patrol, 2. the California State Police, 3. Alcoholic Beverage Control Agents, 4. Fish and Game Wardens, 5. Police Officers of Regional Park Districts, 6. State Fire Marshall, 7. University, State and Community College Police Officers, 8. Probation and Correctional Officers.

There are several categories of "police officers" that have peace officer powers in the performance of the duties of their respective employments. Some of the examples of this group are: 1. Sergeant at Arms of each house of the legislature, 2. Certain persons working for a cemetery district, 3. harbor policeman, 4. special officers of the Department of Airports, 5. certain persons employed by the Department of Transportation.

As indicated, these are only a few of the categories of police officers that are authorized to perform police officer duties in the state of California. For a more detailed examination, the Penal Code Sections indicated above should be reviewed.

Jurisdiction

The authority granted to police officers is derived from the jurisdictions which employ them. The peace officers having general status have that status while performing any duties required of them in the jurisdiction which by they are employed. In addition to this jurisdictional authority, the authority of peace officers is extended to any place in the state of California when one of three specific justifications arise: Penal Code Section 830.1 lists the circumstances under which jurisdiction is extended.

(a) "As to any public offense committed or which there is probable cause to believe has been committed within the political subdivision which employs him." In other words, if a crime has been committed in the city of Los Angeles, then a Los Angeles police officer could travel anywhere in the state of California to apprehend the offender. If a police officer is investigating a crime which was committed in his political jurisdiction, and is required to travel into another city or county to apprehend such an offender, then he would be acting with the same authority granted to him within the city or county which employs him. The police officer, under this condition, would have the same peace officer powers as anyone else in the state of California.

(b) "Where he has the prior consent of the chief of police or person authorized by him to give such consent, if the place is within a city or of the sheriff, or person authorized by him to give such consent, if the place is within a county." If the police officer has the prior consent of the Chief or Sheriff, or another person having the authority to give the consent, then the officer of another jurisdiction would have the same powers as the law enforcement agency which he has entered to perform his duties. There are two important points, resulting from People v. Blake [1] that need to be discussed. First, there is no requirement that the consent be in writing or evidenced in any particular manner. In other words, an informal consent is effective for the purposes of granting police officer powers outside of their jurisdictions. Secondly, the purpose of Section 830.1, subdivision B, is to make sure that a peace officer of one geographical area does not invade a different area without the knowledge and consent of a sheriff or police chief of the latter area. It does not require that where the officer is acting jointly with the sheriff's officers, he must inform wrong-doers that he has the sheriff's consent. Most counties have developed specific policies for granting permission to other law enforcement agencies to enter their jurisdiction for the purpose of performing police functions not otherwise authorized by the Penal Code. For example, the Chief of Police of Los Angeles has designated certain representatives to grant peace officers status to outside agencies. A twenty-four-hour telephone number is available for this purpose. The duration of and the granting of authority will depend upon the information given, and the needs of the officers requesting the permission for peace officer status.

(c) "As to any public offense committed or which there is probable cause to believe has been committed in his presence, and with respect to which there is immediate danger to person or property, or of the escape of the perpetrator such offense."

A police officer, upon witnessing an offense in which there is immediate danger to persons or property, or in which there is danger of the escape of the perpetrator has jurisdiction even though the crime occurred outside his regular jurisdiction. In order to have police officer status, it is only necessary that one of the requirements need be found as described above.

All other catagories of police officers in the state of California will have police officer status only within the jurisdiction which employs them, and only for the purpose for which they have been hired. If they were to leave their jurisdiction then they would act as private citizens with respect to any powers of arrest, etc., except in the three circumstances cited above.

AUTHORITY TO STOP AND QUESTION

The Fourth Amendment prohibits unreasonable searches and seizures. The courts have held that when individuals are stopped for investigation by a peace officer, a seizure has occurred. As a result, there must be a reasonable basis for that seizure. The Fourth Amendment attempts to strike a balance between the individual's right of privacy, and the legitimate need of law enforcement to conduct brief investigations of criminal conduct without the necessity of making an arrest. The laws of stop and question are designed to strike a balance. It must be remembered that a police officer is unable to perform any acts which would restrict the movements of the citizens of the state of California unless there is specific authorization in the law to do so. The courts, through interpretation of various amendments to the constitution and statutes, have extended the definitions of this activity. But unless there is some authorization, police officers are prohibited from interfering with the freedoms exercised by citizens which are contained in the constitution and other provisions.

The following discussion regarding police officers' authority to stop citizens will be based on the mandatory cooperation of those citizens whom the police officers have stopped. (In other words, if a police officer stopped a citizen to carry on an unofficial conversation, the police officer would be acting in the same capacity as any other citizen. It is the situation where the citizen does not wish to converse with the police officer, and the officer demands cooperation that this discussion examines.) Generally speaking, an officer may stop a citizen for an investigation of a crime whenever such a course is necessary for the officer to discharge his duty. There are no hard and fast rules as to what makes stopping a citizen necessary. There are three requirements however, that must be met:

1. There must be a rational suspicion by the peace officer that some activitiy out of the ordinary is or has been taking place. The officer has no right to stop a person who is merely walking down the street or engaging in some other innocent activity.
2. There must be some factor to connect the person under suspicion to the unusual activity. The mere fact that there has been a report of a burglary would not justify the officers in stopping every person within ten miles of the burglary. General discriptions of individuals suspected of criminal activity, specific characteristics of criminals and their method of operations, and evidence to indicate that the individual has been involved in some criminal activity are examples of what is necessary to satisy the above requirements.
3. There must be some suggestion that the activity is related to a crime. Generally speaking, an officer should be able to explain what crime he suspected or distinguished from a vague suspicion. It is not required that the officer suspect the individual of any specific crime, however.

The courts have held the following factors to be significant in determining whether the officers properly stopped an individual. It should not be assumed that any of these factors, standing alone, necessarily justifies stopping an individual. For example, an individual may not be stopped merely because he is present in a high crime area; that fact, though, taken with other factors, may justify the detention. A report of recent crime in the area, the kind of crime reported, as well as how recently it was reported, will be relevant. Other grounds for stopping or detention would be if: (a). It is nighttime. Generally speaking, the courts allow more latitude in detention at night than in day. (b). The place is known as an area of frequent and current crimes, such as the sale of narcotics. (c). There is information that criminal activity was scheduled to take place, and evidence that suspects associated with the activity are in the area. (d). There is knowledge that the suspect was previously convicted of the suspected crime.

In conclusion, the courts have stressed that in justifying a particular detention, the police officer must be able to point to specific facts, clearly expressed, which, when taken together with rational influences from those facts, reasonably warrant the stop and question.

Once an individual has lawfully been stopped, he may be detained for as long as is reasonably necessary to accomplish the purpose for the stop. If, for example, officers stop a vehicle for equipment failure, they could detain the vehicle long enough to issue a citation. If they detain the vehicle for a longer period, in the absence of other evidence indicating the possible commission of other crimes, no evidence obtained during this period is admissable in court. A recent court decision, People v. McGaughran [2], was decided by the California supreme court. The defendant was stopped for a traffic violation by police officers. The officer who made the stop was suspicious of the defendant's activity and returned to his vehicle to make a check for outstanding warrants. The check lasted approximately ten minutes, and revealed an outstanding burglary warrant for the defendant, and two traffic warrants for the passenger. The defendant was subsequently convicted of the burglary. He appealed his case to the Supreme Court of California, which reversed the case. The court ruled that the defendant's initial detention for the traffic violation was proper. However, the scope of that detention was exceeded when the officer ran the ten minute warrant check. Here the officer ran the warrant check both as a matter of routine and due to the suspicious circumstances of the traffic stop. Since neither the officer nor his partner could justify the detention on specific, describable facts, causing them to reasonably suspect that there was in fact an outstanding warrant for the driver's arrest, they could not detain the driver for any longer than was necessary to issue the traffic citation. The court further stated that the routine warrant check of all traffic detainees, regardless of the presence or absence of suspicious circumstances, is constitutionally unreasonable.

Thus, it is constitutionally permissable for an officer to detain an individual for investigation without probable cause to arrest if the officer has reasonable grounds, based on specific clearly expressed facts, that the detention was necessary in the interest of crime detection and prevention. The officer then can stop the individual and question him only to the extent necessary for the performance of his duties. The longer the detention, the more justification the officer will have to give.

PROCESS OF ARREST

Black's Law Dictionary defines arrest as: "to deprive a person of his liberty by legal authority. Taking under real or assumed authority custody of another for the purpose of holding or detaining him to answer a criminal charge." California Penal Code Section 834 specifically defines arrest; "an arrest is taking a person into custody, in a case and in a manner authorized by law. An arrest being made by a peace officer or by a private person." There are two significant parts to Penal Code Section 834: 1. The taking of a person into custody. 2. In a manner authorized by law.

The arrest is accomplished by placing a person under the actual restraint or control of the person making the arrest, or by the person voluntarily submitting himself to the custody and control of a person making the arrest. In other words, it is not necessary that in order for "custody" to occur that the police officer physically restrain the person to be arrested. The mere submission to authority by a person would satisfy the requirements under the law. In order for the arrest to be completed it is necessary that the person arrested know that he is actually under arrest. In some cases it will be necessary for the police officer or other person making the arrest to actually inform the person of his intention to arrest. If the person to be arrested knows that he is being arrested and that the person making the arrest is in fact doing so, then there would be no formal need for the advisement.[3]

Generally speaking, there are four elements of arrest as contained in Penal Code Section 841. 1. The intent to arrest. 2. The reason for the arrest. 3. The authority to arrest. 4. Actual or constructive restraint.

Intent to Arrest

The officer making the arrest must inform the person of the intent to arrest him. A statement to the effect of "You are under arrest," or, "I intend to arrest you," serves to put the person on notice that he is being arrested.

The Reason for Arrest

If a person is committing, or attempting to commit, a crime, he should be aware of his wrongdoings. However, as a matter of courtesy and fair play, he should be told of the cause of the arrest, if he asks. Police officers are under no legal obligation to inform the person who they are arresting of the specific charges against him. However, as indicated above, it is common courtesy that police officers specifically inform the accused of the reason why he is being arrested. There are many occasions when a person may not actually understand why he is being arrested and legitimately wants to know.

Authority to Arrest

Normally speaking, when a person is engaged in a crime, or is attempting to commit a crime, he should be aware that he might be arrested; hence it is neither important, nor is it required, that he be informed that an arresting officer has the authority to do so. An officer in complete uniform, no matter what the circumstances, would automatically display his authority by the mere presence of the uniform. Therefore, he would not be required to specifically inform the person to be arrested that he has such authority. It would be the responsibility of a plain-clothed officer to show his authority by displaying his identification.

Actual or Constructive Restraint

Actual restraint is defined as using physical force in an arrest. Constructive restraint is compelling a person to remain where he does not wish to remain, or to go where he does not wish to go, and may result from the will of the individual, or of both.[4]

Summoning Assistance

As we have seen, the philosophy underlying law and order in this country has been centered around the total population having the responsibility to enforce all laws mandated by society. In support of this philosophy, the Penal Code provides that "any person that is making an arrest may orally summon as many persons as deems necessary to aid him in accomplishing that arrest." [5] It should not be the sole responsibility of one person, or of a few people, to attempt to arrest a suspect or suspects when there are other able-bodied citizens available to accomplish the arrest with the least amount of resistance possible.

There is one other section dealing specifically with police officers requesting assistance in accomplishing arrests. "Every able bodied person over the age of 18 who refuses to assist a lawful request of a police officer in taking or arresting any person or neglecting or refusing to aid and assist in preventing any breech of the peace is guilty of a misdemeanor and can be punished for his refusal."[6] It should be noted that this only applies to police officers making the request. In other words, if a private citizen were to summon the assistance of another person, and that person refused, then there would be no legal consequences that could be attached to the refusal. However, if a person over the age of 18, female or male, is requested by a police officer to assist him in the performance of his duties, and that individual refuses, then the officer could in fact arrest him and that individual could be punished.

Reasonable or Probable Cause

Of the terms which students in law enforcement must understand, the term "reasonable or probable cause" is one of the most crucial. In order for a person to become successful in the field of criminal justice, he is going to have to fully understand the leeways that are granted in the decision-making process, particularly of the laws of arrest. Throughout the statutes, the term "reasonable or probable cause" is

going to be mentioned in relationship to justifying making an arrest. To help understand this concept, it is advisable that the student attempt to categorize probable or reasonable cause in degrees. For the purpose of this discussion, "reasonable" or "probable" cause have the same meaning.

Probable Cause Defined

It is rather difficult to come up with a distinctive definition of probable cause as it is used in the various stages of a criminal justice process. However, one definition seems to be used more often than others; this definition states that probable cause is "such a state of facts as would lead a man of ordinary care and prudence to believe and conscientiously entertain honest and strong suspicion that the person is guilty of a crime."[7] The crux of the definition seems to be that, in analyzing the facts and circumstances which are available to the person making the decision, one concludes that the same decision would be reached by any other person of ordinary care and prudence. In other words, if the facts were available to a group of people of ordinary intelligence who were given the opportunity to vote on what they would do under the circumstances, if the majority would do the same as the police officer did, reasonable or probable cause would have been found. It should be remembered that what an officer does in attempting to justify his actions is based on facts and circumstances which are available to others. He is going to have to articulate those facts and circumstances to the court and jury, and perhaps in a court review later on. If the officer is satisfied that the court and/or jury would act in the same manner as he did, then he should never have any problem with justifying his actions.

Variable Probable Cause

As discussed above, probable cause exists when there are a set of circumstances and facts which can justify the actions of a police officer. What justifies the actions of a police officer in the performance of his duties will depend primarily on the extent to which he was involved. The more restrictions which he places on a citizen, the more justification he needs. Thus the term "variable probable cause" has been identified as a concept which should be taken into consideration. If a peace officer has stopped a citizen for questioning, he would need a certain degree of probable cause to justify his action. This does not imply that he would have the same degree of probable cause as if he were going to arrest that same person. If we were to compare probable cause by placing evidence on a scale, it might be easier to understand; the more evidence that is placed on the scale, the more weight it has, and the more justification the police officer has in depriving a citizen of his constitutional rights. As we go down the list, variable probable cause must be repeatedly shown to justify actions. There must be: 1. Enough probable cause to stop. 2. More probable cause to question and frisk. 3. More probable cause to arrest. 4. More probable cause to book and detain in jail. 5. More probable cause to arraign and set for trial. 6. More probable cause to convict in a court of law.

As can be seen, a police officer could be justified in stopping and questioning a citizen; however, he might not have enough probable cause to go any further. Above all, it must be remembered that any person desiring to satisfy the requirements of probable cause is going to have to substantiate his justifications by setting forth the facts and circumstances which caused him to entertain the strong suspicion that an individual was responsible for some criminal activity. In the final analysis, it will be the tryer of facts who will endorse or deny the feelings of the police officer, or other person, justifying his actions under the term "probable cause."

Accomplishing the Arrest

California Penal Code Section 835 discusses methods of making arrest and the amount of restraint. Before we leave this section, we must also discuss the degree and amount of force that can be used to actually accomplish that arrest. Section 835 states that, "the person arrested may be subject to such restraint as is reasonable for his arrest and detention." This means that any amount necessary to restrain the person may be used, but none greater than what is absolutely necessary. Also, any peace officer who has reasonable cause to believe that the person who, he is arresting has committed a public offense may use reasonable force to effect that arrest, to prevent escape, or to overcome resistance. The officer is under no legal obligation to retreat or desist from his efforts due to the fact that the person being arrested resists or threatens to resist. An officer may use all rights under the self-defense doctrine, and could use any amount of reasonable force to effect the arrest, or to prevent an escape.[8] The law authorizes a police officer to use deadly force in accomplishing an arrest for a felony if it is necessary for him to do so. The law does not allow for police officers to use deadly force in apprehending a person who has committed a misdemeanor.

Duty versus Requirement to Arrest

In the first part of this chapter we discussed the roles and responsibilities of police officers in the criminal justice system. One of those extremely important roles was the apprehension and incarceration of individuals responsible for criminal offenses. This brings us to the discussion of the legal responsibilities of police officers to make an arrest, in addition to those moral and professional obligations that police officers possess. In other words, there are duties and responsibilities that police have which are no different than those of any of the other job functions in any occupation; there are also duties and responsibilities that, if not performed could cause an officer to be responsible for criminal actions. The majority of the laws that police are responsible for enforcing are of the moral and professional obligation categories. There are a few crime situations and various statutes in the state of California that require police to act accordingly; in special situations the officer is legally bound to make an arrest if the crime is committed in his presence, or if some other factors are present which are contained in the specific statutes. These sections and crimes are: 1. Treason Against State of California (Section 37 and 38 of the Penal Code). 2. Gambling (Section 335). 3. Dueling (Section 230). 4. Alcoholic Beverage Control Violations (As stated in 25619 of the Business and Professions Code). 5. Refusing to Receive Arrested Parties Charged with Criminal Offenses (Penal Code Section 142). 6. Refusing to Disperse Rioters (Section 410).

Police Officer and Private Citizen Arrest

California Penal Code, Section 834 states that an arrest can be made by a police officer or by a private citizen. Generally speaking, police officers and private citizens possess the same power in making an arrest. In this section we will discuss the specific authorizations for police officers and private citizens, and distinguish the actual differences between a peace officer making an arrest, and of a private citizen making an arrest.

Arrest by Peace Officers

"A peace officer may make an arrest in obedience to a warrant, or may, pursuant to the authority granted to him by the provisions of Section 4.5 of Title 3 of part 2, without a warrant arrest a person: 1. Whenever he has reasonable cause to believe that the person to be arrested has committed a public offense in his presence. 2. When a person arrested has committed a felony although not in his presence. 3. Whenever he has reasonable cause to believe that the person to be arrested has committed a felony, whether or not a felony has in effect been committed." [9]

Public Offense in his Presence

Penal Code Section 836 subs. 1 has three important phrases: "reasonable cause to believe"; "public offense"; and "in his presence".

Reasonable Cause. In order to justify the arrest, based on reasonable or probable cause, it is necessary that the police officer establish those facts which lead him to believe the person to be arrested is responsible for some criminal activity. For a detailed discussion of reasonable or probable cause, refer back to the section in this chapter dealing with the subject.

Public Offense. Public offense here refers to all crimes committed in the state of California. It should also be noted that this is the only section covering arrests for misdemeanors. Therefore, the only time that a police officer may arrest a person for a misdemeanor is when that misdemeanor has been committed in the police officer's presence. This statement does not include an arrest of a person in obedience to a warrant.

In the Presence of the Officer. A great deal of discussion has been recorded regarding what is meant by, "in his presence." Generally speaking, this term means that the facts ascertained by the police officer in justifying his arrest are gathered through the use of his senses. In People v. Burgess, [10] the court liberally defines the term "presence" as; having reference not merely to physical proximity, but whether the crime was apparent to the officer's senses, including those of hearing and smell; and the public offense may be committed in the officer's presence when his auditory perception is affected by an electronic device." The use of electronic eavesdropping devices has in some cases been authorized by the courts, and would be construed as "in the presence of an officer." The use of a telescope, with which the officer could visually observe the commission of a crime some two-and-a-half miles away, has been determined to be within the officer's presence. Any time that a police officer can smell the commission of a crime, this would be construed to be within the officer's presence.

Misdemeanor Arrests

A police officer may arrest a person for the commission of a misdemeanor based on the probable cause that that individual is responsible for the crime. As long as what the officer senses would cause a reasonable person to conclude that a public offense is being committed, then the courts would agree with the officer's justification.

Since Penal Code 836, subs. 1 is the only section dealing with arrests for misdemeanors, it is necessary to restate the fact that a police officer can only arrest a person for the commission of a misdemeanor in two cases: 1. For a misdemeanor committed in his presence. 2. In obedience to a warrant of arrest.

The only exception to this rule is the result of a vehicle code law that was enacted in 1969 (Vehicle Code Section 40300.5). This section permits an officer to arrest, without a warrant, a person involved in a traffic accident, when the officer has reasonable cause to believe he has been driving under the influence of an intoxicating beverage. This would be the only exception to the misdemeanor arrest rule.

Felony Arrest under Penal Code Section 836, subs. 2

There are two significant phrases under this subsection: 1 "When a person arrested has committed a felony", and, 2 "Although not in his presence". Under this provision there is an absolute requirement that the person who is arrested must have indeed committed a felony. If the person has actually committed the felony, he may be arrested at any place, at any time, with a few exceptions, such as when the defendant is being tried in another court, or for political immunities extended to certain ambassadors, etc. A peace officer may, without a warrant, arrest a person for a felony that has been committed, though not committed in the officer's presence, when a criminal is fleeing from the scene of the crime. Because of the wording in Penal Code Section 836, subs 1 and 836, subs. 3, this section is rarely used. Most arrests for felony offenses would be authorized by subsections 1 and 3.

Felony Arrests under Penal Code Section 836, subs. 3

There are three important phrases contained in subsection 3. They are: 1) "Whenever he has reasonable cause to believe," 2) "the person to be arrested has committed a felony," and 3) "whether or not a felony has in fact been committed." In dealing with the reasonable cause for arrest for commission of a felony, we would again refer back to the section dealing with reasonable or probable cause. The second phrase, means that this section authorizes police officers to arrest for felony offenses only. The most important phrase under Penal Code Section 836.3 discusses whether or not a felony has in fact been committed. If a police officer arrests a person on reasonable cause and discovers, because of information that is obtained at a later date, that a felony was in fact not committed, the police officer would still have acted within the authority granted to him. This subsection protects police officers from criminal and civil litigations as long as they are conducting their activities in a reasonable manner when attempting to execute the arrest of a person for the commission of a felony. As we will see in comparing private citizens' authority to make arrests with police officers' authority to make arrests, the above constitutes a distinct difference; a private citizen does not have this protection. The felony has to in fact have been committed in order for the arrest to be a legitimate arrest.

People v. Ramey

In February of 1976, the Supreme Court of California placed additonal restrictions on police officers in making a warrantless arrest for a felony. The facts of the Ramey case are as follows: police officers, acting on specific information from the victim of a crime, contacted the defendant, Ramey, at his residence. Upon identifying themselves, the police officers entered the residence. Ramey then entered the living room. When the defendant reached behind the bar, one of the officers placed him under arrest. An officer discovered a 45 caliber pistol, and three "lids" of marijuana, in cellophane bags along with other restricted drugs. Defendant Ramey was openly convicted of possession of drugs and other related offenses. He appealed his case to the state Supreme Court, which reversed the conviction, stating that Ramey's arrest, in his residence, as a result of a warrantless arrest, was unconstitutional. The court stated: "The sanctity of a private home is not only guaranteed by the Constitution of the United States and of our own state, but is traditional in our Anglo Saxon Heritage. A man's home is his castle, is and should be, more than an empty phrase," The Supreme Court felt that since there were no emergency conditions existing in this case, the officer should have obtained a warrant from a magistrate to enter Ramey's home for the purposes of arresting him for the felony offense. The court concluded by stating that, "We believe that the 4th amendment prohibits a warrantless entry into a dwelling to arrest in the absence of sufficient justification for the failure to obtain a warrant." The only exception to the above rule is in the case where there are exigent circumstances. The court defined this as an emergency situation requiring swift action to prevent imminent danger to life, serious damage to property, or to forestall the immediate escape of a suspect or the destruction of evidence. [11]

Arrest by Private Citizen

Penal Code Section 837 states that, "A private person may arrest another; 1. For a public offense committed or attempted in his presence. 2. When the person arrested has committed a felony, although not in his presence. 3. When a felony has been in fact committed, and he has reasonable cause for believing the person arrested to have committed it."

Generally speaking, the provisions for private citizens contained in Section 837 are very similar to those for police officers. In analyzing the three subsections of 837, we see, however, that there are some distinct differences which deserve our attention.

In subsection 1, the wording for private citizens is different in that a private citizen, in order to make an arrest for a public offense, must have the crime committed in his presence. Note that the phrase "reasonable cause" is absent for private citizens, where as it is not in the case of police officers. This is the only subsection allowing private citizens to arrest for misdemeanor offenses for private citizens which is substantially the same as peace officers. The only additional wording worth mentioning is that if a public offense is attempted in the presence of a private citizen, than an arrest can be made. Case decisions have supported police officers in making an arrest for an attempted crime, so, from a practical point of view, the two sections do not differ in this respect.

In subsection 2 has wording identical to the peace officer's duties under 836, subs.

In subsection 3 has the most significant difference in comparing private citizens' and peace officers' authority in making the arrests for felonies. There are two significant phrases in 837 subs. 3: 1. "When a felony has in *fact* been committed," and 2."When he has reasonable cause for believing that the person arrested to have committed it." The singularly most important part of this section is that a felony has to have been committed. No matter how good the intentions a private citizen has, even if he strongly believes that a felony has been committed, based on information that is available to him, if it turns out later that a felony had not been committed, then he is subject to criminal and civil liabilities. We saw that if a peace officer was acting under reasonable cause to believe that a felony had been committed, and it turned out that a felony had not been committed, then he was protected under Section 836, subsection 3. This is not the case for a private citizen. It the private citizen believes there is reasonable cause that the person arrested has committed a felony that did in fact occur, then he has some protections under the law. In determining reasonable or probable cause for believing a person to have committed the felony, the same rules would apply as did in the case of a peace officer. As long as the information available to the private citizen would lead a person of ordinary care and prudence to entertain a strong suspicion that that person had committed the crime, then the arrest for probable cause would be legal. It must be emphasized again, however, that in order for the arrest to be legal under section 837 subsection 3, the felony has to, in fact have been committed.

Peace Officer versus Private Citizen Arrest Powers

In comparing the general authorities contained in Sections 836 and 837 for arresting citizens by both peace officers and private citizens, we see that there are basically two distinct differences contained in the sections; only a peace officer can arrest a person in obedience to a warrant for arrest, and only a peace officer can arrest a person for a felony when he has reasonable cause to believe that the person has committed that felony, whether or not a felony has in fact been committed.

In almost all other situations, the private citizen would have fundamentally the same powers of arrest as a peace officer. The private citizen can also use the same amount of force in accomplishing an arrest as that of a peace officer.

Arrests When Made

California Penal Code, Section 840 states that "An arrest for the commission of a felony may be made on any day and at any time of the day or night. An arrest for a commission of a misdemeanor or an infraction cannot be made between the hours of 10:00 p.m. of any day and 6:00 a.m. of the succeeding day unless: 1. The arrest is made without a warrant pursuant to Section 836 or 837. 2. The arrest is made in a public place. 3. The arrest is made when the person is in custody pursuant to another lawful arrest. 4. The arrest is made purusant to a warrant which, for good cause shown, directs that it may be served at any time of the day or night."

This section distinguishes when felony and misdemeanor arrests may be made, and also makes a distinction between warrant arrests and on view arrests. To help the reader understand the provisions of section 840, they will be discussed separately according to when an arrest may be made for a felony, and when an arrest may be made for a misdemeanor.

Felony

An arrest for a felony may be made at any time of the day or night, or any place, with the exception of the Ramey Rule.

Misdemeanor

An arrest for the commission of a misdemeanor may be made at any time of the day or night, or in any place, providing the crime occurred in the presence of the person making the arrest. Otherwise the following conditions for warrants of arrest should be met: The arrest is to be made 1. between the hours of 6:00 a.m. and 10:00 p.m., or 2. The arrest is to be made in a public place, or 3. The arrest can be made when the person is already in custody, pursuant to another lawful arrest, or 4. the arrest is pursuant to a nighttime endorsement.

Basically, Section 840 of the California Penal Code states that, unless the arrest is an on view arrest for a misdemeanor offense, the circumstances are not serious enough to justify making the arrest in the privacy of the person's home between the hours of 10:00 p.m. and 6:00 a.m. The only exception, as indicated above, is when the crime is committed in the presence of the person making the arrest.

Warrants of Arrest

Through Penal Code Section 840 and through various case decisions, such as *People* v. *Ramey*, we have seen that the appellate courts of California place a high degree of importance on police officers obtaining a warrant for arrest whenever possible. The courts prefer that a magistrate review the circumstances for an officer making an arrest whenever possible. In the next section we will discuss the requirements for an arrest in obedience to a warrant as well as the specific provisions for the warrant itself and for obtaining a warrant.

Since the only time a person can be arrested for a misdemeanor is when the crime occurs in the presence of the arresting person, a large percentage of the arrests will be in obedience to a warrant. Oftentimes, even though a police officer could make an arrest under Section 836, subs. 3 of the California Penal Code for a felony not committed in his presence, he will often secure the support of the district attorney and courts through the obtaining of a warrant.

Procedure

Normally the first step in obtaining a warrant is to complete the necessary investigation and to establish the specific facts which would justify the issuance of a warrant in the minds of the prosecutor and the judge. Upon consulting with the prosecutor, the police officer will then request that a warrant be issued. The prosecutor then files an accusatory pleading in the form of a criminal complaint with the court. At the same time he requests that a warrant of arrest be issued against the accused. A warrant of arrest is a written order signed by a magistrate directed to a police officer, commanding him to arrest a person.[12] Since a warrant is a written order that is signed by the magistrate, the officer is acting merely as an agent of the court, and is following out the orders of the court in making the arrest of the person whose description is contained in the written order itself. For this reason a warrant of arrest assures the highest degree of protection on the part of the officer, and in the majority of cases, an arrest in obedience to a warrant would prohibit any subsequent civil litigations against the officers for faults or mistakes regarding the warrant.

California Penal Code, Section 813 also provides that a Superior Court judge be required to issue the warrant as requested once he is satisfied from the complaint that the offense has been committed and that there are reasonable grounds to believe that the defendant committed it. On the other hand, a Superior Court judge must concur with the district attorney before the warrant will be issued.

Form of a Warrant

In order for a warrant to be "valid upon its face," specific information has to be contained in the warrant. The following information is critical in this respect:

1. Name of the Defendant. If the defendant's name is unknown, it is proper for the warrant to designate the individual by a nickname, alias, or other form of identification. If there is no proper name for the accused, then it is necessary that a complete description be included on the warrant so as to avoid arresting the wrong individual. California has never allowed so-called John Doe warrants; that is, it would be improper for a warrant to be issued without a name or description of the person, a fact which prevents a police officer from serving the warrant on anyone whom he desires. However, as long as there is some type of identification or description of a person, and it is reasonable to assume that the person arrested is the same as the one described on the warrant, then this particular part of the requirement would be satisfied.

2.   Time of Issuance. It is absolutely necessary that the time of issuance of a warrant be included on the face of that warrant. We will find that there is a statute of limitations for all offenses in the state of California. If the statute of limitations expires prior to serving the warrant, then the warrant would be void and no longer legal.

3. City and County where Issued. Warrants can be effectively served anywhere in the state of California. A defendant could conceivably be arrested hundreds of miles away from where the crime occurred and from where a warrant for him was issued. For this reason it is absolutely necessary that the city and county of issuance be included in the warrant so that the defendant may be returned to that jurisdiction for prosecution.

4.   Signature of Issuing Magistrate. The only authorized individual who can issue a warrant is a magistrate. If the signature of the magistrate was not included on the warrant, then the warrant would be void and illegal.

5.   Amount of Bail. The United States Constitution and the California Constitution basically provide that a defendant be allowed to be released upon submitting the proper amount of bail for the appropriate offense.   Because the defendant is innocent until proven guilty, he should have the opportunity to remain free if he is willing to post the amount of bail prescribed on the warrant. A great deal of time could elapse before the arrested person is actually brought before a magistrate and therefore would have to remain in custody until the magistrate sets bail. Having the provision that bail be included on the warrant therefore eliminates the necessity of having the defendant be brought before a magistrate.

In the Justice Court of _____ Judicial District
County of Shasta, State of California

The People of the State of California,   Plaintiff,

vs.

....

....

....

....

Defendant ...

Defendant is to be admitted to bail in the sum of $ ....

....

Judge of the Justice Court of ....

Judicial District County of Shasta, State of California.

Warrant of Arrest
PENAL CODE SECTIONS 814, 1427, & 840

The County of Shasta, The People of the State of California,

To any Peace Officer of said State, or of the County of Shasta:

Information on oath having been this day laid before me, by ....

.... **that the crime of**

....

....

....

....

....

has been committed, and accusing ....

....

thereof, YOU ARE THEREFORE COMMANDED forthwith to arrest the above-named ....

....

and bring .... before me at my office in .... **Judicial District,**

or, in case of my absence or inability to act, before the nearest or most accessible Magistrate in this County.

I direct that the service, under this warrant, may be made by telegraph.

Dated .... this .... day of ....

one thousand nine hundred and ....

WITNESS my hand this .... day of .... A. D., 19..........

....

Judge of said Judicial District

For misdemeanor offenses only: For good cause shown I direct that the arrest, under this warrant may be made at night.

....

Judge of Said Judicial District

I certify that I received the above warrant on the .... day of ...., 19........,

and served the same by arresting the above-named ....

....

hereon .... on the .... day of ...., 19...... ,

and bringing .... into court this .... day of ...., 19........

....

....

....

The said defendant ......, having been brought before me under this warrant declare ....

.... true name .... to be ....

....

and ...he.... hereby committed to the Sheriff of the County of Shasta until ...he.... can be examined on said charge, and ... he .... admitted to bail in the sum of $ ....

.... and stand committed until ...he.... give such bail.

Dated ...., A. D., 19 ......

Judge of said Judicial District

6. The Crime. The defendant has the right to know what he is being arrested for. Therefore, it is essential that the specific crime be included on the face of the warrant so that he can be informed of it by the person making the arrest.

Service of Warrant

As indicated above, the warrant of arrest, when issued in California, can be effectively served anywhere in the state of California. It should be noted that a warrant could not be served outside the state due to the reason that any authority for issuing a warrant outside the state of California must come from the originating state. A police officer is the only person authorized to serve a warrant in the state of California. Even if an officer does not have the warrant in his possession the officer can legally arrest a person under the warrant's authority. If the person arrested requests to see the warrant, then he would have the right to see it within a reasonable amount of time after the arrest. [13]

Abstract Warrant

Once a warrant of arrest has been issued by a judicial district in the state of California, it is permissible to make telegraphic copies or abstracts of that warrant in order to send it anywhere in the state. An abstract or telegraphic copy, in the hands of a peace officer, is as effective as the original warrant itself. The purpose of authorizing an abstract or telegraphic copy of a warrant is to provide a more efficient and effective way of quickly notifying police officers anywhere in the state of California of the existence of a warrant for arrest of a specific person. If a peace officer has reasonable cause to believe that a warrant is in effect, he may contact the agency issuing that warrant to obtain confirmation that the warrant is in effect and is valid. Once this is done, an abstract of that warrant can be sent through a teletype network in a matter of minutes to the agency making the actual arrest. Therefore, the arrest can be consummated in a short period of time.

A proper abstract must contain the following information: 1. The charge (felony or misdemeanor) and the specific offense. 2. Court of issuance. 3. The subject's name, address, and description. 4. The amount of bail. 5. The name of the issuing magistrate. 6. The warrant number.

If a person is arrested in a county other than where the warrant was issued, then it is the responsbility of the arresting officer to inform the defendant of his right to be taken before a magistrate in the county of the arrest. The purpose of this hearing is to determine the legality of the arrest and to ensure that the defendant is informed of his constitutional rights. The accused will then be informed of the time and location for the court dates in the jurisdiction where the crime was committed.

He will be given the opportunity to be released on bail if this has not already been done. If the accused wishes to be immediately released, then he can put up the amount of bail indicated on the warrant. In this case, the jailer or other custodial officer would inform the defendant of the time and location for his next court appearance in the jurisdiction where the offense occurred. The defendant must be given a minimum of ten days after being released on bail to return to the jurisdiction for his court appearance.[14] If the defendant has not posted bail, then the arresting officer must notify the law enforcement agency requesting the arrest; that agency must then take custody of the defendant within five days after the arrest. If the five days elapse, then the defendant could request that the court release him on a writ of habeaus corpus.

The defendant has the option to waive his right to be taken before a magistrate if he is arrested on a warrant outside of the county where the crime occurred. If he signs a waiver indicating his desire not to be taken before the magistrate, then it would be the responsibility of the arresting officer to allow the defendant to be released on bail upon his being booked into jail, or to have the agency requesting the accused be arrested to pick him up within the statutory time.

In the event the warrant is executed in the county for which it is issued, the requirement would simply be that the arrested person be taken before a competent court, either the court issuing the warrant, or another competent court, for the purpose of arraigning him on the charges indicated on the warrant.

Once a warrant has been issued by a competent court it is necessary that the warrant be served as soon as possible. Even though a warrant is in effect until it is served or recalled, it would be improper for an officer to hold the warrant until it is convenient for him to serve it. In one case a police officer kept the warrant until such time he felt the accused was in possession of certain illegal contraband. It was established that the officer had the warrant for several weeks and could have served it on numerous occasions, but neglected to do so until such time that he was assured that the accused had the contraband mentioned. Upon arresting the defendant, the accused was searched as part of the booking procedure, and the evidence was discovered. The officer then rearrested the defendant for the possession of the contraband and attempted to convict him of same in court. The court reversed the case, stating that the evidence was obtained illegally and that the officer should have served the warrant at a more appropriate time.[15]

Bench Warrant

Before we leave the subject of warrants, a distinction should be made between a warrant and a "bench warrant." The bench warrant is simply a warrant that originates from a magistrate, rather than from a police

SUPERIOR COURT OF THE STATE OF ANYSTATE

FOR THE COUNTY OF MYCOUNTY

The People of the State of Anystate)
)
                     Plaintiff,   )   NO.
)
             vs.   )   BENCH WARRANT
)
)
Bill Blaylock   )
                     Defendant.   )
)

DA File # 80 F 257
SO # 80-9118B, 80-9118C

THE PEOPLE OF THE STATE OF ANYSTATE

TO ANY PEACE OFFICER IN THIS STATE:

An Indictment having been found on the ___15th___ day of
___April_____ , 19_80_, in the Superior Court of the State of Anystate,
for the County of Mycounty, charging   Bill Blaylock
with the crime of FELONY, IN TWO COUNTS,   to-wit:
SALE OF HEROIN, in violation of § 11352, Anystate Health and
Safety Code.

YOU ARE THEREFORE COMMANDED FORTHWITH to arrest the above
named defendant and to bring him before this Court to answer said
Indictment, or if the Court be not in session, that you deliver him into
the custody of the Sheriff of the County of Mycounty.

The defendant shall be admitted to bail in the sum of
Five Thousand and no/100 - - - - - - - - - - - - -DOLLARS ($5,000.00).

GIVEN UNDER MY HAND with the seal of said Court affixed this
_15th_day of ___April_____ , 19_80_ .

Hon. John Jones
JUDGE OF THE SUPERIOR COURT

officer or a prosecuting attorney. The magistrate, in order to require the attendance of certain individuals in court, has to have a process whereby he can compel their attendance; a bench warrant serves this purpose. If a defendant refused to appear in court when he had been so ordered, or if a witness who had been subpoenaed failed to appear on the date indicated on the subpoena, then the magistrate would issue his "bench warrant," which would then be served in the same manner as any other warrant. The bench warrant would be given to a peace officer, who would then arrest the person named on the warrant and bring him before the magistrate for the purpose of explaining why he had failed to abide by the order of the court.

Citations in Lieu of Arrest

Several California statutes authorize the issuance of a citation in lieu of taking an arrestee into custody for a misdemeanor or minor infractions. In some cases the officer would not have any other choice, and would have to release the accused with a written notice to appear. A citation is often referred to as a summons, and simply is a written notice to a person suspected of committing an offense; it directs him to appear at a specific time and place to answer for a specific charge. The significance of a citation is that it does not compel the officer to transport the accused to jail. In effect, the accused is released immediately upon arrest, as soon as he promises that he will take care of his obligations by appearing in court when directed to do so. The defendant need only promise to appear by signing his name to the citation.

There are several advantages to the misdemeanor citation procedure. One of the main reasons for issuing a citation, instead of placing an individual in jail, is the cost and time factors. It is extremely costly to engage a police officer and his patrol car for the amount of time necessary to transport an individual to jail; the same holds true for jail custodial people who are responsible for supervising him while he is in the jail facility. The expense involved is astronomical when the total amount is figured in terms of man hours and housing costs. Also the advantage to law enforcement agencies is that the officer has more time to patrol if he issues a citation rather than going through the process of booking the accused. It takes only a few minutes to issue a citation, whereas it could take up to three or four hours to book that same individual into jail. The advantage to the accused is extremely important as well. The defendant is not subjected to any more restrictions on his freedom than is necessary. As soon as he signs the citation he is free to go until such time as he is ordered to appear before the court. He is under no financial strains since he does not have to post bail or hire an attorney to get him out of jail. The only problem with the issuance of a citation is that before a defendant can be released he must sign the citation. Some people have been under the impression that signing the citation is an admission of guilt. The fact that a defendant signs a written notice to appear does not in any way indicate his involvment in a criminal activity. By signing this citation, he is merely agreeing that he will take care of the responsibilities required under the law.

The specific provisions for the issuance of a citation for a misdemeanor offense are contained in Penal Code Section 853.5 and 853.6. They are as follows:

1. The officer upon arresting the accused gives him the opportunity to be taken forthwith to a magistrate. If not:

2. The police officer decides that the accused will take care of his obligation and should be released with the written notice to appear in court.

3. A written notice to appear containing the name and address of the person, the offense charged, and the time and place where such person shall appear in court is prepared.

4. A minimum of five days must be given in order for the defendant to appear in court after his arrest.

5. The officer must order the person to appear before the court having proper jurisdiction.

6. A copy of the written notice to appear shall be given to the defendant along with a copy to the magistrate.

In the event the subject failed to appear in court at the time and date indicated, then a bench warrant would be issued by the magistrate commanding him to be brought before the magistrate without unnecessary delay. In this case the accused would be arrested, booked into jail, and then processed accordingly.

It must be noted that not all persons who are arrested for misdemeanor offenses would be eligible for release with a written notice to appear. Obviously, if the person arrested was so intoxicated that he was a danger to himself or to others, he would not be allowed to be released, but would be placed in jail or some other facility until he had sobered up. There are other examples of offenses and conditions that would prohibit the release of accused persons with a written notice to appear. For specific information the student should read section 853.6 of the California Penal Code.

Duty to Take Accused Before a Magistrate on Arrest Without a Warrant

Penal Code Section 849 states:

When an arrest is made without a warrant by a peace officer or private person, the person arrested, if not otherwise released , shall, without unnecessary delay, be taken before the nearest or most accessable magistrate in the county in which the offense in triable. The complaint stating the charge against the arrested person must be presented to the magistrate. Any peace officer may release from custody, instead of taking such person before a magistrate, any person arrested without a warrant whenever:

1) He is satisfied that there are insufficient grounds for making a criminal complaint against the person arrested.

2) The person arrested was arrested for intoxication only, and no further proceedings are desirable.

3) The person is arrested only for being under the influence of a narcotic drug, or restrictive dangerous drug, and such person is delivered to a facility or a hospital for treatment and no further proceedings are desirable.

4) Any record of arrest of a person released pursuant to paragraphs on entry of subdivision 2 shall include a record of release. Thereafter, such arrest shall not be deemed an arrest, but a detention only.

Subsection a of 849 requires that upon arresting a person for an alleged crime, it is the responsibility of the police officer to take him before a magistrate without unnecessary delay. For the purposes of this statute, this would normally be the next judicial day or would be the next time a magistrate is sitting before the court for the purpose of arraigning persons arrested for criminal offenses. Common practice with most law enforcement agencies is to place a defendant in jail and then, as a normal procedure, to take the accused to court along with other arrested individuals at times which have been set aside for the purpose of arraignments.

Section 849, subs. (b) (1) authorizes police to release a person for a crime for which they have been arrested when the officers are satisfied that there are insufficient grounds for filing a criminal complaint. If the officers acted with reasonable cause and then discovered that their information was inaccurate, this section would allow them to release the accused without any further proceedings.

Section 849, subs. (b) (2) and (3) have to do with being under the influence of alcohol, narcotics, or any other drug. If an officer arrests a person solely for intoxication, and does not wish to prosecute the individual in court, then as soon as this individual is sober the officer could release him without any further action. In the case of narcotics or drugs, if the person is delivered to a proper facility or hospital for treatment and the officer desires not to prosecute, then he could drop the charges without any further action necessary.

As indicated, subsection (c) of 849 states that in the event a person is released under subsection (b) (1) and (b) (2), then the arrest must be deemed as a detention, rather than as an arrest, for all record keeping purposes.

RESPONSIBILITY OF ARRESTEE

It is an established fact that a police officer who peacefully makes a lawful arrest cannot lawfully be resisted. When the arrest is valid, the officer may use reasonable force to effect the arrest, to prevent escape, or to overcome resistance. There is generally no statutory limit on the amount of force that an officer may reasonably use to effect such an arrest.[16]

Section 834 a states that a person who knows that he is being arrested by a police officer has the duty and the responsibility to refrain from using any force or any weapon to resist that arrest. Also, Penal Code Section 148 makes it a crime to willfully resist, delay, or obstruct a police officer in discharging of his duties. A citizen has the duty to submit to the lawful arrest of a police officer. Generally speaking, the statutes mentioned deal with some type of active resistance. For example, a person who goes limp therefore requires the arresting officer to drag or bodily lift and carry him in order to effect the arrest. Although this is a passive action, it could constitute an active delay and obstruction to a lawful arrest.[17] We should distinguish between some types of resistance and mere argument or verbal disagreement with the officer. Arguing with the officer about the validity of an arrest or some other police action is not prohibited under existing California statutes. Obstruction statutes are not intended to make simple interruption or distraction a criminal offense.

It is generally the responsibility of a citizen to go peacefully along with the officer upon arrest. If, however, the police officer uses unlawful force, then it would be justifiable for the private citizen to protect himself. To this point, a private citizen should not use any more force than is necessary to protect his own life. Unless the person being arrested is being physically abused and is attempting to protect himself against the unlawful abuse, it is his responsibility to submit peacefully to the arresting officer, regardless of whether or not the arrest is unlawful. It is the responsibility of the judicial system to decide whether or not the officer was acting improperly or illegally in accomplishing the arrest. If we were to allow arrested persons to analyze the arrest, and make a judgment as to whether or not in his mind the arrest was lawful or not, there could be serious problems between the arrested person and the law enforcement officer. It is therefore in the best interests of the citizen to submit peacefully to ensure that he is not injured; a police officer is equipped and trained to accomplish the arrest and therefore, in all probability, the citizen will end up becoming injured in the arrest process. If the officer is wrong, the citizen will get redress in court. A police officer making an arrest is civilly liable to the arrestee if he employs unreasonable force. California follows the general rule in the United States of holding law enforcement officers personally liable for wrongful acts which have caused personal injury or death. Thus, in one case—in which an officer beat an arrestee while holding him in a helpless position on the ground—both compensatory and punitive damages were properly awarded.[18]

THE UNIFORM FRESH PURSUIT ACT

The Uniform Fresh Pursuit Act was established in 1937 in California. The act is contained in Chapter 5a of the Penal Code, commencing with Section 852. We must remember that in California a police officer has the power of arrest along with other powers, as discussed previously, within his political jurisdiction. The power to arrest extends outside of his political jurisdiction to any area in the state of California whenever the officer is attempting to overtake a person who has escaped, or whenever he is trying to arrest a citizen for an offense that was committed within his jurisdiction. California law cannot authorize a police officer to leave the state of California and still maintain the powers authorized from the state; conversely, the same is true of any peace officer entering from another state into the state of California. An officer would not possess any powers unless they were granted by the state which he enters. For this reason, the Uniform Fresh Pursuit Act was established throughout the United States. It is the responsibility of whatever state an officer enters to authorize that officer to have peace officer powers. All of the states surrounding California have initiated the Uniform Fresh Pursuit Act or something similar to it. Penal Code Section 852.2 states that "Any peace officer of another state, who enters this state in fresh pursuit and continues within this state in fresh pursuit of a person in order to arrest him on the grounds that he has committed a felony in another state, has the same authority to arrest and hold the person in custody, as peace officers of this state having to arrest and hold a person in custody on the ground that he has committed a felony in this state". There are four key requirements to the Uniform Fresh Pursuit Act which need to be clearly defined: "any officer from another state"; "fresh pursuit"; "felony"; and "the same powers of arrest."

The first requirement is that an officer entering California must be a duly sworn police officer of a political subdivision of the state which he is leaving.

When a police officer from another state enters this state in pursuit of a person who committed a felony in his state, the pursuit must be "fresh." *Black's Law Dictionary* defines fresh pursuit as, "a pursuit instituted immediately and with intent to reclaim or recapture after an animal escaped, a thief flying with stolen goods, etc." The intent of this definition is to allow police officers to pursue someone when they are "fresh on the trial" of that individual. It is not necessary that the police officer be in direct sight of the person he is pursuing; he could be only hours behind him, but it is enough that the officer is pursuing him with fresh information. Normally speaking, fresh pursuit will be within a short period of time after the officer has last seen the person he is pursuing.

In order for the officer to have police officer status in California it is absolutely essential that the person he is pursuing have committed a felony. If it is any other type of offense, the officer would cease to have any police officer powers whatsoever, and could be subject to statutory violations that he might have committed once he entered the state. It should be noted that the statute provides that, as long as the felony is in fact a felony in the state where it was committed, then the requirements of the law would be satisfied. As long as the crime is a felony in that state it is immaterial how the offense is classified in California.

Police officers working on or near the state borders throughout California have a particular problem in apprehending some criminals, particularly for misdemeanor offenses. If they are in hot putsuit of a person who has committed a misdemeanor, and that person crosses the state line, then they would be required to stop at the border, allowing the suspect to escape. Agreements have been worked out between bordering cities in the same state whereby police officers who were in pursuit would radio ahead and have the police officers of the neighboring city apprehend the violator so that the person could be arrested. If there is no such arrangement then it would be the responsibility of the officer to stop the pursuit, allowing the person to escape.

If an out-of-state police officer makes an arrest in the state of California under the Uniform Fresh Pursuit Act, there are certain steps that he must follow upon making an arrest which he would be responsible for adhering to.

1. The officer would be required to immediately take the prisoner before a magistrate in the county in which the arrest was made. This is necessary because the local magistrate has the responsibility to ensure that the arrest was proper and that the accused was informed of his constitutional rights. If the officer failed to follow this step and instead returned the accused to the place where the crime was committed, the officer could be guilty of kidnapping under Penal Code Section 217.

2. A magistrate, upon reviewing the case, will make a determination as to whether or not the arrest is lawful. If the arrest was unlawful then he has the responsibility to discharge the person from custody. If the magistrate determines that the arrest does appear to be in order, then he must commit the prisoner to jail pending further actions by the state where the crime was committed. Once the arrest has been determined to be lawful, extradition procedures will commence.

On some occasions a magistrate will determine that it is appropriate to set bail for the defendant. If this is the case, the defendant will be allowed to return on his own to the state where the crime occurred without the necessity of following the extradition process.

EXTRADITION

Extradition is a legal process for returning a person for trial in the state or country where the crime was alleged to have occurred. It is also used to return from such foreign jurisdicition a defendant who has escaped from confinement or who has violated the terms of his bail, parole, or probation. Due to increasing mobility and the transitory nature of today's communities, it is extremely easy for a person charged with a crime to leave the jurisdiction of that court, thereby making it rather difficult to prosecute him. Once the person has been arrested or located in a particular state, it is necessary to bring him back to the state where the crime was committed. We have learned in previous chapters that it is necessary to try an accused person for a crime in the jurisdiction where the crime was committed.

International and Interstate Extradition

Generally speaking, there are two types of extradition: international, and interstate. International extradition is basically an agreement between two countries to returning accused persons to the country where the crime was committed. The agreement usually depends on some kind of treaty or other type of formal arrangement made between those countries. The type of crime suitable for extradition is usually specified by the treaty. Normally the crimes are few and only include the most serious ones. One element that is usually uniform in international extradition agreements is that the person who has been extradited can only be prosecuted for the offense that he has been charged with in the extradition papers.

As can be seen, in international extradition there is no requirement that a country return a person who has fled to that country. Due to diplomatic relations and other political implications, one country can merely ask another for the return of the person who fled when extradition is requested. Interstate extradition is based on revised federal statutes and also supplemented by the Uniform Criminal Extradition Act. In excess of forty states have adopted this act. Under it, a person can be extradited for both a felony and misdemeanor, depending on the policy of the state which requests the extradition. There is no limitation as to what the person extradited can be charged with once he is brought back to the state for prosecution.

Procedure

In California, extradition originates with the district attorney of the county where the prosecution is desired. By this point the entire investigation process has been completed and the accused person has been identified. A criminal complaint has been filed and a warrant has been issued for the arrest of the person charged with the offense.

When it is determined that the individual is no longer in the state, the district attorney will present to the governor a written application for a requisition for the person. The application for a requisition must contain the following information: the name of the defendant, the crime, the date and time of the occurrence, the circumstances of its commission, and name of the state where the defendant is located. The application is filed with the secretary of state, along with all extradition papers. The extradition papers would include pertinent information about the local officials, including the confirmation and status of the district attorney, the superior court judge, and other officials who are involved in the certification of the local government. Generally speaking, the attorney general or other designated person will review all the papers and supporting documents to ensure that a crime has indeed been committed and that it appears likely that the defendant committed it. When he is thus satisfied, he will recommend extradition to the governor. The governor will then issue a warrant (which is called a 'warrant of rendition') under the seal of the State of California. The warrant is directed to the local agency where the original crime was committed, and it commands that agency to bring the defendant back to the state.

The agent of the state of California, having in his possession a warrant, an extradition application, and other papers, will proceed to the state where the person is located. Upon his arrival, the agent will present the extradition material to the governor of that state, or to his executive, who will then issue an official warrant, sometimes called an 'executive warrant,' which is the actual authorization to make the arrest and return the person to the state of California.

ARRAIGNMENT ON WARRANT

Once the accused has been arrested under the authority of the executive warrant, it is necessary that the individual be taken forthwith before a magistrate in the jurisdiction where the arrest occurred. It is the responsibility of the magistrate to inform the defendant of his rights, the crime with which he is being charged, and the reason for extradition. The accused may request a reasonable amount of time to review the legality of the extradition proceedings, and to obtain a counsel to assist him in arguing against the return.

The magistrate may keep the subject in jail in the jurisdiction where he was arrested until the court hearings have been concluded and it has been determined that the individual should be returned to the state where the crime was committed. Once the hearings have been completed, the agent will then return the subject to the original state for trial.

It is possible that a person can waive the entire extradition process upon his arrest. If this occurs then it is not necessary that the governors of the two states be involved. It would only require that the magistrate inform the defendant of his rights, and explain the extradition procedure along with any other pertinent information. If the accused wishes to waive his extradition right, he would be returned to the original state without any further action. It is also possible that the local magistrate may release the defendant on bail and allow him to return to the state, ensuring that the accused will meet his responsibilities and return to the state for court action.

SUMMARY

In this chapter we have discussed the overall police function and process as it relates to the administration of justice. We began with a discussion of the police role, and identified the major responsibilities of the police in California. We explicitly discussed the roles of crime prevention, the protection of lives and property, the discovery of evidence, the suppression of crime, and the identification, apprehension, and incarceration of suspects. We then identified the powers of the police, indicating that the specific powers authorized are derived from the philosophy that all citizens in a jurisdiction have a responsibility to provide law and order. Over the years this responsibility has been delegated to a specific agency which normally has jurisdiction within a specific political subdivision. We saw that police officers normally do not have extensive powers beyond those which any private citizen has. There are some areas where the authority of the police is extended, due to the nature and responsibilities of the job.

In discussing the authority of police officers, from the initial stop and question of a citizen through to the actual arrest and detention of a citizen, we indicated that the police must justify their actions according to the amount of liberties that they remove from the citizen. Variable probable cause was defined and discussed, and it stated that the more rights police take from citizens, the more justification is in order.

The specific sections in the Penal Code and other codes were discussed in relation to the process of arrest. The distinction between police officer arrests and private citizen arrests was identified, indicating two major differences: only police officers have the power to arrest under authority of a warrant; and police officers may arrest for a felony when they have reasonable cause to believe that the person committed that felony, whether or not the felony was in fact committed. In other words, a private citizen can only arrest a person for a felony when that felony was in fact committed, regardless of their good intentions.

Also discussed in this chapter was the proper time for making specific arrests, both for misdemeanors and felonies. We discussed the Ramey Case, which restricted police from arresting private citizens in their homes for felonies unless there were emergency conditions which would justify relieving the officer of the requirement to obtain a warrant.

The responsibility of the arrestee included the duty to refrain from resisting arrest, even if it appears likely that the arrest is unlawful. A private citizen has the opportunity to object to the manner and legality of the arrest when he goes to court, and this is the proper time for objecting to that arrest, rather than at the time that the arrest is made. It was pointed out that the police officer is trained to handle resistance, and he has the necessary equipment to execute an arrest even though the arrest may be unlawful. For this reason the citizen would be in a dangerous position and could be severely injured by the officer. The officer is liable both civilly and criminally for any unlawful acts he commits in an arrest, and he can be punished accordingly when a legitimate court has made the decision that the arrest was, in fact illegal.

We found that police officers may enter another state, and officers of another may enter this for the purpose of pursuing an accused person who has committed a crime in their jurisdiction. The requirements are that the offense must be a felony, and the pursuit must be fresh. Once the accused has been arrested in another state, established extradition help to return the person to the state where the crime was committed. The procedure for obtaining extradition papers and returning the person was described.

DISCUSSION QUESTIONS

1. The roles of the police in today's society have more than one interpretation. Identify the roles as seen by law enforcement. What are the opposing views?

2. Distinquish between the powers which police officers have compared to those of private citizens. What was the intention of the legislature when additional powers were given to police?

3. Reasonable or probable cause are terms which must be thoroughly understood by a police officer. Define the terms. What does variable probable cause mean?

4. What powers of arrest do police officers have which private citizens do not?

5. Discuss the reason that the courts prefer arrests by warrant whenever possible.

6. Describe the specific step-by-step procedures for interstate extradition and international extradition.

REFERENCES

1.   21 Cal. App. 3d 211, 98 Cal. Rptr. 409 (1971).

2.   People v. McGaughran, 22 Cal. 3d 469, 149 Cal. Rptr. 584, 585 P. 2d 206 (1978)

3.   California Penal Code, Section 841.

4.   People v. Agnew, 16 Cal. 2d 655, 107 P. 2d 601 (1940).

5.   California Penal Code, Section 839.

6.   People v. Kilvington, 104 Cal. 86, 37 P. 799 (1894).

7.   People v. Kilvington, 104 Cal. 86, 37 P. 799 (1894).

8.   California Penal Code, Section 835a.

9.   California Penal Code, Section 836.

10.   170 Cal. App. 2d 36, 338 P. 2d 524 (1959).

11.   16 Cal. 3d 263, 127 Cal. Rptr. 629, 545 P. 2d 1333 (1976).

12.   California Penal Code, Section 813.

13.   California Penal Code, Section 842.

14.   California Penal Code, Section 822.

15.   Rost v. Municipal Court, 184 Cal. App. 2d, 507, 7 Cal. Rptr. 869 (1960).

16.   California Penal Code, Section 834a.

17.   In re Bacon, 240 Cal. App. 2d 34, 49 Cal. Rptr. 322 (1966).

18.   People v. Curtis, 70 Cal. 2d 347, 74 Cal. Rptr. 713, 450 P.2d 33 (1969).

4

The Coroner

CHAPTER OBJECTIVES

Upon reading this chapter, the student will be able to:

1. Delineate the present authority and role of the coroner in California.
2. Define the legal authority and responsibility of the coroner.
3. List the major types of deaths that the coroner is responsible for investigating.
4. Explain the purpose of the autopsy and the inquest.
5. Discuss the combination of the coroner position with other county positions.

This chapter is devoted to the study of the office of the coroner of the State of California. The coroner plays a very important role in the administration of justice, and yet is very often overlooked by most practitioners. Since many times little attention is given to the coroner's functions and responsibilities, this chapter hopes to bring into focus the duties performed by the coroner, and the coroner's relationship to the many agencies and departments within the State of California.

We learn in this chapter that there is a definite benefit to coordination and cooperation between the various law enforcement agencies and the coroner's office of each county. The functions of the coroner sometimes overlap with law enforcement functions and sometimes animosities develop between the various agencies.

We will learn in this chapter that the role of the coroner is one of the oldest 'law enforcement' functions in existence. Many changes have taken place over the years to define and redefine the responsibilities and functions of the coroner. We will see that the coroner has the primary responsibility of investigating the causes and circumstances of unexplained or questionable deaths in the state. He has sole authority to take custody of a deceased person and determine the cause of death. We will see that for all intents and purposes, nearly all deaths occurring in California must be reported to the coroner for his investigation and the determination of the cause of death.

Lastly, in this chapter we will discuss the combined responsibilities of the coroner with the duties of other county officers within each county.

HISTORY OF THE CORONER

Though the duties of the coroner were modified by the California Legislature in 1876, the office itself is most ancient, and stems from English Common Law, from which many of our laws were derived. The office of the coroner is so old, in fact, that the actual date of its origin is unknown. It is one of the many old Saxon institutions which were adopted by the Normans after their conquest of England and which then found their way into the English statute books.

The original title, *Custos Placitorium Coronal* ("Keeper or Guardian of the Crown") was eventually, through various transitions, changed to 'Coroner' in the fourteenth century. The Coroner served as an agent of the crown, and he was one of the first of the king's legal assistants. Back in those early days, the coroner was charged with many duties (including inquiry into certain crimes, bringing criminals to justice, and the pronouncement of judgments), some of these duties having been taken away from the sheriff. The police duties were eventually returned to the sheriff, and other duties, such as the pronouncement of judgments, were returned to other officers of the crown, leaving the coroner with

his present-day duties.   These include the inquiry into, and determination of, the causes and modes of certain deaths, and their classification
(i.e., natural, accidental, suicide, or homicide).

Another interesting note is that the coroner, many years ago, was
responsible for carrying out regulations concerning *deodands*—that is to
say, the thing or chattel which caused a death by misadventure, such as
an ox that killed a man. It was the coroner's duty to seize the deodand
and have it or its monetary value forfeited to the king. If a man drown-
ed at sea, an entire vessel might be forfeited. As late as 1838, a coroner's jury levied a deodand forfeiture of £1500 on the boiler of the S.S.
Victoria, which had exploded, causing the death of one of the sailors.
These forfeitures were generally bestowed upon the church, in the
manner of alms, for the good of the souls of the persons deceased. This
legal principle and its legal sequence of compensation represents the
beginning of our present—day system of workman's compensation.

LEGAL CONSIDERATIONS

Medical certification of medico—legal cases is necessary in approximately
one—third of all deaths in the United States. It is easy to understand
that an objective, impartial governmental body must function to determine the causes and modes of such deaths. Herein lies the basic authority of the coroner, making him as important to society in the protection
of decedents' rights as the police department is in apprehending the
criminal, the district attorney in prosecuting a criminal, and the courts
in assuring justice.

Coroner's cases are not limited to deaths from violence and suspected
violence; they involve many deaths from natural causes. Jurisdictional
laws for the coroner's office are mainly derived from the Government
Code, and the Health and Safety Code of the State of California. In
concert with the concept of the unification of statutes policy and
practice relating to state medico—legal activities, the State of California
has put into action the recommendations of the United States National
Committee on Vital and Health Statistics.

DUTIES OF CORONER

The coroner is directed by law to: administer and direct objective investigations in cases which come under his jurisdiction; direct medical
personnel to establish medical facts pertaining to each case; and to direct
other scientific personnel, when required and when deemed necessary, to
provide information in questionable cases. In those cases which come
under his authority, the coroner must certify the cause and mode of
death, which shall be based upon medical and scientific facts.

Deaths Reported to the Coroner

The deaths which are to be reported to the coroner are stated in the Government Code Section 27491. Generally speaking, it is the responsibility of the coroner to investigate nearly all deaths occurring in the county for which he has jurisdiction. The degree and detail of the investigation by the coroner as to the cause of death will vary with the circumstances. As can be recognized, if the death is unexplained or there are any suspicious circumstances regarding the manner or cause of death, then a thorough investigation will be conducted by the coroner. Otherwise, a superficial or preliminary investigation would be conducted, and that would be the extent of the coroner's involvement.

Deaths investigated by the Coroner's office are classified according to the International Classification System, which is used the world over by medical records personnel.

The California Government Code directs the coroner to inquire into and determine the circumstances, manner, and cause of death in the following cases which are immediately reportable:

1. No physician in attendance.
2. No medical attendance within 24 hours of death.
3. Wherein the deceased has not been attended by a physician in the 10 days prior to death.
4. Physician unable to state the cause of death (unwillingness does not apply).
5. Known or suspected homicide.
6. Known or suspected suicide.
7. Involving any criminal action or suspicion of a criminal act.
8. Related to or following known or suspected self-induced or criminal abortion.
9. Associated with a known or alleged rape or crime against nature.
10. Following an accident or injury (primary or contributory, occurring immediately or at some remote time).
11. Drowning, fire, hanging, gunshot, stabbing, cutting, starvation, exposure, alcoholism, drug addiction, strangulation, or aspiration.
12. Accidental poisoning (food, chemical, drug, therapeutic agents).
13. Occupational diseases or occupational hazards.
14. Known or suspected contagious disease and constituting a public hazard.
15. All deaths occurring in an operating room.
16. All deaths where a patient has not fully recovered from an anesthetic, whether in surgery, recovery room, or elsewhere.
17. All deaths in which the patient is comatose throughout the period of a physician's attendance, whether in the home or a hospital.
18. In prison or while under sentence.

19. All solitary deaths. (Unattended by physician or other person in period preceding death.)
20. All deaths of unidentified persons. [1]

The Necessity for Autopsies

Approximately one-third of all county deaths fall within the jurisdiction of the coroner. Since the nature of the coroner's work mainly constitutes unknowns or unsolved questions, it can easily be seen that an accurate cause of death cannot be reached unless an autospy is conducted, followed by any necessary technical studies. The law makes it mandatory that the coroner furnish an accurate cause of death, either by autopsy, or by medical information as provided by acceptable medical practice and within the requirements for accuracy described by the Division of Medical Statistics of the State Department of Public Health. At the conclusion of all of these medical and scientific studies, it may then be known with certainty that the death was from an exact cause in almost every case.

Results of the investigation by a coroner's office may greatly aid law enforcement, as well as surviving relatives. In deaths occurring within a forty—eight—hour period of a motor vehicle accident, the determination of blood alcohol concentration is made, in addition to analysis for barbituates and dangerous drugs, when indicated. In all single—car motor vehicle deaths, a determination of carbon monoxide concentra-

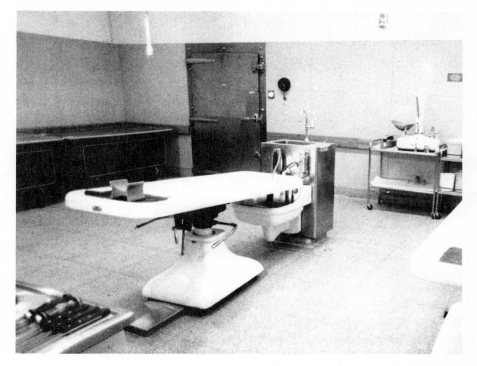

tion is made in addition to other studies. Specific analyses for specialized drugs are made in any kind of circumstances which warrant suspicions.

Although there are many so-called natural causes of death that could be certified as such, medical facts may substantiate that a suicide actually took place, or that an undiscovered accident occurred prior to death which was the actual factor. It is not enough to say that a man who was fatally injured in an automobile accident died solely from the injuries sustained simply because the appearance of this person may indicate a traumatic death. This person might have suffered a stroke, a heart attack, gone into a diabetic coma, or might have suffered a spontaneous hemorrhage or rupture of some internal organ prior to death, thereby causing the accident.

In cases of unknown causes of death where a contagious disease is suddenly discovered through the autopsy and attending studies, it is vitally important to family members and to those who came into contact with the disease to know of the exact cause of death so that they may take preventive measures. Diseases of a hereditary nature may be discovered in autopsies, which may then be important to the living blood relatives. An accurate cause of death by means of autopsy certification may absolve a mother or relative or the decendent from any responsibility in causing the death, thus preventing a family member from continuing through life with a guilt complex.

In instances where accident benefits are provided in a life insurance policy, the beneficiaries will know they are entitled to this benefit after the coroner's office has completed a thorough investigation. On the other hand, if an "accidental death" is subsequently found to be caused by natural causes, the insurance company would not be required to pay accident benefits, and would affect the type of claim that the life insurance policy owners could make.

The autopsy may be compared to an operation which is carefully and respectfully done. The autopsy does not interfere with preservatives or enbalming procedures, and will at times provide means for improving the preservation of a body. After the body has been prepared properly by a mortician, there are no aftereffects which could be seen in the customary viewing practices of our society.

Investigation, Examination, Identification, Removal of Deceased Persons

Government Code Section 27491.2 states that, "The Coroner or his appointed deputy, on being informed of a death and finding it to fall in the classification of deaths requiring his inquiry, may immediately proceed to where the body lies, examine the body, make identification, make inquiries into the circumstances, manner, and means of death, and, as circumstances warrant, either order its removal for further investigation or disposition, or release the body to the next of kin. For the purposes of inquiry, the body of one who is known to be dead under any other circumstances enumerated as deaths reportable to the Coroner, shall not be disturbed or moved from the position of place of death without permission of the Coroner or his appointed Deputy."

The above section contains several extremely important legal points which the reader should be aware of. For example, it is the primary responsibility of the coroner to examine the scene where a death occurred and make a preliminary investigation of the cause and circumstances of the death prior to the scene being disturbed in any way. Law enforcement officers are required to protect the scene as best as possible and prevent the removal of the body so that the coroner can examine the body in the original state in which it was found. It is the sole responsibility of the coroner to order the removal of the body for investigation or disposition, or to release the body to the next of kin. If there is any question as to whether or not the victim is still alive or not, it is the primary responsibility of the police officer and anyone else initially at the scene to seek medical assistance to attempt to protect the life of this individual. Because of the sometimes overlapping responsibility between law enforcement officers and the coroner's office, it can be seen that some conflicts could develop regarding who is responsible for the preservation and collection of evidence surrounding the scene of a crime where a death has occurred. As long as it is remembered that the coroner has the primary responsibility for dealing with a deceased person, and that only he can move the deceased, law enforcement can work around this provision and still protect the scene of the crime to the extent provided by law.

Government Code Section 27491.3 states "In any death into which the Coroner is to inquire, he may take charge of any and all personal effects, valuables and property of the deceased at the scene of the death and hold or safeguard them until lawful disposition thereof can be made. He may, in his discretion, lock the premises and apply a seal to the door or doors prohibiting entrance to the premises, pending arrival of a legally authorized representative of the deceased, provided that this shall not be done in such a manner as to interfere with the investigation being conducted by all other law enforcement agencies. Any costs arising from the premises being locked or sealed while occupied by property of the deceased may be a proper and legal charge against the estate of the deceased."

As can be seen by the above section, the coroner again has the primary responsibility for taking charge and handling all the personal effects, valuables, and property of the deceased at the scene of the death. When there appears to be no criminal involvement, this requirement poses no problems or conflicts between law enforcement and the coroner. However, in those cases where the cause of death is question-able, whether it is by criminal means or not, specific conflcts between law enforcement and the coroner could develop. Law enforcement agencies desire to preserve and collect all of the possible items that can be considered as evidence in the discharge of their duty to investigate the cause and circumstances of the death. On the other hand, the coroner, because of the above section, is required to take charge of those effects. The coroner will normally cooperate with law enforce-ment agencies and allow the agencies investigating the death to collect any evidence that they feel would be pertinent to their investigation. At a time when the law enforcement agency decides that any items that they collected do not have a bearing on the criminal investigation, they will normally turn them over to the coroner for his care. In support of the above statement, the same section of the Government Code states that, "Any such property or evidence related to the investigation or prosecution of any unknown or suspected criminal death may, with knowledge of the Coroner, be delivered to a law enforcement agency or district attorney, receipt for which shall be acknowledged." The law enforcement agency would then be required to give the coroner a receipt for the property which they have in their possession, thus satisfying the requirements of the law.

Other privisions in the Government Code prohibit the removal of any papers, monies, valuable property, or weapons from the person of the deceased, from the premises prior to the arrival of the coroner, or when the coroner has not given his permission. The only exception to this rule is when a law enforcement investigation is necessary. In the case of such an investigation, then the primary responsibility for the belongings and related evidence is with the law enforcement agency. The coroner then would have a legal responsibility not to further or willfully disturb the body or any evidence until law enforcement agen-cies have had a reasonable opportunity to respond to the scene and make a preliminary investigation.

MEDICAL DUTIES

As stated in previous sections, the necessity for autopsies falls within the responsibilities and medical duties of the coroner. In most large counties, the coroner is generally a medical doctor who, specialized in pathology. Because one of the major functions of the Coroner's office is to examine the deceased and determine the cause of death, it only follows that a person trained in performing autopsies and understanding the human anatomy will be most qualified to act as a coroner. How-ever, it should be noted that the law does not require that a person be licensed as a medical doctor in order to become a coroner of the county.

Since the coroner is elected, he need only convince the voters of his interest and ability to carry out the functions of the coroner. In those cases where the coroner is not a medical doctor, then he has the authority to hire a pathologist to perform autopsies as required by the law.

Government Code Section 27491.4 states, "For purpose of inquiry the coroner may, in his descretion, take possession of the body, which shall include the authority to exhume such body, order it removed to a convenient place, and make or cause to be made a post-mortem examination or autopsy thereon, and made or cause to be made an analysis of the stomach, stomach contents, blood, organs, fluids, or tissues of the body." The coroner also has the right to retain those tissues removed from the body at the autopsy for the purpose of identifying his findings.

The detailed medical findings resulting from an autopsy are required to be reduced to writing and permanently preserved as part of the record. This record then becomes the primary authority for the determination of the legal cause of death.

The Inquest

After an examination of the body has been made, the usual procedure for the coroner is to call a special type of jury, which is known as a 'Jury of Inquest'. The inquest is a coroner's court, held at the coroner's discretion before a jury, in accordance with the provisions of California state law, to bring forward facts and to fix responsibility in questionable cases. Usually a good investigation by both the coroner's and peace officer investigators will be sufficient to provide information necessary in any given case. National authorities on the subject state that a thorough investigation is superior to an inquest. Occasionally, however rarely, factual evidence may be withheld or unavailable by usual means to the investigating officer. If the latter is true, an inquest certainly would be in order.

Years ago it was the practice of the coroner to hold an inquest immediately at the scene of an accidental or violent death. The coroner's jury would be made up of witnesses at the scene and a verdict would be sumarily rendered. At the present time, evidence is collected, witnesses subpoenaed, and an inquest held one or more weeks after the death, and almost always after the body has been buried. In some jurisdictions the coroner's entire case is investigated only by means of this delayed inquest. Based on the way evidence is presented and the attitudes reflected by witnesses, coroner's juries are known to render emotional verdicts rather than verdicts based on inquest facts. The inquest, then, is a mechanism to resolve a case that is too weak to prosecute, from a district attorney's standpoint, and too notable to dismiss without the rendering of an opinion or verdict by a group of citizens acting as a coroner's jury.

Since he has the responsibility for inquests in California, the coroner acts as an investigator and quasi—judicial officer. This quasi—judicial responsibility is derived from the fact that he is established in a some-what limited judicial role when he summons jurors and holds an inquest, as described above. Although the purpose of the inquest is investiga-tional in nature, the coroner does make recommendations as to the cause and circumstances of the death. Law enforcement agencies are under no responsibility to prosecute a case based on information that is found at the coroner's inquest. It must further be noted that it is not the procedural responsibility of the inquest to determine who is respon-sible for committing an alleged homicide. The coroner limits the testimony of witnesses and other persons involved in the death of a person solely to the determination of the cause and circumstances of that death.

Also, as stated above, the coroner has the authority to summon jurors. Normally the jury would not have less than nine, nor more than fifteen members. Coroner's jurors may be selected according to the procedures established by the coroner. These jurors are not selected with the same legal restraints as trial jurors; the courts are not as con-cerned with who is going to be on the jury and how it is drawn, since an issue of guilt or innocence is not in question. Only the cause of death is the issue, so the only requirement for selection would be whether the prospective jurors can intelligently interpret the evidence, and make a recommendation based on the facts. They need not be screened for biases or prejudices, as do trial jurors.

DEATHS REPORTABLE TO THE CORONER

Because of the importance of the specific deaths that are to be reported to the coroner, we will now discuss in some detail the more common types of deaths that must be reported and investigated, and the signifi-cance of the coroner's investigation.

1. *Homicide or Suicide* These types of deaths must be reported for obvious medico—legal reasons. When there is even the slightest indica-tion of either, a person having knowledge of such death shall be expected to notify the coroner's office immediately for a thorough investigation.

2. *Accident or Injury* When a death has occurred through an accident or an injury, the death must immediately or as quickly as possible thereafter be reported to the coroner. Regardless of whether the accident or injury was of a grave nature or only slight, as long as it is the opinion of the attending or reporting physician that the accident or injury might have contributed to the death in any degree, then the

death is reportable. If the injury is to be listed anywhere on the death certificate, the case must be reported to the coroner. If there is any question as to the cause of death—that is, whether or not the injury was responsible or contributed to the death—a coroner would normally be consulted and will make the ultimate decision as to whether any criminal, civil or other legal considerations would enter into the case to require his further investigation.

3. *Criminal Action or Suspicion of a Criminal Act* This group of deaths revolves around instances where there is gross evidence of criminal involvement, suspicion of a criminal abortion, euthanasia, or questionable results of auto accidents.

4. *No Physician in Attendance* As provided in the law, if there is no physician in attendance, then it is the responsibility to bring in the coroner for his examination. Such instances include those where there is no history of medical attention of the deceased, or when what attention there was has been so remote as to afford no knowledge or relation to the cause of death.

5. *In the Continued Absence of the Physician* The provisions of this statement vary through interpretation throughout the state of California. However, in most counties it is the policy that if a physician has not seen a patient within twenty days before the death, then such cases should be reported. If a physician has not seen a patient during the twenty days before death, such cases are reportable to the coroner and the death certificate shall be signed by the coroner.[2]

6. *Physician in Attendance less than 24 Hours* When the death occurred in a hospital then the case is reportable. The coroner, in consultation with the physician, will determine whether the individual's case properly falls within the court's jurisdiction. Frequently the coroner may learn of another physician who was very recently in the close attendance of the patient and who is in a position to provide such information which will remove the case from the coroner's jurisdiction.

7. *Physician Unable to State the Cause of Death* There seems to be little confusion in this category of deaths. When the physician states, or the evidence indicates that the physician is unable to establish a cause of death, then the coroner will initiate an investigation. On many occasions physicians will be unwilling to state the cause of death because of uncertainty. The coroner's office in most counties is willing to accept the full responsibility for investigating any cases when there is sufficient ground to legally authorize the coroner to do so. If there appears to be any question as to the cause of death, then the coroner may have the ultimate responsibility for analyzing and making a final statement as to the cause and circumstances of that death.

8. *Poisoning* This section includes all food, chemical, drug, and therapeutic agent poisoning. Deaths wholly or partly due to industrial

agents or toxic agents, ordinary food poisonings, household medicaments, prescribed pharmaceuticals and biologicals, etcetera, are reportable when they in any way contribute to the death, or when there is sufficient evidence to reasonably suspect that they contributed.

9. *Occupational Deaths* When a death is clearly known to be due to an occupational disease, or when there is reasonable ground to suspect that the death resulted in whole or in part from an occupational disease, then that death is reportable.

10. *Operating Room Deaths* Any type of death occurring in the operating room is reportable to the coroner. Regardless of whether the death was expected or not, the case is still reportable. Depending upon the nature of the patient's condition, the reason why he is being operated on, the time and manner of the death, etcetera, the coroner will determine whether the case needs to be investigated fully.

11. *All Solitary Deaths* When a person has not been under the medical care of his physician, or when a responsible family member was not on the premises during the time that the death occurred, the death would then be categorized as a solitary death and is reportable to the coroner. Thus, in instances where persons are found dead in, for example, hotels, or rooming houses, such deaths are reportable, even though a physician may know of some previous existing illness. Similarly, if a person should be found dead in his home and no family member was on the premises during the time that the death occurred, the coroner would investigate to assure that no mishap or misadventure transpired, and such deaths are reportable even though a physician may have known of some preexisting illness.

12. *All Deaths of Unidentified Persons* In all cases where the decendent is unknown or unidentified, the coroner must be notified immediately. The coroner is charged with the responsibility of identtifying all unknown dead. He must also fingerprint persons over sixteen years of age and send copies of the fingerprints to the California Identification and Investigation Bureau in Sacramento. It is also the coroner's responsibility to notify the next of kin concerning the deaths under his jurisdiction.

COMBINED RESPONSIBILITIES
OF THE CORONER AND OTHER COUNTY OFFICERS

Government Code Section 24300 covers the consolidations authorized. The coroner's duties can be combined with those of the public administrator, the district attorney and the sheriff, or any combination thereof. The two duties combined most often are those of the public administrator—coroner and the sheriff—coroner. Normally this will occur in small counties where there is little responsibility in carrying out each of the individual functions. There are several small counties in the state of California that have combined the public administrator and coroner duties. Because of this combination, we will describe some of the major responsibilities of the public administrator and how that functions relates to the coroner. Generally speaking, one of the most common duties of the public administrator as it relates to the duties of the coroner is that the public administrator is responsible in certain cases for the personal property of the deceased.

Jurisdiction of the Public Administrator

The public administrators of the various counties in California function by virtue of the authority vested in the office by sections of various California codes, most notably the California Probate Code. The public administrator acts most often in the following cases:
1. When the next of kin or family cannot be found.
2. When there is no known will, no known heirs, or when the heirs cannot be located.
3. When the heirs cannot serve as executors or administrators of the estate; for example, they may not be residents of the state, may be incompetent, or may refuse to serve as such.

Another one of the more important responsibilities of the public administrator is to ensure that the property of the deceased is released to the proper person. The public administrator would take charge of the property and determine the proper heirs.

In general, it is the duty of the public administrator to determine, if possible, the whereabouts of heirs, the existence of a will, and to completely investigate and safeguard all assets belonging to the decedent. If a matter comes within the jurisdiction of the public administrator, it is necessary for him, in the absence of responsible heirs or next of kin, to make arrangements for a funeral and to dispose of the remains according to the standards of living of the person prior to death. The public administrator must: secure the assets of the decedent; secure letters of the administration; liquidate the assets or arrange for their storage; see that all judgments are paid; file all income tax returns for the decedent; pay any inheritance tax; and arrange for the distribution of the balance of the estate to those entitled thereto.

Sheriff—Coroner

Another fairly common role combined with the coroners is that of sheriff. As we learned in Government Code Section 24300, the consolidation of the coroner and the sheriff roles can occur when it is felt that there is an insufficient workload to justify having both offices. Again, this normally occurs in the small counties in the state of California.

This consolidation seems to work very effectively due to the fact that many of the functions of the coroner are tied into the functions of the sheriff.

Because of the diversity of interests and qualifications of the two public offices, most often the primary responsibility of the combined offices will be towards law enforcement. This means that the main interests and qualifications of the person elected will be in the area of law enforcement. As we learned in previous sections, it is perfectly legal and acceptable for a coroner to be a 'layman' with respect to medical training. It is not necessary that this person be a licensed physician or patholohist, or to have a degree in medicine. The sheriff—coroner, in this case would contract with local pathologists to perform the necessary medico—legal autopsies and the other various functions which would normally be required of a physician. The sheriff—coroner then acts as an administrator, overseeing the duties of the coroner. This combination works very well, providing there is not too much of a work-load for either of the public offices.

In summary, we have seen that the coroner plays a truly important role in the administration of justice in each of the counties in the state of California. Since the coroner has law enforcement responsibilities, he is involved in the investigative steps for determining the causes and circumstances of a death. It is extremely critical that the coroner work very closely with law enforcement agencies, and that a cooperative attitude exists between both.

SUMMARY

In this chapter we learned that the coroner in the State of California receives authority from the legislature, dating from 1867, when the office of coroner was established. We also found that the office of the coroner has been in existence since prior to the conquest of England by the Normans.

In excess of one third of all deaths in the United States come within the jurisdiction of the coroner, medical certification of the medico—legal causes of these deaths are necessary. The coroner's cases are not limited to deaths from violence or suspected violence, but may involve many deaths from natural causes.

We learned the importance of the coroner's autopsy, and that, in order to accurately determine the cause of death, a medico—legal autopsy needs to be performed on the deceased. The Government Code requires that the coroner be informed of all unexplained or questionable deaths within the county in which he is employed. It is his responsibility to determine the causes and circumstances of those deaths and to report his findings to the state. The coroner has the authority to remove the body for investigation, for disposition, or to release the body to the next of kin. It is also the sole responsibility of the coroner to handle and take charge of all personal effects, valuables and property of the deceased at the scene of a death.

It is not a legal requirement that the coroner be a practicing physician or have an extensive background in the medical field. However, in large counties, the coroner generally is a medical doctor specializing in pathology. In those counties where the coroner is a lay person, he will hire a pathologist to perform autopsies as required by law.

The inquest is a coroner's court, held at the coroner's direction before a jury for the purpose of bringing forward facts on the cause and circumstances of a death, and fixing responsibility in questionable cases.

Lastly, we discussed the combination of responsibilities of the coroner with other duties of certain county offices. We indicated that in some rural counties such offices as the sheriff, public administrator, and district attorney can be combined with that of the coroner. The most common combination is the public administrator—coroner, due to the fact that the public administrator is responsible for dealing with the California Probate Code, ensuring that the property of the deceased is released to the proper person.

It is hoped that the reader fully understands the importance of the coroner's office and has realized that it is an extremely important resource to law enforcement agencies. Those who work in cooperation with the coroner's office can further benefit the administration of justice.

DISCUSSION QUESTIONS

1. How has the role of the coroner changed in this country, compared to its original role in England?

2. Why is it important for the coroner to have the authority to perform autopsies on deceased persons in California?

3. List and discuss the functions of the coroner which sometimes conflict with law enforcement functions.

4. List the positions in county government which can be combined with the office of the coroner, and discuss why the law authorizes this procedure.

REFERENCES

1. Government Code, Section 27491.
2. Government Code, Section 27491.

5

Related State Agencies and Regulatory Commissions

CHAPTER OBJECTIVES

Upon reading this chapter the student will be able to:

1. List four specific state agencies having a major impact on the criminal justice system, as well as define their major roles and responsibilities.

2. Identify one California regulatory commission, listing the specific responsibilities and duties in terms of regulation with California.

3. List and describe five federal regulatory commissions, indicating their major functions and responsibilities, as well as defining their source of authority.

4. Define and list the specific differences between regulatory commissions on the state and federal levels and know of specific criminal justice agencies in California.

The principles and procedures of the justice system consist of a very large and complex network of criminal justice and related agencies. It is extremely important to recognize the role that some of these agencies and commissions play in the criminal justice system. A great deal of emphasis is placed on the role of the major 'actors' in the system, such as the law enforcement sector, prosecutors, and defense attornies, as well as the subsystems, including the grand jury, trial jurors, and the like.

In this chapter we will be identifying some of the more frequently mentioned state agencies that play an important role in the principles and procedures of justice system. It is impossible to thoroughly discuss all of the state agencies in the state that do have a role; therefore, it is necessary to single out some of those agencies that will be utilized more frequently by the criminal justice community. On the state level we will discuss the Department of Alcoholic Beverage Control, the Department of Motor Vehicles, the Department of Justice, and the Resources Agency, which in recent years has become more and more important to the citizens of California. In addition, we will examine one of the many regulatory commissions in the State of California. The Public Utilities Commission plays an extremely important role in the regulation of specific privately owned utilities and transportation companies within California.

Since the turn of the century, federal regulatory agencies have played an important role in the supervision and regulation of the private sector in the United States. Citizens understood very little of the background, functions and performances of these commissions. It is important to the student that they respect and understand the role that each of the regulatory commissions plays on the federal level.

We will discuss five of the major regulatory commissions that have been in existence since the early 1900s. The student should pay particular attention to the agencies listed in this text, understanding that there are many more commissions which have not been discussed at all. In this chapter we will discuss the Civil Aeronautics Board, the Federal Communications Commission, the Federal Trade Commission, the Interstate Commerce Commission, and the Security and Exchange Commission.

RELATED STATE AGENCIES

Alcoholic Beverage Control

The Department of Alcoholic Beverage Control derives its authority from Article 20, Section 22 of the California Constitution. The Department of Alcoholic Beverage Control in the State of California has the exclusive responsibility for issuing licenses for the distribution and sale of any alcoholic beverages in California. In addition to determining who should receive a license to sell, the Department of Alcoholic Beverage Control also has responsibility to enforce all provisions in the Business and Professions Code, and other related codes, dealing with the sale and distribution of alcoholic beverages.

The majority of the laws relating to alcoholic beverage control are contained in the Alcoholic Beverage Control Act, which is Division Nine of the Business and Professions Code. As previously discussed, the Department of Alcoholic Beverage Control has the sole responsibility for licensing individuals in the state of California. Prior to issuing a license, the department will conduct a thorough investigation to determine whether the applicants and premises meet the qualifications which have been established by the constitution and the legislature in the State of California. The investigators employed by the Department of Alcoholic Beverage Control will be involved in complete investigations of the licensing, as well as enforcement of, the ABC Act.

Types of Licenses. The licenses issued by the Department of Alcoholic Beverage Control are generally divided into two broad categories: retail licenses and wholesale licenses.

The retail licenses are divided into two groups: off sale and on sale licenses. Both of these groups are further divided into specific types of offsale or onsale licenses. These licenses authorize sales directly to the consumer. The onsale license authorizes persons to sell alcoholic beverages on the premises for consumption on the premises. The offsale license is restricted to individuals buying alcoholic beverages and removing the beverages from the premises prior to consumption.

The wholesale class may be divided into three general groups: wholesale distributors, manufacturers and producers, and importers. Each of the three groups divide into specific types of licenses covering various privileges. Generally, the licensees in this category sell the alcoholic beverage specified in the license only to another licensee for resale. As a rule, no licensee holding a wholesale license can hold or have any interest in any retail, onsale, or offsale general license.

Every person who seeks to secure a license must file an application at one of the offices of the Department of Alcoholic Beverage Control. Upon application, the department will conduct a thorough investigation of his background and financial status. If, after the investigation, the department officer is satisfied that the applicant meets the minimum qualifications that are established, he will then recommend the issuance of the license.

Enforcement Responsibilities. In addition to the primary responsibility for investigating potential applicants for Alcoholic Beverage Control Licenses, the Deparment of Alcoholic Beverage Control is also an enforcement agency. Section 25755 of the Business and Professions

Code states that all persons employed by the Department of Alcoholic Beverage Control are peace officers and have peace officer powers for the enforcement of the penal provisions of the various codes dealing with alcoholic beverages. The agents for the Department of Alcoholic Beverage Control will normally concentrate on enforcing the laws relating directly to the licensing of premises. Since it is a specialized law enforcement responsibility, Alcoholic Beverage Control agents rarely involve themselves in criminal investigations other than when offenses fall within the provisions of the Business and Provisions Code.

Subsequent appeals may be taken to the state Court of Appeals and on to the U.S. Supreme Court. Since the department does not have legal authority similarly to revoke or suspend a license, this sometimes results in continued operation of a license long after offenses have been detected.

Law Enforcement Agencies. Section 21619 of the Alcoholic Beverage Control Act provides that every peace officer and district attorney in California shall enforce the provisions of this act. With approximately 57,500 licensed premises and only 200 special investigators in the department, it is obvious that diligent enforcement of the act by every peace officer in the state is necessary for proper regulation of the industry.

Section 24202 of the ABC Act provides that, "all state and local law enforcement agencies shall immediately notify the department of any arrests made by them for violations over which the department has jurisdiction which involve a licensee or licensed premise. The department shall promptly cause an investigation to be made as to whether grounds exist for suspension or revocation of a license or licenses of a licensee."

As we learned in Chapter 3, failure to enforce the provisions in the Alcoholic Beverage Control Act is a misdemeanor, and police officers who willfully refuse to abide by the provisions contained in sections 25619 and 24202 of the Alcoholic Beverage Control Act can be charged and convicted of a misdemeanor.

ABC Structure. The director of the department is appointed by the governor. The director appoints a deputy director and two area assistant directors, one each to be in charge of the northern and southern halves of the state. These areas are served by district and branch offices which are responsible for the licensing and enforcement duties prescribed in the Alcoholic Beverage Control Act. The district offices maintain complete files on the investigations of applicants and licensees and reported violations on licensed premises. Any person who is denied a license or subjected to disciplinary action by the department as a result of a violation may demand a hearing. If the department's recommendation is unfavorable to him, he may appeal to the Alcoholic Beverage Control Appeals Board.

California Department of Motor Vehicles

The Department of Motor Vehicles is a service agency that performs three major functions.   The responsibility for registering vehicles falls within the Division of Registry.

Registration of Motor Vehicles   Nearly every city in the state of California will have a Department of Motor Vehicles office.   Since all vehicles that are registered on the roadway have to be licensed, the primary responsibility of the Department of Motor Vehicles will be to maintain adequate registration records, and to be responsible for collecting fees for the vehicles on the roadways in the state of California.

The Division of Registration maintains in its Sacramento files a history of every motor vehicle registered in the past year and for the three preceeding years, a total of about 16,667,887 records.   The files are maintained in three separate systems: under the registered owner's name (in alphabetical order); under the license number; and under the serial or identification number of the vehicle.   As an added service, a duplicate license number file is maintained in Los Angeles due to the volume of information requests in the southern part of the state.   Funds derived from registration fees are generally allocated for highway purposes, except such amounts as are necessary to support the department of the California Highway Patrol.

The license plates issued by the Department of Motor Vehicles are retained for the vehicles for which they were issued for a period of five years or longer.   In the years between the distribution of plates, a validating device for updating the license plate, usually a reflective sticker which is affixed to the rear plate, is issued annually to each registered owner.

Testing and Licensing of Drivers.   This responsibility is assigned to the Division of Drivers Licenses, the second major function of the Department of Motor Vehicles.   Since it is considered a privilege to drive a motor vehicle in the state of California, only those persons who can adequately demonstrate their proficiency and ability will be allowed to drive.   The Department of Motor Vehicles is the sole agency responsible for the licensing of drivers in the state.   Each department office in the state of California will be responsible for giving written examinations to determine the competency of a prospective driver, as well as giving field examinations to determine competency behind the wheel.   The department will collect all fees for licensing drivers of the state of California.   The   Department of Motor Vehicles also maintains a complete file of all drivers in the state of California who possess licenses.

This file is kept in a central location in Sacramento, and is available to any law enforcement agency or other agency having a valid reason for obtaining any information from those files.

As indicated above, one of the major responsibilities of the Department of Motor Vehicles under the Division of Drivers Licenses is the issuance and renewal of drivers licenses, and the maintenance of adequate records of all drivers, including their driving histories.

The division is also charged with the revocation or suspension of the driving privileges of those whose records show them to be negligent or unsafe drivers. These actions cover two categories: mandatory revocation or suspension after court convictions for serious traffic violations; and discretionary or driver improvement actions. Under the driver improvement classification, the division deals with those drivers who are habitual violators of the law, those who are accident prone, or those with physical or mental disabilities that affect their ability to drive safely. In these dealings, the division has recourse to reexaminations, interviews, investigations, warnings, and hearings before a referee. A specially trained staff of driver improvement analysts is maintained for this purpose. In its endeavors to correct bad driving habits and attitudes, the division makes liberal use of its power to improve conditions of probation on drivers with poor records.

Administration of Financial Responsibility Laws. This responsibility concerns consumer protection. Because of the financial impact of maintaining and operating a motor vehicle in the state of California, the Department of Motor Vehicles has undertaken the responsibility of consumer protection. Complete records are maintained of all individuals possessing drivers licenses and motor vehicle registrations, and their responsibilities under the financial laws. For example, it is illegal for a person to operate a motor vehicle in the state of California unless he has proper insurance or has demonstrated financial responsibility.

The Department of Motor Vehicles also investigates certain aspects of the operation of vehicles in the state of California. For example, the following areas, in some limited degree, would be within the jurisdiction of the Department of Motor Vehicles: theft of vehicles; unlawful ownership transfers; altered license plates; forged or counterfeit registration or drivers licenses; and the licensing of auto dealers and dismantlers. Other law enforcement agencies will have an active role in one or more of the areas outlined above.

California Department of Justice

The Department of Justice is headed by the Attorney General of the State of California. The Attorney General is the chief law enforcement officer who oversees the law enforcement agencies in all fifty-eight counties. He has jurisdiction over district attorneys, sheriffs, and police chiefs.   The Department of Justice consists of five divisions: 1.   The Division of Civil Law 2.   The Division of Criminal Law 3.   The Division of Special Operations   4.   The Division of Administration   5.   The Division of Law Enforcement

Division of Civil Law.   The Department of Justice is responsible for the prosecution or defense of most of the civil laws brought by or against the State of California, its agencies, officers and employees. The department provides legal opinions for the governor, legislature, state officers, state agencies, district attornies and county councils. The Division of Civil Law is divided into the: Tax law section; the Professional and Vocational Administrative Law section; the Public Administrative Law section; the Public Welfare Law section; the Government Law section; the Business Law section, and the Torts and Condemation Law section.

Division of Criminal Law.   The Division of Criminal Law represents the state in appeals from convictions in criminal cases in the state appellate courts, as well as the state Supreme Court. It processes writs of habeas corpus and other extraordinary writs involving criminal cases in both the state and federal courts. It also processes all extradition requests to and from the state.

Division of Special Operations.   The Division of Special Operations is composed of four sections: public resources; environmental and consumer protection; land law, and special statutory complaints. Much of the work of special operations derives from the common law power of the attorney general to protect the public in the areas of consumer protection, antitrust suits, and the environment. The division represents numerous state agencies involved with the regulation of land and resources in legal actions.

Division of Administration.   The Division of Administration is concerned with all administration and budgetry matters of the Department of Justice. The Division maintains the law library in the attorney general's office and has the responsibility for allocating manpower in the office. The special legal services section has the responsibility for reviewing and publishing the official attorney general's official opinions on state legal matters.

Crime Prevention Unit. This unit was established in 1971 for the basic function of developing, implimenting and coordinating effective crime prevention programs throughout California. The Crime Prevention Unit conducts educational programs in California schools aimed at reducing crime among juveniles. The unit also sponsors senior citizens' seminars to train elderly persons in effective crime control.

Division of Law Enforcement.   Under constitutional and statutory provision, the attorney general is required to provide services to federal, state and local criminal justice agencies in the areas of investigation, organized crime, criminology, narcotic enforcement, statistics, identification and information, communications, and data processing. These activities are performed by the Division of Law Enforcement, which consists of four branches: Enforcement and Investigation; Investigative Services; Organized Crime; and Identification and Information.

Enforcement and Investigation Branch. This unit is composed of two bureaus: narcotic enforcement, and investigation. The Bureau of Narcotic Enforcement has the primary function of enforcing of the State Narcotic Act. Liaison is maintained with other law enforcement agencies in coordinating and conducting investigations. The Bureau of Investigations is staffed with special agents and maintains four field offices, and two resident agent offices in the state. The agents provide investigative field assistance to local law enforcement agencies in the solution and prosecution of major crimes.

Investigative Services Branch. This branch includes the Criminalistics Laboratory System. Its services are available to local law enforcement agencies which do not have laboratory facilities. The criminalistics laboratories under the Department of Justice are located throughout the state of California, and provide scientific investigative and analysis services to aid in the detection and apprehension of criminals throughout the state of California.

Organized Crime Unit and Criminal Intelligence Branch. This branch combats organized criminal groups by providing a strategic intelligence system to satisfy the investigative, prosecuting, and regulatory needs of criminal justice agencies. It provides training programs for local law enforcement agencies, and develops special investigative and prosecutive techniques.

Identification and Information Branch. This branch provides identification and criminal information services to all law enforcement agencies through three sections. The Bureau of Criminal Statistics gathers, analyzes, interprets, and reports the major facts on crime and delinquency in California. The Automated Information Services provides data processing services to all divisions of the Department of Justice, and statewide information services to criminal justice agencies. The Bureau of Identification maintains a fingerprint section which processes criminal fingerprints. It maintains criminal history files on all persons arrested in California.

Commission on Peace Officers Standards and Training. In 1959 the Department of Justice established the Commission on Peace Officers Standards and Training, which consists of ten members appointed by the governor. The attorney general is an ex officio member. Six members are peace officers in city police departments or county sheriffs offices, one must be below the rank of sergeant, two are elected officers or chief administrative officers of cities, and two are similar personnel from counties. The commission is authorized to adopt rules on the standards of physical, mental, and moral fitness which are to govern the hiring of police officers and their training in those cities and counties which receive state aid under the law.

The commission is also empowered to develop programs to improve the effectiveness of law enforcement, and conducts management surveys of police agencies upon the request of local jurisdictions. The commission is authorized to allocate funds to cities and counties which voluntarily agree to adhere to the standards of hiring and training of peace officers. The commission reimburses cooperating agencies for a percentage of the salary of the officers who train in approved facilities, and for a portion of their living expenses. The commission is empowered to determine conformity with cooperating agencies.

Resources Agency

Departments within the Resources Agency include the Departments of: 1. Forestry, 2. Fish and Game, 3. Parks and Recreation, 4. Water Resources, 5. Navigation and Ocean Development, 6. Conservation. The departments within the Resources Agency are all concerned with California's natural resources. They are all dedicated to the betterment of California's environment through conservation and the prudent use of the state waters, soils, fish and wildlife, recreational facilities, forests and minerals.

Division of Forestry. The Division of Forestry is responsible for the protection and conservation of privately and state owned forests, brush and grass lands. These lands provide food, water and forest products, and are environmental necessities for clean air, fish and wildlife habitat, recreational areas, and open space. The division's functions include: fire protection; fire prevention, fire suppression, resources management; forest practices; state forests; forest nursuries; forest advisory programs; range and watershed management; conservation, and ecology camps.

Department of Navigation and Ocean Development. The Department of Navigation and Ocean Development is the state agency responsible for boating safety, boating facility development, and beach erosion control programs of the state.

Department of Fish and Game. Within the Resource Agency the Department of Fish and Game and its personnel are charged with the administration and enforcement as dictated by the Fish and Game Commission. The functions of the Department of Fish and Game include inland fisheries, operations research, marine resources, wilderness management, wildlife protection, environment services, planning, and special units. Of all of the units of the Department of Fish and Game, the most visible and most recognized are the wilderness management and wildlife protection units.   Wildlife management primarily functions: to maintain a continous survey of game and non-game wildlife species; to work on the improvement and preservation of wildlife habitats; to prevent wildlife losses from pesticides and disease; to work on public access projects; and to recommend regulations for the use of game population in accordance with modern game management principles, based on their accumulated knowledge of California wildlife.

Wildlife protection functions to carry out the law enforcement work of the Department of Fish and Game to protect fish and wildlife resources, and to prevent violations before they occur. Fish and Game wardens throughout the state report to patrol lieutenants or patrol captains, who in turn report to patrol inspectors in charge of law enforcement in each region. The wildlife protection branch also enforces the laws and regulations governing the transportation on possession of exotic species, and conducts California hunter safety programs.

California Public Utilities Commission

The California Public Utilities Commission is a judicial and administrative agency comprised of five members appointed by the Governor, and approved by the senate. Its duty is to regulate specific privately owned utilities and transportation companies, and to secure for the public adequate services and rates which are just and reasonable. The law prohibits variation from established rates and discrimination by companies. The commission has both legislative and judicial powers, and the authority to take testimony. It issues decisions and orders, may cite for contempt, and may subpoena the records of regulated companies.

The Public Utilities Commission regulates the rates and services of more than 1,500 privately owned utilities and transportation companies. These include gas, electric, water, telephone and telegraph companies; railroads, buses, trucks, airlines and vessels transporting passengers or freight in intrastate commerce; wharehousemen, wharves, pipeline companies, household goods, carriers and others. There are also more than 18,000 highway carriers who have permits to transport property for the public for hire.

FEDERAL REGULATORY AGENCIES

Regular agencies have been called the fourth branch of government. Citizens generally have little knowledge of the background, functions and performance of these agencies. Even politically aware people often maintain sketchy and inaccurate images regarding the commissions and boards which are charged with regulatory responsibility. It can be said that at the federal level, especially, independent regulatory agencies have low visibility. While they are often mentioned in the news media, and while many of us are very familiar with the titles (such as FTC, ICC, FAA etc.), we often harbor distorted information on their true nature.

Structure of Regulatory Agencies

In examininig the legal basis for regulatory agencies, we find that while they were created and funded by Congress, they are staffed by Presidential appointees for varying terms. Through congressional actions, regulatory commissions have acquired a great deal of power. Many of them have the unique role of performing the three major functions of government. Their primary role is to control the myriad processes between business and the public. In doing so, they have a great influence on economics and other related matters. [1]

FEDERAL INDEPENDENT OFFICES AND ESTABLISHMENTS

ACTION
Administrative Conference of the U.S.
American Battle Monuments
  Commission
Appalachian Regional Commission
Board for International Broadcasting
Canal Zone Government
Civil Aeronautics Board
Commission of Civil Rights
Commission of Fine Arts
Commodity Futures Trading
  Commission
Community Services Administration
Consumer Product Safety Commission
Environmental Protection Agency
Equal Employment Opportunity
  Commission
Export-Import Bank of the U.S.
Farm Credit Administration
Federal Communications Commission
Federal Deposit Insurance Corporation
Federal Election Commission
Federal Home Loan Bank Board
Federal Maritime Commission
Federal Mediation and Conciliation
  Service
Federal Reserve System Board of
  Governors of the
Federal Trade Commission
Foreign Claims Settlement
  Commission of the U.S.
General Services Administration
Indian Claims Commission

Inter-American Foundation
International Communication Agency
Interstate Commerce Commission
National Aeronautics and Space
  Administration
National Credit Union Administration
National Foundation on the Arts
  and the Humanities
National Labor Relations Board
National Mediation Board
National Science Foundation
National Transportation Safety Board
Nuclear Regulatory Commission
Occupational Safety and Healty
  Review Commission
Overseas Private Investment
  Corporation
Panama Canal Company
Pennsulvania Avenue Development
  Corporation
Pension Benefit Guaranty Corporation
Postal Rate Commission
Railroad Retirement Board
Renegotiation Board
Securities and Exchange Commission
Selective Service System
Small Business Administration
Tennessee Valley Authority
U.S. Arms Control and Disarmament
  Agency
U.S. Civil Service Commission
U.S. International Trade Commission
U.S. Postal Service
Veterans Administration

Inputs into regulatory agencies come from many directions: commission appointments by the executive branch; rulings and legal interpretations from the judicial branch; laws from the legislative branch; lobbyists and experts from the industry; and suggestions, requests and proposed directions from consumers. As a result, policy formulation is influenced not only by congress, but also by the aforementioned in varying degrees, and in many ways. It would be reasonable to say that it is congress, and specifically, the congressional committee, that are most effective in influencing policy formulation through legislation and appropriation. However, we cannot overlook the fact that, because of the appointment powers of the president, influential interests can at time infiltrate the regulatory body itself.

Examination of some of the specific federal regulatory agencies having a major influence on the citizens of the United States is in order. There are seven regulatory commissions which have the most impact on the regulation and control of the private sector in the United States today. They are: 1. The Civil Aeronautics Board, 2. The Federal Communications Commission, 3. The Federal Maritime Commission, 4. The Federal Power Commission, 5. The Federal Trade Commission, 6. The Interstate Commerce Commission, 7. The Securities and Exchange Commission.

The "Big Seven," as they are often labeled, have a special prominence in economic regulation because of their established nature, the importance of the functions they perform, and the political controversy which often surrounds them.[2]

Each of the seven agencies is engaged in complex regulatory, and, in some instances, promotional tasks. Some of the agencies regulate entry, prices, financial arrangements and control, business conduct, and competitive prices in the public sector. The Civil Aeronautics Board has jurisdiction over civil air transportation; the Federal Communications Commission exercises control over common carriers employing wire or the radio spectrum; the Interstate Commerce Commission oversees various forms of surface transportation. The Federal Trade Commission involves the economy as a whole in regard to corporate structure and competitive practices. In addition, it provides particular protection for consumers in such things as credit practices, and in textiles, labeling flammable fabrics. The Securities and Exchange commission regulates the operations of the securities industry in order to protect investors, principly through the mechanism of disclosure. It would be in order to examine five of the seven agencies listed above and discuss them in more detail.[3]

Civil Aeronautics Board

Over the years the Civil Aeronautics Board has developed a more and more important role in the regulation of activities of the private sector in the United States. Over a period of years the federal government has taken the initiative to control and supervise all interstate aviation and commerce. All foreign commerce is exclusively under federal control. Two agencies, the Civil Aeronautics Administration, and the Civil Aeronautics Board, supervise civil aviation and administer regulations. The Civil Aeronautics Administration is executive in character, and enforces the rules of the Civil Aeronautics Board. It directs the federal aid program with the ultimate purpose of providing a national airport system.[4]

The Civil Aeronautics Board is an independent Board of five members who are appointed by the president with the senate's approval. It makes civil aviation rules and regulations, determines rates, adjudicates differences, and performs investigations and other functions essential to the promotion of air transportation, the postal service, and national defense. It issues certificates of convenience and necessities, and furnishes permits to foreign carriers.

Federal Communications Commission

The Federal Communications Commission was created by an act of congress in 1934 to regulate communications by wire and radio in interstate and foreign commerce. Its jurisdiction includes telephone, telegraph, submarine lines, radio and television. The regulation of these forms of communication are assigned to the commission by congress, and are intended to secure adequate facilities, assure reasonable charges, promote safety measures, and advance the national defense. The commission consists of seven members appointed by the president, subject to confirmation by the senate. The term of office is seven years, and the president designates the member who will serve as chairman. The commission exercises general supervision over telegraph and telephone companies and can require an extension of services, maintenance of reasonable rates, and forbid special benefits or favors. In the field of radio, the commission regulates not only broadcasting, but also public and private communication by radio. The commission: awards licenses to broadcasting stations; assigns frequencies; determines the location of stations and their power; provides the regulations respecting the operation of the actual stations; participates in determining international agreements relative to broadcasting; and, while freedom of speech cannot be abridged, can forbid the use of profane and obscene language over the air, and require that advertising meet certain broad standards.

Federal Trade Commission

Satisfaction with the administration of the Sherman Act was largely responsible for the creation of the Federal Trade Commission in 1914. An agency was created, at first, to prevent the formation of monopolies and, second, to protect competing businesses from practices which might prove detrimental to their businesses.

The purpose of the Federal Trade Commission is to foster and protect free competition, subject to certain exceptions. The Federal Trade Commission is an independent regulatory agency consisting of five members, appointed by the president with Senate confirmation, for terms of seven years. Basically, the commission engages in two types of activities.[5] The first, which is legal in nature, is to ensure compliance with fair trade practices, rules, and regulations; the second is to make studies and investigations of certain business conditions, and to issue reports for the use of both government and individuals.

Interstate Commerce Commission

The Interstate Commerce Commission is composed of eleven members with terms of seven years. Its function include the regulation of not only railroads, but also interstate trucking, water and pipeline transportation, Pullman service, and express companies. Because of the increased duties and responsibilities assigned by congress, the ICC now requires a staff number of over 2,000.

One of the major functions of the commission is to determine the rates to be charged by railroads. In addition, the commission is responsible for the enforcement of safety regulations, promotion of safety programs, and the maintenance of statistics. Another responsibility is to see to it that the railroads offer proper service. This has proven to be difficult with respect to the passenger service on local lines, which is often insufficient to pay the costs of operation. The commission may authorize the construction or abandonment of particular lines, the curtailment of train service, the joint use of terminals, or may take other action for the improvement of service.

The Interstate Commerce Commission regulates motor transportation in the same manner as rail. Unfair practices like rebates and other descriminations are forbidden. Licenses to operate must be secured, rates set, and standards provided.[6]

Securities and Exchange Commission

The Securities and Exchange Commission was created shortly after the stock market collapse in 1929. Due to complaints from citizens, Congress felt the pressure to protect the investor from salesman and promoters who used unethical, dishonest, means of selling securities. The Securities and Exchange Commission thus was created in 1934 as a supervisory agency over the entire security market. Members of the five member commission are appointed by the president with the approval of the Senate for a term of five years. The commission is located in Washington, but there are several regional offices scattered over the United States. The work of the commission is to administer acts of Congress, and to provide for regulation of the issuance and sale of securities and the control of holding companies.

SUMMARY

In this chapter we have analyzed some of the more recognizable state agencies having a primary function in the criminal justice system. As indicated, this list does not include all of the criminal justice agencies in the system.

We discussed the Department of Alcoholic Beverage Control, stating that the department received its authority from the California Constitution. The Department of Alcoholic Beverage Control has exclusive responsibility for issuing licenses for the distribution and sale of any alcoholic beverage in California. The majority of laws relating to ABC are contained in the Alcoholic Beverage Control Act in the Business and Professions Code. The responsibilities of the ABC consist of licensing and enforcement. Since the sole responsibility of the ABC is to license distributors of alcoholic beverages, a large percentage of time is devoted to investigating and recommending approval or denial of specific license requests. Of the licenses required in California, we learned that retail licenses are the most frequently requested, and are divided into two groups: off-sale and on-sale licenses. In terms of enforcement responsibilities, we indicated that the ABC agents perform these functions as peace officers, to serve as defined by the State of California.

The Department of Motor Vehicles has three major functions; one is the registration of motor vehicles. This function includes the registering of all motor vehicles in the state, as well as maintaining proper records or their identity and ownership. Information on the vehicles is filed in three separate categories: by the names of registered owners, by license numbers, and by serial or identification numbers. Another important responsibility is the testing and licensing of drivers. A third responsibility of the Department of Motor Vehicles is the administration of financial responsibility laws. This responsibility concerns liability and consumer protection, as laws in California require a person operating a motor vehicle to possess proper insurance, or to demonstrate financial responsibility.

The Department of Justice has five divisions, each of which performs specific functions within the state of California. We discussed each of those divisions, including the Division of Civil Law, the Division of Criminal Law, the Division of Special Operations, the Division of Administration, the Crime Prevention Unit, and the Division of Law Enforcement. Commission on Peace Officers Standards and Training was discussed. We indicated that the most recognized division was the

Division of Law Enforcement, which has the responsibility for enforcement and investigation. For example, the Bureau of Narcotics Enforcement is included within this branch, and has the function of enforcing the State Narcotics Act. The Criminalistics Laboratory, branches of which are located throughout California, is also under this division, as well as the identification and Information branch.

The Resources Agency, which is becoming more and more important in the state of California due to conservation efforts, was discussed. Included in the Resources Agency are the Forestry Department, Fish and Game Department, Parks and Recreation Department, Water Resources Department, Navigation and Ocean Development Department, and Conservation Department.

The last section of this chapter was devoted to the state and federal regulatory commissions. We discussed the California Public Utilities Commission, and emphasized the important role it plays within the state. We indicated that the commission regulates the rates and services of more than 1,500 privately owned utilities and transportation companies, and that there are more than 18,000 highway carriers, which it also supervises, who have permits to transport property for hire. On the federal level, we indicated that there are more than eighty regulatory commissions controlling and supervising some aspect of the private sector. We discussed in detail five of the more important commissions which are most frequently recognized. Specifically, we discussed the Civil Aeronautics Board, the Federal Communications Commission, the Federal Trade Commission, the Interstate Commerce Commission, and the Securities and Exchange Commission.

DISCUSSION QUESTIONS

1. Why is it necessary for the State of California to create a special agency, such as the Department of Alcoholic Beverage Control, to regulate and control alcoholic beverages in California?

2. Briefly discuss the five divisions within the California Department of Justice, indicating what is, to you, the most important division and its responsibilities. Justify your choice.

3. List the responsibilities of the Commission on Peace Officer Standards and Training and discuss the role which the commission plays in the regulation and control over peace officers in the state. Has the role changed over the past five years?

4. List and identify the six specific departments contained within the Resources Agency, identifying two of the six which play an important role, and indicate their duties and responsibilities. Justify your choice.

5. Identify one state regulatory commission and describe the various companies which it regulates and controls. In your own words, defend or attack the importance of this commission.

6. Identify two federal regulatory commissions, indicating their specific duties and responsibilities, including the areas which they supervise and regulate.

REFERENCES

1. Wilborn, David M. "Governance of Federal Regulatory Agencies."

2. Wilborn, David M. "Presidents Regulatory Commissionars and Regulatory Police" (Journal of Public law 15 number 1, 1956).

3. Commission on Organization of Executive Branch of the Government, Task Force Report on Regulatory Commissions, (Washington D.C. and U.S. printing office).

4. Crampton, Roger C. "Regulatory Structure and Regulatory Performance: a Critique of the Ash Counsel Report(, Public Administration Review 32 (July/August, 1972).

5. Bernstine, "Regulating Business By Independent Commissions".

6. Robinson, Glen O. "Reorganizing Independent Regulatory Agencies" Virginia Law Review, 1971.

6

The Legal Profession

CHAPTER OBJECTIVES

Upon reading this chapter, the student will be able to:

1. Write an essay that outlines the history of the United States legal profession.

2. Compare the past education and training of lawyers in the United States to the present standards.

3. Describe the roles and responsibilities of various criminal justice professionals within the legal profession (i.e., judges, prosecutors, and defense counselors).

4. List some of the various professional associations that lawyers might belong to on a local, state, or national level.

5. Identify the services provided to the community by the legal profession.

6. Realize the importance of the United States legal profession to the operation of the criminal justice system.

There is probably no other group of professionals in the United States, or the world, who have had a greater impact upon the criminal justice system than the legal profession. When speaking of the U.S. legal profession, one not only speaks of the lawyers who prosecute or defend criminal cases, but also of the judges who sit as the triers of law in those cases. Additionally, one must remember the many legal societies and associations whose purposes are to provide services to their communities and their profession. A full understanding of the U.S. legal profession is necessary in order for any student of criminal justice to more truly recognize the workings of the criminal justice system. Lawyers, judges, and legal educators are concerned with more than just the criminal law. However, for the purposes of this chapter, we shall limit our inquiry to those matters which are primarily concerned with the criminal law, its enforcement, application, and adjudication by members of the legal profession.

No study of the U.S. legal profession would be complete without an inquiry into the history of that profession and its changing roles, from its early formations in this country, to the present. Furthermore, an inquiry into the training and education of the members of the legal profession in our country as it has developed is necessary. Finally, a thorough study of the roles and responsibilities of the various members of the U.S. legal profession is necessary, as these people play important decision—making roles in the criminal justice process. Our study shall include an examination of the office of the prosecutor at federal, state, and local levels. The office of the public defender shall be examined as well as the legal societies whose function is to defend the criminally accused as well. A brief study of the various professional associations, which are dedicated to furthering the professional development of the legal profession, will also be made. It is hoped that, with this background, the student will more fully understand the profession's role in the criminal justice system.

HISTORY OF THE LEGAL PROFESSION

The early history of our country had a great impact upon the formation and characteristics of the fledgling American legal profession. The American colonies, in the early days, were primarily settled by colonists who were familiar with a common law tradition—that is to say, colonists from Great Britain. Many of these colonists left the old world because of their dissatisfaction with the law and its adverse effect upon their lives. In the earliest of our colonial days, the need for a highly sophisticated and organized bar was absent; legal problems were few and far between. When they arose, they could generally be solved within the community, without the need for a trial. This was in great contrast to the specialized legal system of England. In England, the traditional division of the bar into those, who practiced before the courts, and those, who prepared the legal paperwork necessary to practice before the courts was a way of life. This division was recognized by the creation of what we called members of the bar (or barristers), and solicitors (who created societies of solicitors). This division of labor might well have suited the needs of England at the time, but the need for lawyers and any such division of the bar was nonexistent in America in those early days. As a matter of fact, lawyers were not particularly desired; there was not a great need for complicated legal documents or for sophisticated arguments before learned judges. In many of the settlements founded upon religious beliefs, the law, in fact was considered to be unnecessary; rather only the law of God was necessary, and not the law of men. However, things were to change as our country grew, prospered, and became more complicated. The point is that early on, the law and the legal profession were not welcomed with open arms.

In the early days, lawyers had no law schools to go to. Many young Americans who desired to study law had to go to England to obtain a proper legal education. Most of those who remained in America obtained their training as apprentices under the guidance of a practicing attorney or tutor. With the coming of the eighteenth century, and with a steady increase in our population, the number of lawyers in the colonies also grew. Many of the early legal scholars and practitioners in our country were some of the leading revolutionaries of the day, and were the men who led our fight for independence.

Of the fifty-six signers of the Declaration of Independence, approximately twenty-five of them were attorneys, so we can see that the power, influence, and significance of the legal profession, even in the early days of our country, was great. This still holds true today as one can see from the number of lawyers or legally trained persons who are members of the various representative governmental bodies and who hold other executive—type offices.

The development of the legal profession took various approaches, depending upon the colony in which they were in; however, it became clear by the middle of the eighteenth century that lawyers were here to stay. The need for the distinction between solicitors and barristers apparently never took firm hold in the new world. Rather, the idea of barristers, with their fancy white wigs and gowns, became more of a representation of the old ways, for which, during this period of our history, there was little acceptance, as revolution was in the wind. Legal education likewise had developed only in insignificant ways. Many of the leading barristers or lawyers were attending or had attended college, at for example, Harvard College in Massachusetts; however, the most common background that any of the early members of the profession had was that they had studied with lawyers who had either received their education in Europe, or somehow had become recognized in their field in America. By this time, we see that the legal profession obviously did not develop in exactly the same way as it had in England. That is to say that, compared to the Inns of Court for purposes of study for the barristers, and the various legal societies for the solicitors, things here seemed to have been comparatively lax and easy. The American bar had been born with no stringent requirements of any kind, either on a colonial or national level.

Naturally, with the coming of the revolution, anything that reflected an English quality was not held in the best of respect; this lack of sympathy was particularly true for the English law that had been brought to America, and one supposes for the legal practitioners, also. Thus, during the period immediately after the American Revolution, not only had we lost many distinguished attorneys because of political differences, but also because of war losses. There was a need to establish some kind of guidance as to how the legal profession would grow, and what direction it should take. Little help was to be found. In fact, during this time there was great backlash; anything reflective of the English Common Law was rejected, and lawyers in many situations

Daniel Webster arguing before John Marshall and other Justices of the Supreme Court in the famous Dartmouth College Case. Courtesy of the Trustees of Dartmouth College.

"THIS, SIR, IS MY CASE! IT IS THE CASE NOT MERE-LY OF THAT HUMBLE INSTITUTION, IT IS THE CASE OF EVERY COLLEGE IN OUR LAND!...IT IS, SIR, AS I HAVE SAID, A SMALL COLLEGE. AND YET..."

were restricted from referring to any cases decided under the common law prior to the Declaration of Independence in 1776. There were virtually no American judicial reporter systems which could accurately reflect what was taking place in the American courts; these precedents at least could have been used by the lawyers in the various states. In fact, it seems that about the only reliable document that was used which tied the American legal profession to its roots in England as the Commentaries of Blackstone.

Another one of the early problems that the legal profession faced was, what amounted to a decline in professionalism. Various states in the new nation in the early part of the nineteenth century began to open the courts to every citizen who wished to present his case, thereby eliminating the necessity that one be represented by a member of the bar. This democratization of the legal process caused a decline in the professional quality of those who appeared before the bench. Citizen lawyers did not need to have a legal education; in some instances, they were only required to have read law for a few years. Generally, taking into consideration our frontier attitude, it was looked upon as the right of any man to represent himself. There was no great call made to have an organized bar. This led to many of the problems that the legal profession had in later years in achieving significant levels of control over the quality of members of the bar. It wasn't really until the dawn of the twentieth century that legislatures began to take a closer look at the right of the average citizen to appear in court by himself without qualified counsel.

During this era, in which the legal profession was controlled by the legislature, dominated most of the latter two–thirds of the nineteenth century. It wasn't until the twentieth century that the control of admission into the bar became a judicial function, rather than a legislative function. The same impact that the early legislative control had over the bar could be witnessed also in the judiciary, which, during the latter part of the nineteenth century, was opened up to the electoral process. All of this led to a disintegration of efforts to improve the legal profession in America. This early opposition to an educated, adequately trained bar, and a permanent judiciary, left permanent scars on the history of the U.S. legal profession.

The latter one third of the nineteenth century marked the lowpoint in the organizational efforts of the U.S. legal profession. Lawyers were scattered widely over dozens of states; there was no centralized body, such as the Inns of Court, or the Law Society in England, exercising any kind of control or leadership. There were virtually no standards of legal education or qualifications for admission to the bar. Thus, the early history of the U.S. legal profession was marred by several factors: the rejection of the English system as a result of our revolution, and the ensuing democratization of the legal profession and judiciary by the legislatures in the nineteenth century. The final straw was the lack of any professional organization which could lead those who called themselves lawyers.

The foundations of our contemporary bar associations were laid in the early part of the nineteent century by the formation of the Philadelphia Bar Association, which did much to uplift the standards of that particular bar. Also, the formation of the Association of the Bar of the city of New York in 1870 did much to give guidance to future bar associations. It developed a fine library, and a committee structure to deal with the problems of organizing a bar in a city the size of New York. This, in many ways, led to the formation of the American Bar Association, the first national association of lawyers, which was organized in 1878 at Saratoga Springs, New York. While it was at first a fairly conservative organization reflective of its membership, it grew over the years. By 1900 it had became a leading force in its attempt to professionalize and regulate the members of the bar throughout the country, in every regard, through its leadership position. Needless to say, there exist today in the United States, as a direct result of these founding efforts, bar associations in virtually every state of the union, and bar associations at the county and city levels in most parts of the United States. The sheer number of lawyers entering the legal profession in itself places a great responsibility upon the bar associations and the judiciary in regulating this profession, and the task is not an easy one.

TRAINING AND EDUCATION OF THE LEGAL PROFESSION

As was pointed out earlier, the training and education of this group of professionals departed from the traditional British model fairly early on. In the beginning, the apprenticeship system was the system of legal education for young lawyers in early America. This was much in the character of the English system, some of which still is present today. The English system combined the work-study idea of apprenticeship with formal schooling at either the Inns of Court or Law Societies. Further, one could study law at the university level. However, in the United States, because of the absence of any formal Inns of Court or schools of law for either the barrister or the solicitor, the apprenticeship was much more a true apprenticeship here. Reading the law was just that—a study with a practicing member of the profession while reading certain subjects under his guidance. Much earlier the training and education of our professionals was modeled on the English system for education. In fact, many Americans studied law at Cambridge, Oxford, and the various Inns of Court in England prior to wider acceptance of the apprenticeship program as the American method of legal education.

By the middle of the eighteenth century, the apprenticeship program was the method of legal education; there were no universities or professional schools that could provide this kind of training and education. In the late eighteenth and early nineteenth centurys, however, several of our leading universities did incorporate law professorships into their programs. These were at such institutions as the University of Pennsylvania, the University of Virginia, and Harvard. But, these law professorships were limited to the study of law as part of the undergraduate curriculum, and not as a separate and independent law school, such as we know today. Many of the leading professors in these early years were former members of the judiciary and were respected members of the bar. However, given the general apprenticeship background, the fact that very few persons attended universities, and the apparent unwillingness to accept university law education as a prerequisite to practicing law, the study of law as an undergraduate subject never really grew in great popularity. It became just one of many courses that one could study at the undergraduate level.

One of the first real law schools in the true sense of the word that began during this time was the Litchfield Law School. Here we see, in New England, the beginning foundations for the truly independent law school. A practicing attorney, by the name of Tapping Reeve, was called upon quite often to serve as the master for various persons who wished to study the law. Then, as his reputation grew, and the number of students increased, he decided to open a school of law, with the students actually staying near his home and studying law full time. The Litchfield School of Law was outstanding in several ways. First, probably a greater percentage of its graduates went on to take leadership positions in the American society than any other school since its time. Secondly, it was probably the first true professional law school in America. It existed from the 1780s to the 1830s, and then went out of existence, but for fifty years served as the prototype of what was to come.

One of our most important early law schools was Harvard Law School. In approximately 1815, Harvard College, later to become known as Harvard University, established its first professorship of law. Isaac Parker, the Chief Justice of the Supreme Judicial Court of Massachusetts, was the first professor. Here again, law was taught as part of the regular undergraduate curriculum; however, Parker had great desires to make the school into a separate school of law at the graduate level. Several years later, the Harvard Corporation went along with his ideas, and in 1817 the Harvard Law School was established, but only as an undergraduate institution.

The Harvard experiment during this period of time (1815-1830) was not highly successful in terms of its program or of the number of students enrolled.   But then Joseph Story was to come along and change this picture significantly. Story was appointed professor of law and he took on the job of reorganizing the Harvard Law School. Because of his national fame as a leading jurist on the Supreme Court of the United States, the school was immediately a success and became, in a sense, the first national law school.   Students came, during Story's tenure, from all regions of the United States. Shortly after his death, the school fell again into a period of decline. It should be noted that during Story's tenure as head of the law school, a great percentage of the students were graduate students. It was not required that one should be a graduate, but, of course, it was encouraged. It was a purely professional school. Again, with Story's death, as had been the case in the past at various law schools, once leading figures departed from the scene, standards began to fall. So it was with the Harvard Law School, which up until the 1870s became a rather pathetic school of law. Its curriculum and student body went into a period of qualitative and quantitative decline.

The really important change in American legal education came with the appointment of Mr. Christopher Langdale, in 1870, to the Harvard Law School faculty. Langdale was appointed as the Dean of the Law School, a first for the law school up to that time. Numerous changes were introduced.   The major change was the special—course study method of law schools, as differentiated from most other faculties and facilities. Dean Langdale brought in the casebook method of instruction. Prior to this, most law studies had centered around an analysis of Blackstone's Commentaries, and a rather ineffective method of apprenticeship to learn certain information about the law. With the creation of casebooks, which contained the latest and most significant cases in each of the areas of study, and the socratic method of teaching, Harvard began to lead a new wave of teaching law. It wasn't long before it would come to pass that everyone had to be a university graduate before one could become a student at the law school, too. The law school had finally achieved status as a graduate program and was characterized by its case method study.

Thus, we see that the Harvard Law School came to be the forerunner of the legal educational institutions of today. Presently, in the United States, all accredited schools of law (as certified by the American Bar Association or the Association of American Law Schools), are graduate programs. One studies law as a three year, full-time program after having obtained a bachelors degree. In some instances one might be allowed to enter into the law school after successful completion of all but the senior year at some institutions. In any case, the normal course of study for a student of law in the United States now is four years of undergraduate study in any field of interest, followed by three years of study at the graduate level law school. There are also Master of Law programs which take the student of law even further into specialized areas after successful completion of the law degree. The birth of the American Bar Association and the American Association of Law Schools gave guidance to the curriculum, development, and the establishment of basic standards for American law schools. The vast majority of law schools strive for this accreditation as the key to recognition in the legal field of training and education.

All the bar associations themselves, county, state, and national, present various training programs for their members. These programs vary in success and complexity from state to state, city to city, and depending upon their size. Some of the earliest examples of the success of local bar associations can be traced to New York and Philadelphia, where substantial, strong local bar training programs were established. The creation and establishment of the American Bar Association gave great national impetus to improving the standards of training and education within the legal profession throughout the entire nation. Law students today come from virtually every ethnic, cultural, and religious background. Law students tend to be the sons or daughters of those who had been professionals before, as could be expected; but more and more, we see minorities entering into the study of law, because this is considered one of the leading ways in which to achieve what one may conceive to be the proper ends of social justice. Law students, while they tend to be from middle class homes, have more and more in recent years come from a variety of backgrounds. Minority programs have, of course, stimulated this development.

ROLES AND RESPONSIBILITIES OF THE LEGAL PROFESSION

Let us now examine some of the roles and responsibilities that members of the U.S, legal profession have accepted in our society. The early history of the profession shows its involvement in many aspects of the political and judicial life of the people. Because their training and education gives them both a well—rounded undergraduate education, as well as a specialized professional preparation, there can be little doubt of the value of these people in our society. However, there are some distinctive legal roles which members of the U.S. legal profession play. They serve as prosecutors at federal, state, and local levels throughout the United States. They serve also to defend those accused of crime in our society, both as public and private defenders, either through systems such as the public defender's office, or privately, through their own practice respectively. Furthermore, they serve as members of legal societies, representing and providing legal services for various groups. They also play a significant role in our society through their various

American Bar Association
Code of Professional Responsibility

Preamble

The continued existence of a free and democratic society depends upon recognition of the concept that justice is based upon the rule of law grounded in respect for the dignity of the individual and his capacity through reason for enlightened self-government. Law so grounded makes justice possible, for only through such law does the dignity of the individual attain respect and protection. Without it, individual rights become subject to unrestrained power, respect for law is destroyed, and rational self-government is impossible.

Lawyers, as guardians of the law, play a vital role in the preservation of society. The fulfillment of this role requires an understanding by lawyers of their relationship with and function in our legal system. A consequent obligation of lawyers is to maintain the highest standards of ethical conduct.

In fulfilling his professional responsibilities, a lawyer necessarily assumes various roles that require the performance of many difficult tasks. Not every situation which he may encounter can be foreseen, but fundamental ethical principles are always present to guide him. Within the framework of these principles, a lawyer must with courage and foresight be able and ready to shape the body of the law to the ever-changing relationships of society.

The Code of Professional Responsibility points the way to the aspiring and provides standards by which to judge the transgressor. Each lawyer must find within his own conscience the touchstone against which to test the extent to which his actions should rise above minimum standards. But in the last analysis it is the desire for the respect and confidence of the members of his profession and of the society which he serves that should provide to a lawyer the incentive for the highest possible degree of ethical conduct. The possible loss of that respect and confidence is the ultimate sanction. So long as its practitioners are guided by these principles, the law will continue to be a noble profession. This is its greatness and its strength, which permit of no compromise.

Canon 1. A Lawyer Should Assist in Maintaining the Integrity and Comtence of the Legal Profession

Canon 2. A Lawyer Should Assist the Legal Profession in Fulfilling Its Duty to Make Legal Counsel Available

Canon 3. A Lawyer Should Assist in Preventing the Unauthorized Practice of Law

Canon 4. A Lawyer Should Preserve the Confidences and Secrets of a Client

Canon 5. A Lawyer Should Exercise Independent Professional Judgment on Behalf of a Client

Canon 6. A Lawyer Should Represent a Client Competently

Canon 7. A Lawyer Should Represent a Client Zealously Within the bounds of the Law

Canon 8. A Lawyer Should Assist in Improving the Legal System

Canon 9. A Lawyer Should Avoid Even the Appearance of Professional Impropriety professional associations, such as the American Bar Association, The National Lawyers' Guild, The American Civil Liberties Union, and through all of the state, local, and county bar associations. They act also as members of the judiciary. An examination of some of these major roles and responsibilities is necessary in order to round out our understanding of the U.S. legal profession. Let us first look at the office of prosecutor.

Prosecutors

The prosecutors are the true managers of the criminal justice system today. They have the unique role of deciding and managing criminal justice resources, especially when it comes to enforcing criminal law through the prosecution of individual criminal acts. Needless to say, not all criminal acts can be prosecuted, and not all efforts are worth the time. For these reasons, the job is an extremely difficult one in our criminal justice system. Let us look at some of the foundations of the office of prosecutor.

Naturally, being a common law society, we looked to the English system of prosecution for guidance in the creation in our own. In England, crimes were originally prosecuted by individuals who were, in a sense, seeking vengeance for a crime against them or their family. Because this inconsistency often worked against the purposes of the criminal law, the king eventually took over the duty of prosecution because of the greater public interest. Major crimes were delineated, and the office of the attorney general was eventually created. Thus, we see that prosecution for criminal wrongs, in its earliest development, was done on a personal basis, and eventually developed into prosecution for and on behalf of the king, or the society as a whole. In England, quite early on, the office of the attorney general was created, and much later an office for a director of public prosecutions. This creation of state offices or a sovereign office representing the King and/or the people became the fundamental guideline for the American office of prosecutor. It differed from our English forefathers' system only in the sense that we divided the tasks and responsibilities for prosecution into three distinct levels: the federal, state, and local levels; whereas, in England, they were all at a national level only. In the United States today, the prosecutor at the federal level is the United States Attorney General. He has representatives throughout the United States to prosecute violations of the federal law. At the state level there is usually a legal officer known as the attorney general, responsible for prosecution of all violations of state law. Here again, the workload is decentralized through district attorneys serving throughout the state. At the local level, there is either a city attorney or a prosecutor who represents the city for the enforcement of its local ordinances.

At the federal level, the U.S. Attorney General is a member of the president's cabinet, and is the head of the Department of Justice. Under him there is the office of the Solicitor General, and nine deputy attorney generals for various special branches. The largest of the subdivisions are the Anti-Trust Division, the Civil Division, and, of course, the Criminal Division. The U.S. Attorney General is responsible for the prosecution of all violations of federal law, and represents the United States in all cases of interest. The U.S. attorney general not only prosecutes violations of federal criminal statutes, but represents the United States in all civil actions, and as well, runs the federal correctional institutions. Of the nine divisions, each headed by one of the deputy attorney generals, the largest is the Criminal Division, which has by far the largest number of attorneys actively engaged in the prosecution of cases. There are ninety-three U.S. district attorneys throughout the United States, each of whom is responsible for prosecuting federal violations in his district. Because of the federal nature of the office of the U.S. Attorney General, there are obviously far more opportunities for coordination of law enforcement efforts and consistency of prosecutional discretionary action than one would find on the state or local level.

At the state level, the organization of the office of the Attorney General may vary, but the basic function is similar to that of the U.S. Attorney General; that is to say, he represents the interests of the given state in both civil and criminal actions. Normally, he divides his workload and enforcement duties on some kind of geographical basis. Major qualifications for the office are usually that one be a member of the bar, be experienced, have a proper legal education, and fulfill other criteria.

At the city level, not only does the title of the prosecutor vary, but his criminal responsibility is much less significant than at either the federal or the state level. This is so primarily because criminal statutes are enforced on a state—wide basis, and are based upon a state criminal code, rather than on varied codes from city to city. Normally, prosecutions for criminal activities at the city level include only minor criminal infractions, generally those of the misdemeanor type. Again qualifications for city attorney may vary from city to city, but generally most candidates are qualified members of the legal profession.

Thus, we see the organization and structure of the office of prosecutor, from its earliest beginnings through to today, in both England and in the United States.

The primary responsibility that the prosecutor has is the decision on whether or not to prosecute, based upon the information that has been provided to him by the law enforcement and investigative agencies. Additionally, he must take into consideration matters of public policy, and the simple logistics of the numbers of cases that can be prosecuted by his staff in a successful and worthwhile manner. Needless to say, economics is not a minor consideration in terms of the enforcement of the law. He is, in fact, a manager of criminal justice resources. The prosecutor represents the interests of the people at all stages of criminal prosecution, be it preliminary hearings, pretrial negotiations, screening decisions, or the actual trial.

Defense Counsel

Another significant role which members of the U.S. legal profession play in our criminal justice system is that of the defense counselor. They take on this responsibility in several different ways; we have the public defender's office operating at both federal and state levels, and private attorneys engaged in law practice defending those accused of violations of our criminal law. Additionally, we have various types of legal aid societies, whose purpose it is to provide defense counsel in civil and criminal cases for indigent persons. Also, judges may assign local counselors to criminal cases under the assigned counsel system established by that court. Again, we see a significant role that a member of the U.S. legal profession plays in the criminal justice system. Structurally, one can serve in the role of defense counselor from either a public or private prospective. The responsibilities of the defense counsel are extreme. He has the duty of defending the guilty, as well as the innocent, from prosecution for alleged violations of the criminal law. Perhaps one of the most difficult concepts for the average citizen to understand is the idea that, under our system of constitutional law, a person, even though guilty, has the right to be fully and vigorously defended. This role and this responsibility have been accepted by the U.S. legal profession.

Significant case decisions highlight our constitutional right to counsel under the Sixth Amendment of the U.S. Constitution. The right to counsel's impact is manifested in other ways too, such as in our Fifth Amendment right to remain silent. This right would be of little value without the advice of counsel concerning its use. Because of *Gideon*,[1] *Escobedo*,[2] *Miranda*,[3] and other decisions by the U.S. Supreme Court, we have seen a great growth in the role of defense counseling in the criminal justice system in the last fifteen to twenty years.

The public defender's system is largely the result of the creation of the Office of Economic Opportunity, and other federal projects, with funds and aims designed to help the accused in the criminal justice system. The public defender can be likened in many ways to the prosecutor at the trial level, in the sense that he is the prosecutor's counterpart. His responsibility, however, instead of prosecuting, is to defend. His training is comparable to that of the prosecutor. He is employed by the state and his duty is, instead of to the state, to his client. The private defense counselor is compensated for his fee, and is also called upon to take on cases on a voluntary, no-fee basis. This was the case prior to the creation of large public defender's offices in most of the major cities. Legal societies also have come to the fore in providing legal advice and protection for those accused of crimes, as well as to advocate other positions in the law. Such free legal aid societies have grown throughout the United States, particularly in light of the lack of response at one time by the collective bar to the needs of the indigent criminal.

Assigned counsel systems can and have been established in the various trial courts of our nation at the local, state, and federal levels. This was the major way of handling indigent cases prior to the creation of the public defender's office and legal aid societies. In that system, local attorneys were appointed or assigned by the court to defend various indigent clients who had that need. Unfortunately, the assigned counsel system has never really worked out well in our country. There have been various successes in different cities, where the response of the bar has been adequate, but by and large, it has been an unsuccessful system. This method is perhaps most well suited to rural or smaller areas, where the sense of obligation to the community is more prevalent. In large urban areas, the sheer number of cases that come up requiring counsel

Ernesto Miranda (right) was convicted for a second time although his first conviction was overturned by the Supreme Court. Courtesy UPI

without a fee or with a minimal fee places extreme burdens upon those active members of the bar willing to support such a system. Furthermore, judges must be careful about how they assign cases to 'qualified' members of the criminal bar.

One of the noticeable changes in the legal profession in recent years is the real establishment of what one might call a criminal bar. Because of the licensing procedures required to practice law throughout the United States, it is not unheard of to have somebody directly out of law school take on a major felony case without a great deal of either trial practice or criminal experience. Quite often now, states are certifying certain members of the bar who have experience, and who have chosen the criminal bar as their field. We find the bar is labeling these lawyers as members of the criminal bar, to differentiate them from other specialized areas of practice, such as tax, patent, or international law. This is good in the sense that it will hopefully delineate those who are qualified from those who are not, to take on major criminal trials.

As mentioned above, another source of defense counsel would be the various legal aid societies that have been in existence in various forms throughout the history of our country. These societies began, in some instances, in attempting to unify and defend various members of different cultures and races. Today they represent one common denominator, that is, those who are indigent and unable to defend themselves, or unable to hire a well qualified attorney to defend them. Through the legal services programs started by the Office of Economic Opportunity, a great many legal aid programs were created, and serve to this day to provide legal services to the indigent community. The members of such legal aid societies are generally members of the bar who volunteer their time. In a great many instances, law students, authorized under the rules of the court of various states, may represent clients even though they are not fully qualified members of the bar. This is not possible in cases where extremely serious crimes are being prosecuted; there, of course, a qualified member of the bar must control the case.

Judiciary

Another area in which members of the U.S. legal profession have taken on roles and responsibilities of great significance in our society is in the judiciary. Almost all judges in the United States are lawyers by training, education, and professional background. The role of the judiciary in our society is extremely significant. A well educated bar and an extremely efficient law enforcement system would do no good were there not an effective and respected judiciary to which to bring the criminal defendant accused of a violation of the law. Throughout the history of our country, U.S. lawyers have played a dominant role in the establishing a great status and respect for the judiciary of the United States. The role that they fulfill is that of the judge; that is, the trier of law in cases in both civil and criminal courts. The judges could range from magistrates and traffic court judges, all the way through to members of the supreme courts of the various states, and of the U.S. Supreme Court. Most judges are chosen because of their experience, character, integrity, and professional expertise. The system of selection varies from state to state. Some are appointed on a purely political basis, some on a merit system, and others are elected by the public. Whatever the method, their important role in our criminal justice system is clear. Once having obtained this office, the responsibilities are immense. There is the difficulty of ruling on the ever–changing laws and the precedents provided by higher courts, and also the burden of the imposition of an appropriate and just sentence for those convicted by the criminal process.

California Code of Judicial Conduct

Preamble

The Conference of California Judges, mindful that the character and conduct of a judge should never be objects of indifference, and that declared ethical standards should become habits of life, adopts these principles which should govern the personal practice of members of the judiciary. The administration of justice requires adherence by judiciary to the highest ideals of personal and official conduct. The office of judge casts upon the incumbent duties in respect to his conduct which concern his relation to the state, its inhabitants, and all who come in contact with him. The Conference adopts this Code of Judicial Conduct as a proper guide and reminder for justices and judges of courts in California and for aspirants to judicial office, and as indicating what the people have a right to expect from them.

CANON 1.   A Judge Should Uphold the Integrity and Independence of the Judiciary

CANON 2.   A Judge Should Avoid Impropriety and the Appearance of Impropriety in All his Activities

CANON 3.   A Judge Should Perform the Duties of His Office Impartially and Diligently

CANON 4.   A Judge May Engage in Activities to Improve the Law, the Legal System, and the Administration of Justice

CANON 5.   A Judge Should Regulate His Extra-Judicial Activities to Minimize the Risk of Conflict with his Judicial Duties

CANON 6.   Compensation and Expense Reimbursement for Quasi-Judicial and Extra-Judicial Activities

CANON 7.   A Judge Should Refrain from Political Activity Inappropriate to his Judicial Office

Professional Associations

One final area which we should look at in terms of the roles and responsibilities that the members of the U.S. legal profession have taken on in our country is their own professional associations. These associations provide guidance, standards, and training to the profession as a whole. The associations are organized on local, state, national, and international levels. The paramount organization would be the American Bar Association; also significant are the local bar associations, and such other national legal associations as the American Civil Liberties Union, the National Lawyers' Guild, and the Federal Bar Association, to name a few. Through these professional associations, the bar has succeeded in improving the standards for admission in the various states, and in providing important training and seminar programs for the improvement of the general quality of the bar. Furthermore, they provide guidance in establishing standards for law schools, court performance, and various areas of legal specialization.

SUMMARY

The role of the U.S. legal profession in the criminal justice system has played a significant part in the history of this country. From its beginnings and its common law traditions, the law and the legal profession had to adapt to the American way. This was seen in various ways in the early history of our nation. First and foremost was the fact that for many years there existed no legitimate process by which one could become a member of the legal profession. In fact, because of our revolutionary attitudes, and later, our separation from Great Britain, it was quite difficult for the American people to accept a legal profession based upon the English model; and it was sometimes difficult for the people to accept man-made law in the early colonial times. Be that as it may, eventually the American lawyer emerged, at first in a British form, but with definite American characteristics. His training and education in the earliest of days was a transposition of the English system. Many of our lawyers, in fact, obtained their training and education in England itself. But, because of the distance from the motherland, and of parochial desires on the part of the American people, the apprenticeship system of training and education of the bar was prevalent in the formative years of the legal profession. After the revolution, many of the English ways were discarded. Because of the decentralization of power which was vested in the state level, there was no national guidance, no national law school, and no national basis for admission to practice before the bar. This caused many problems, but it was soon apparent that the apprenticeship program was to be the way of basic legal education and training for the first hundred years or so of our nationhood.

There was, however, some university activity in the field of legal education which had various successes and failures. It wasn't until the twentieth century really, that the law school came into its own and provided the American people with a fully educated and trained graduate student of law, who was then prepared for admission to the bar. The roles and responsibilities that these new members to the bar had to choose from varied. We saw that the office of prosecutor was created under our system of government at the national, state, and local levels. It is a significant office, with great discretion and responsibility, and is primarily occupied by members of the U.S. legal profession. Hand in hand with the need for the office of prosecutor is the need to defend the criminally accused. This, in the early days, was taken care of by those in private practice, or on an assigned counsel basis for those who the court felt needed counsel. Also, early in our history, various legal societies were formed to aid various groups, generally along ethnic lines. Eventually, with the arrival of the twentieth century, we saw the creation of the public defender's system. We discussed the members of the judiciary, who also come from the ranks of our law graduates, and who fulfill another role and responsibility which the U.S. legal profession has readily taken on. Because of the general political nature of the American lawyer, candidates have sought offices in the judiciary on the basis of their credentials and experience. Finally, we saw and briefly examined the role of professional associations, such as the American Bar Association, the local bar associations, and such specialized groups as the American Civil Liberties Union. These associations did and do much to enhance the professional development of members of the bar, and create basic criteria and standards of excellence for law schools and for professional practice.

From all of these roles, and the significant responsibilities included therein, we can see that the legal profession has an essential and important function in the criminal justice process. Through training and education, lawyers are well prepared for their managerial and discretionary roles, although in some instances in the past they were not as well prepared as we might have wished. This profession always has and still does play a most significant role in American society. The U.S. legal profession has done its job, and done it well, despite its growing pains and historical obstacles. One can only hope that this profession will be blessed continually in the future with great legal servants, as it has been in the past.

TOPICS FOR DISCUSSION

1. Why did the American lawyer fail to emerge with the same education, training, and background as his English counterpart?

2. What was it about the American form of government that caused organizational problems here for the early legal profession?

3. What was the typical education and training of the American lawyer of the past, compared to today?

4. Compare the role and responsibilities of the prosecutors at all levels in the United States.

5. Why was the public defender's system established?

6. What is the general purpose of the various professional associations that American lawyers have established?

7. Has the U.S. legal profession had much of a role to play in the judicial area?

REFERENCES

1. Gideon v. Wainwright, 372 U.S. 335, 83 S.Ct. 792 (1963).

2. Escobedo v. Illinois, 378 U.S. 478, 84 S.Ct. 1758 (1964).

3. Miranda v. Arizona, 384 U.S. 436, 86 S.Ct. 1602 (1966).

7

The Court
and Its Officers

CHAPTER OBJECTIVES

Upon reading this chapter, the student will be able to:

1. Outline the structure of the federal court system in terms of appellate courts and trial courts, indicating the work or jurisdiction of each component.

2. Complete a chart or diagram showing the state equivalents of the various levels of federal courts, and indicate the work or jurisdiction of each component.

3. Compare and contrast the federal and state judiciaries in terms of methods of selection, tenure in office, and procedures for discipline or removal.

4. Discuss the judicial process in terms of decision making, rules, facts, and discretion.

5. List and briefly describe the importance of the major tasks of the court support staff and court enforcement officers.

6. Identify and comment knowledgably on the following topics: the dual structure of the appellate courts and inferior courts; Gordon v. Justice court; court unification; referees; commissioners; court use of computers; court administrators; super-secure courtrooms; and witnesses protection.

Having considered the American legal profession in the last chapter, the stage is set for an examination of the American court system, or, more precisely, the court systems. The place to begin is with a review of the structure and organization of the federal court system, and of the diverse state systems. In this portion of the chapter, students will do well to carefully note the distinctions between appellate and trial courts, and between superior and inferior trial courts.

Previous chapters have discussed the part that discretion plays in the roles of law enforcement officers, prosecutors, and others. Here, too, discretion will be considered in connection with the judge and his decision-making process. The student will find that while all judges share the same general process in making decisions, the men who make them are selected by very different methods. Similarly, there is a great variety in the methods that have been devised for the discipline and removal of judges.

Since the most important function of a court is to make decisions, the judges are by far, the single most important element; however, no judge works alone in the courthouse, or even in the courtroom. The presence of his clerk, his bailiff, and often a stenographer is a reminder that the courthouse is a complex set of people, procedures and equipment, all dedicated to supporting the decision-making function of the court. Consequently, the work of the clerical staff will be considered in terms of what these people do in order to support the judge's work, and to move cases through the system. Additionally, the chapter will devote some attention to the uniformed or sworn courthouse staff—the court enforcement officers—in hopes of shedding some light on the ways in which their work supports the same objective.

The power of the courts is enormous. In a real sense, they may be thought of as the fulcrum of the criminal justice system because they have the power to intervene directly into the activities of other system components, such as corrections and the police. Hence, it is not remark-able that serious issues surround the courts in terms of their efficiency and image. The reader is encouraged to be alert to these issues and controversies which are noted throughout the chapter.

COURT ORGANIZATION AND STRUCTURE

When the thirteen American colonies separated from Great Britain and became independent states, each of them already had a system of courts, a system completely independent of and unrelated to the others. The thirty-seven states that have since been created sustain this indepen-dence. But beyond the state courts, the Constitution, which created the federal union of states, allowed for the creation of a separate national judicial branch. Such a dual system of tribunals is often thought to be a necessary ingredient in any workable federal system of government. We can see by referring to our neighbor, Canada, however, that a dual system is not the case. Under the Canadian federal system, the Dominion Supreme Court is virtually the only federal adjudicating body. All matters arising under provincial or Canadian federal law are tried by the provincial courts. Certain classes of cases may be appealed from the highest court of a province to the Dominion Supreme Court. Obviously then, Canada has no dual system of federal and state courts.[1] It is the dual arrangement of our courts, along with the great diversity of the state systems, that make the American judicial system somewhat complex.

Federal Court Structure

The United States Constitution commands the establishment of only one court, the United States Supreme Court.   However, Congress is

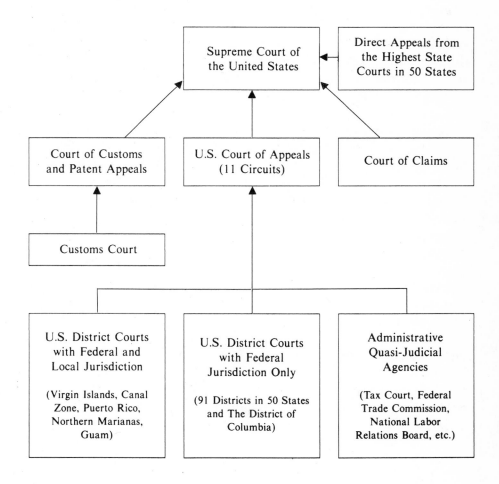

empowered to create other national courts as it sees fit. Theoretically, at least, the legislators could have formed the high court and then simply allowed state courts to try matters arising under both state and federal law. Instead, the decision encompassed by the Judiciary Act of 1789 favored the creation of a separate system of federal courts that has continued, with periodic modification, to this day. The basic unit within this system is the dictrict court. There is at least one such unit per state. Populous states, with their heavy caseloads, may be divided into several districts, each with its own court. For example, New York, Texas, and California are each split into four districts. The number of judges within a district ranges from one to more than twenty, depending upon the caseload.

Each district court houses a clerk's office. It also serves as head-quarters for a United States marshal, as well as for the prosecutor (the United States attorney for the district). In addition, each court maintains one or more bankruptcy referees, United States magistrates, court reporters, and probation officers. In courts having a high volume of criminal cases, a full time public defender is available. The jurisdiction of this court includes both civil and criminal trials, with bankruptcy and civil suits by far the most numerous. Criminal violations tried by the district courts include offenses such as embezzlement, fraud counterfeiting, forgery, interstate auto theft, and alcoholic beverage violations. The district courts for the Canal Zone, Guam and the Virgin Islands have not only the authority to hear cases involving federal law, but also matters of local or territorial jurisdiction.[2]

Of particular interest are the roles and responsibilities of United States magistrates (formerly titled United States commissioners). Magistrates are appointed by the district's judges to act for the court in the capacity of lower court judges. In civil cases, the magistrates are permitted to hear pre-trial motions, and to make recommendations to the judges for a ruling. In criminal matters, the magistrate is allowed to attend to a wide variety of tasks preliminary to trial. He may hear and grant requests for search warrants if probable cause is found. Further, the law requires that persons accused of a federal offense be brought before a United States magistrate for an inquiry as to the probable cause of the arrest. If the charge is a felony, a second hearing may be held before the magistrate to determine whether or not there is sufficient evidence to proceed to trial. The magistrate is allowed to set bail, rule on motions for the transportation of an accused person to another district, and to hear prisoner petitions. Finally, he is permitted to try cases classified as minor or petty offenses. Under federal law, these classes of cases involve fines of less than one thousand dollars, or sentences of less than one year. Since trials before a magistrate occur without a jury, the consent of the accused is required before such a trial.[3]

An individual involved in a civil suit in federal court or charged with a federal crime can appeal his case at two levels. The first resort is to the United States Court of Appeals. Whereas trials are normally conducted by one judge or one magistrate, an appellate hearing ordinarily involves three judges who as a unit, or *en banc*. Trial court decisions may be affirmed, modified, reversed, or ordered retried by the appellate courts. Just as the district court serves a specific geographical area, so does the court of appeals. The fifty states, territories, and the District of Columbia are organized into circuits, called so because they were formerly served by traveling justices of the United States Supreme Court. All of the circuits include three or more states, with the exception of the court that serves the District of Columbia. The court of appeals has two important purposes; it can correct errors made at the trial level, and it can assure uniformity in legal interpretation by reviewing cases where two or more courts have reached different conclusions on the same issue.

The United States Supreme Court serves as precisely the same purposes, but speaks with the ultimate authority. The Court's nine justices are appointed for life by the president with the advice and consent of the Senate. The court meets on the first Monday of October each year for a session that normally continue until June. Since the Supreme Court hears only cases of great national significance, several thousand petitions will be rejected and only some two—hundred to two—hundred and fifty matters will be formally heard by the Court. Of all the federal courts, only the Supreme Court will ordinarily hear an appeal from one of the state courts. Normally, such an appeal involves a matter of great importance that has been appealed from the highest tribunal of one of the states.[4]

The reader will have noted that the criminal jurisdiction of federal courts is very limited. Most federal law violators have become somehow involved with the national government's authority to collect taxes and to regulate interstate commerce. While there are some offenses that equally involve federal and state law, by far the largest number of criminal offenses—an estimated ninety-five percent—clearly belong to the state courts. The structure of the court systems of the various states is generally similar to that of the federal courts. Most states have the two levels of appellate courts. For example, California is divided into five districts, each with its own district court of appeals. The California State Supreme Court is the state's court of last resort for hearing both civil and criminal matters.

At the level of trial courts, the federal two-tiered pattern is usually found. Generally this involves a "superior court" of general or unlimited jurisidiction, and an "inferior court" of limited jurisdiction. In this pattern the superior court resembles the federal district court in having the authority to try both felonies and civil cases involving unlimited sums of money. The lower courts are limited to conducting the preliminaries for felony cases, and to trying misdemeanors and minor infractions. However, unlike the federal magistrate, the state lower court judges are typically permitted to try lesser civil cases involving sums of money limited by law. Finally, it is not unusual for the state systems to provide for at least two types of inferior courts: a rural justice of the peace, and a municipal court designed to serve cities and suburban areas. In these respects, California's court system is fairly typical.[5]

California Court Structure

The constitution of California provides that each county be served by a superior court of one or more judges. Jurisdiction of the superior court extends to felonies, civil suits without monetary limit, and to juvenile, probate, and other civil matters. For the purpose of organizing lower courts, each county is divided into districts. Those having more than 40,000 residents are supplied with a municipal court. Jurisdiction of these courts includes misdemeanors, infractions (most traffic offenses), local ordinance violations, small claims cases, and civil suits involving sums of not more than five thousand dollars. Municipal court judges are permitted to arraign persons accused of a felony and to preside over the preliminary hearing. Both superior and municipal court judges must be lawyers, and have at least ten or five years of experience, respectively.

Districts within the county having less than 40,000 inhabitants are served by a justice court. The judges are elected to their posts, as are the judges of the superior and municipal courts. Justice court jurisdiction is virtually the same as that of the municipal court, with one important exception; in 1974, the California Supreme Court ruled in Gordon v. Justice Court[6] that these courts may not try misdemeanors which involve the prospect of incarceration. The decision was based on the presumption that the non-lawyer judges who commonly served the justice courts would be unable to provide a fair trial in accordance with all of the due process safeguards that now apply. The United States Supreme Court refused to hear an appeal on Gordon in 1975. Thus did California end over a century of misdemeanor trials by popularly elected non-lawyer judges. The Gordon case is of interest not simply because it forced California's rural areas to find lawyer—judges, or to make some arrangement for circuit-riding, but because it exemplifies the nation's continuing concerns about the lower courts.

Courts of general jurisdiction, or superior courts, tend to be adequately financed, dignified, and generally meticulous in their handling of civil and criminal matters. In contrast, the lower courts have often been underfinanced and overburdened with cases. Historically, they have tended to be noisy, undignified, crowded, and have lacked support services. The accusation implicit in *Gordon* has been frequently heard; that is, that the lower courts provide skimpy attention to due process and the rights of defendants. Consequently, for more than seventy years court reformers have lobbied in behalf of various schemes intended to improve the performance of the nations's lower courts.

One aspect of the reform effort has involved a drive to upgrade the lower courts by establishing requirements that all the judges have formal legal training. The other major thrust of the reformers involves changes in court structure. Often this thrust has taken the form of a drive to unify or combine the courts of general jurisdiction with the lower courts in an effort to raise overall standards. A unification of this type

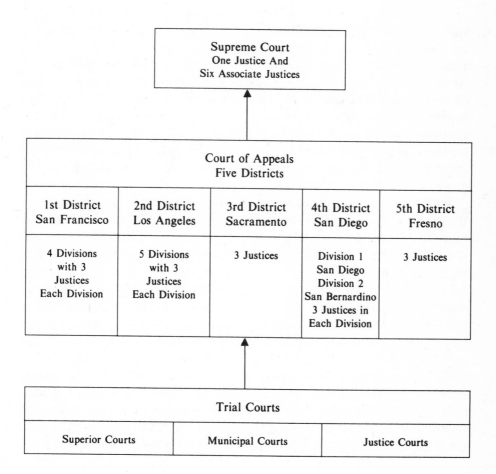

occurred in Illinois in 1974. [7] More decisions on the order of *Gordon*, and structural changes tending toward unification can be expected in the future.

JUDGES, MAGISTRATES AND REFEREES

Federal Judges

Judges of the federal courts are appointed by the president with the advice and consent of the United States Senate. The senators are generally accorded the privilege of nominating individuals for district court judgeships that become available in their states. If a senior senator and the president are of the same political party, and the senator's nominee meets with the approval of the attorney general, an appointment is virtually assured. The American Bar Association has attempted to exercise a consultative function in this process by rating candidates by ability. However, the association's recommendations have sometimes been ignored.

The Constitution guarantees a newly-appointed judge that his salary will not be reduced during his term of office. Furthermore, the judge has his position "during good behavior"; he can be removed only by a vote of impeachment in the senate, and then only if convicted of treason, bribery, or other serious crimes. So difficult is the process, and so obscure the language, that "good behavior" means virtually a lifetime tenure. Territorial judges (the Canal Zone, the Virgin Islands, and Puerto Rico) are an exception, and have only a tenure of eight years. Because of their security of salary and office, the federal judiciary is both extremely independent and quite capable of attracting talented candidates.[8]

Without a real threat of removal, there is little that can be done in the way of disciplining federal judges. Decisions can be reversed or modified on appeal, but serious problems of misbehavior, disability, or low productivity can usually only be handled by suggestions of retirement. A judge who is a sufficient embarrassment to his peers might be assigned to the least desirable facilities in the courthouse, or to the most unattractive cases. Magistrates do not share the "good behavior" tenure of the district court judges. They are appointed and serve "at pleasure," meaning that they can be dismissed at any time.[9]

Party politics are less important (though not absent) in the selection of judges for the court of appeals. New justices of the United States Supreme Court are selected on the basis of complex political, regional, philosophical and ethnic considerations. Retirement benefits for the federal judiciary members are quite generous and are structured in such a way as to encourage retirement or limited service after age seventy.

State Judges

Like the state court systems, the methods of selecting state court judges are extremely varied. In some states, judges are appointed by the governor with the approval of one or both houses of the legislature. A much more common method of selection is by popular election. Judges run for their offices in two different ways. The candidates may be listed on the ballot by their party affiliation. In such a partisan contest, judges are frequently swept into office on a party victory, or ousted in the party's defeat. The non-partisan method calls for candidates to appear on the ballot without party designation. Further, the prospective candidate may not participate in political activities such as soliciting funds, endorsing other candidates, making contributions, or serving on a party committee. While the latter selection process is viewed as a means of political involvement, it should be noted that unless the voters are completely inattentive, political affiliation will play some part in the election. Terms vary widely and tend to be longer for elected appellate judges than for trial judges.

All of the above mentioned methods of selection, in common with the federal appointment process, have political elements. None but the politically active or the politically connected have much prospect of service on the bench when such means of selection are used. In addition, while the field of choice is thus narrowed, there is absolutely no assurance that the best qualified individuals from the field will be selected by the people or the party managers. Three major efforts to surmount this problem have been tried so far. The so-called Missouri Plan was adopted by that state in 1940. Here nominations are made by a non-partisan board consisting of three laymen, three lawyers, and the chief justice of the state supreme court. The board solicits candidates through newspaper advertisements, reduces the ensuing list to three names, and submits it to the governor. The individual selected by the governor serves for a year, and then runs unopposed in an election where the issue is simply whether the candidate should be retained. If the result is an affirmative majority, then the individual serves a full six or twelve year term.

In California, the governor nominates an individual to fill a specific vacancy. The nominee's name is then presented to the state's Commission on Judicial Qualifications. Included as members on the commission are the chief justice of the California Supreme Court, the attorney general, and the presiding judge of the appropriate district court of appeals. Approval by the commission allows the nominee to serve for a year, and then to run unopposed, as in Missouri. Finally, merit schemes similar to the Missouri Plan have in effect been created by the executive decrees of various governors and mayors. The problem with these arrangements is that they are not sanctioned by law, and hence may be revoked at the whim of any successor. [10]

It appears likely that experimentation will continue the effort to lessen political influence in the process of selecting judges. The merit system is one of the primary articles of faith among court reformers. Many Americans find it hard to be comfortablé with the idea that a judge must owe something to his sponsor or sponsors. Accusations of favoritism were recently leveled at a California judge, who dismissed five counts of rape and accepted plea bargains of guilty to one count of robbery and one of rape for each of the two defendants. The sentences handed down were probation for one defendant, and fifty-two weekends in confinement for the other. The judge was censured and the judgment reversed on appeal, but more importantly, local newspapers took up the issue and helped to defeat this judge's bid for re-election in January, 1975.

This example raises the question of removal from office; obviously, there must be some method of removing judges who are corrupt, disabled, or those whose conduct toward others is not in keeping with high standards. The three traditional remedies are impeachment, resolution, and address. All are implemented by the state legislature, and none of them have been utilized very often or with much success. Elected judges may be recalled in some states, and in others there is the possibility of a vigorously contested election. However, the current trend toward a solution for this problem involves plans developed by California and New York. In 1976, an arrangement became effective which provided New York with a Court on the Judiciary. Composed entirely of judges of the state's court of appeals and the appellate division of the supreme court, this body has the power to remove or retire judges for cause, or for mental or physical disability. California's Commission on Judicial Performance is empowered to make recommendations of removal or censure to the state's supreme court. The California agency is considered very effective because it has a permanent investigating capacity, and it has been successful in forcing individuals to resign rather than to face charges in the supreme court.[11]

In addition to the judiciary roles that have been examined, it is fairly common practice for states to provide for lesser judicial officials, often known as referees or commissioners. Many times these officers are like federal magistrates, appointed by the judges and hold their posts "at pleasure." Generally, the work of these subordinate judicial officers is limited to an area of special expertise or to duties of a very specific nature. Particular commissioners may be employed in juvenile courts because of their skills in dealing with young people; others are utilized by domestic relations courts for similar reasons. Finally, at the lower court level, referees may be assigned to hear traffic matters. There is a growing feeling that most traffic matters are not worth the considerable expense of court processing. Following the lead supplied by New York, California is now experimenting with assigning minor traffic hearings to an administrative agency, the Department of Motor Vehicles.[12]

Judicial Decision Making

Any discussion of judges would be incomplete without some reference, however brief, to the process of judicial decision-making. In criminal cases, trial judges make decisions at every stage of a case. Requests for search warrants, wire-taps, or arrest warrants may be made even before any arrest has taken place. At the arraignment stage, decisions involve such issues as probable cause, bail, various waivers, and informing the defendant of his rights. If there is a preliminary hearing, the judge decides whether the evidence is sufficient to proceed to trial. Next there may be motions for the discovery of or suppression of evidence, continuance, change of venue, or various kinds of examinations. Should the defense and the prosecution strike a plea bargain, the judge will ordinarily be compelled to review its terms, and to ascertain if the plea is made with the defendant's full understanding. If the matter goes to trial, more decisions have to be made involving jurors, evidence and testimony. Finally, a judgment of guilt or innocence may be required, as well as a determination of an appropriate sentence. Over and over again, the judge faces the agony of choosing between valid possibilities.

Judicial decisions are controlled by two components: the rules and the facts. The rules involve all of the possible laws that might be applied to a specific case. Rules, then, might include such elements as constitutional law, statutory law, case law decisions, procedural rules, etcetera. The facts would include every piece of information that might be brought forward about the defendant and the events that led him to be charged.

The judicial process consists of selecting the appropriate rule at many points along the way. Often the judge will find it necessary to select the appropriate rule from several possibilities suggested by the contesting attorneys. Facts determine what rule applies to a situation. Conversely, rules determine the admissability and weight of facts. At some point, the judge may be on his own to discover the facts in testimony that might be self-serving, hostile, incomplete, confused or perjured. Like the rest of us, he may be forced to depend on his own perceptions regarding the credibility of a certain individual. Since the perceptions, logic, experience and learning of any one judge will naturally vary from that of another, no two judges will follow precisely the same path through the dozens of decisions involved in a case. At some points, a judge will have considerable discretion in making a choice between alternatives. On other occasions he will find no room to maneuver or choose.[13] At present there is a growing tendency to reduce judicial discretion in some areas, such as in sentencing.

The process of judging is both abstract and complex. Furthermore, it tends to be obscured by the whole panoply of symbols and customs that surround the judicial process: the bench, the black robe, the archaic language, the ceremonial quality of the proceeding, the deference accorded to the judge.   In the end, we return to the question with which we started—how do we get our judges?   As one observer puts it,

> It is the men who count. Men through the agony of resolving human conflict, make a judicial system what it is. Their quality and character, intelligence and dignity, make the law a living, vital entity . . . to the end that men shall know justice. [14]

Now, let us examine the kinds of support that judges receive from the rest of the court staff in the performance of their decision-making function.

COURT SUPPORT PERSONNEL

Within the justice system we tend to emphasize the roles of individuals who have powers of discretion—that is, those with the ability to make choices that will affect the outcome of a case. This focus on discretion is natural because it explains, at least on one level, how the criminal justice system works. However, if we move to a bureaucratic description of how the criminal process works, it becomes obvious that for a case to move through the system, a large number of tasks must be accomplished by the court's clerical or support personnel. Unlike the judges described previously, these individuals exercise little or no discretion in the handling of a particular case.

Court Clerk and Deputies

The court's support personnel are referred to by many different titles. Generally, the staff is headed by a clerk of the court who provide direction to deputy-clerks. The deputies may have job titles based on their specific function. What makes the support staff's work significant is the reality that the court's process may be challenged as irregular or inadequate, and hence, unfair to a particular person. Prosecutions can be dropped or cases lost if there is a discernible failure at a critical step in the criminal process. Just as the court's employees have a responsibility to correctly perform the tasks necessary to move an individual case with justice, they also have a duty to prevent the system from backlogging and falling into error. In order to see the work of the clerical staff in some detail, let us follow an imaginary case through a large California metropolitan court.

One January morning a police detective approached the division chief of the criminal department at the municipal court. From some hastily scribbled notes a clerk was able to prepare for the officer a search warrant for the premises of one John Dealer, the chief suspect in a narcotics investigation. The officer, with his warrant and affidavit, was ushered in to see Judge Law, who signed it. The following day the detective returned to the criminal division in the company of a deputy district attorney. At their direction, a criminal complaint was typed up. Since Dealer had been arrested as a consequence of the search, there was no need to prepare an arrest warrant. The accused was in custody, and was scheduled to be arraigned in municipal court the following day.

A case file folder was prepared for Dealer. Into the folder went the warrant and the complaint. John Dealer was entered into the defendants' index of the court's computer, and various documents were file-stamped. That day's work ended with Dealer's name and the charges against him being typed onto the calendar for Judge Law's arraignment session. The judge's courtroom clerk, Mr. Trusty, picked up the file folder along with others before the morning session. After Trusty called the case, he made entries in his record, the docket or minutes, regarding the charges and the intruction of rights by the judge. Dealer went back to the lock-up, and Trusty returned the file to the clerk's central records area.

Two days later the accused reappeared at the municipal court for a preliminary hearing. Trusty was kept busy marking and labeling various items that had been mentioned in the search warrant, and which were now entered by the prosecutor as exhibits. Included were packages of narcotics and a revolver, as well as various notes and business records. The courtroom clerk swore in the arresting officer before he testified, and prepared documents so that Dealer could be released on a bail bond. After the hearing, Trusty shipped the file and the exhibits upstairs to the superior court. The accused had been remanded for trial on several felony charges.

Before Dealer and his attorney ever set foot in superior court, clerks were preparing for his next appearance. The exhibits custodian, Mr. Locker, logged in and securely stored the revolver, the narcotics, and the records, thereby preserving the chain of evidence. The case was calendared for Judge Scholar's arraignment session. At this appearance, Scholar's courtroom clerk, Miss Reliable, accepted written motions for suppression of evidence and reduction of bail. These motions went into the file folder. Reliable was not surprised when the judge denied both motions. The denials were entered into the minutes, along with Dealer's plea and waiver of a speedy trial. Reliable was not present when Judge Scholar met with the deputy district attorney and the defense counsel at a pre-trial conference. However, she had scheduled this effort to spare the expense of going to trial. Since no plea bargain could be worked out by the three, the courtroom clerk was instructed to get a jury trial date from the master calendar clerk.

Mr. Manager, the superior court administrator, never took direct notice of Dealer's case, but he did bring up the problem of the glut of jury trials at a meeting of the judges in early March. Based on a computer simulation that Manager presented, the judges agreed to try several measures aimed at preventing the backlog from growing. Most important of these measures was a new policy on continuances (postponements of hearings usually made at the request of attorneys). Meanwhile, metropolitan court deputy clerks were subpoenaing witnesses, arranging for a jury panel to be called on the date set, and preparing forms, such as the jury instructions and verdict sheets.

The entire office worked meticulously and on the morning of the trial Miss Reliable had everything in readiness at her desk in front of the bench. When the jury assembly clerk brought her the panel of jurors, the computer was already preparing checks for the panel's jury fees and mileage.

Miss Reliable was kept busy with her forms, exhibits, and minutes during the trial. When the jury found Dealer guilty late that May afternoon, she was directed by the judge to enter a date for sentencing. At this hearing Reliable placed the probation department's pre-sentence report in the folder and recorded a sentence to state prison in the minutes. Judge Scholar never saw Dealer again, but clerks typed up the commitment forms and then packaged up the records, exhibits and trial transcript for the court of appeals. Long after Dealer's appeal had failed, the clerks had occasion to be reminded of the case. They were reporting the outcome of People v. Dealer to the state Bureau of Criminal Statistics and the judicial council. The records were sent off to be microfilmed, while Mr. Locker had the narcotics destroyed. As state law provides, the revolver was sent off to a foundry to become part of a new city manhole cover. [15]

While no one took much notice of the work of the clerical personnel, it will be apparent that there were plenty of opportunities for the smooth functioning of the criminal process to fail. What has been described here reflects a high degree of specialization on the part of the staff. In a smaller court the many functions described would have to be handled by a much smaller team. Clerks in the civil divisions of both the municipal and superior courts perform very similar tasks, but handle a much higher volume of cases.

The *Dealer* case illustrates two recent developments related to the way that court staffs do their jobs. One of these developments involves the computer which logged the defendant's name when the case began.

The same machine was later used to prepare checks for the jury fees, and to simulate a solution to the backlog problem. American courts differ considerably in their willingness and ability to utilize such sophisticated equipment. Encouragement from the last two Supreme Court chief justices, along with financial resources from the Law Enforcement Assistance Administration, have been crucial in the adoption of the new technology. In addition to their capacity to process huge quantities of data at high speeds, computers may be used in the courts for any or all of the following purposes:

1. To store, organize and index information in order to make it available for the use of participants in the court's process.
2. To schedule cases, facilities, conferences, and the appearances of defendants in custody.
3. To simplify and speed-up juror selection and utilization.
4. To manage financial accounts.
5. To centralize information for the use of other criminal justice agencies, including state and federal organizations.
6. To provide control over the flow of cases and to simulate the results of adjustments related to caseflow.

Obviously then, computers have the capability to absorb much of the drudgery of the court's activity, and to improve upon the manual processing methods that have traditionally characterized American courts.[16]

A second innovation that entered our imaginary case involved Mr. Manager, the superior court administrator. The theory behind the increasing use of such officers is, "that 'experts' thoroughly schooled in judicial procedures and modern administrative techniques will imbue courts with the managerial competence they have traditionally lacked . . . judges will be freed from time-consuming non-judicial activities." [17] One activity that occupies many court administrators is caseflow management. This term is used to describe the coordination of resources (judges, staff, jurors, finances, space, etc.) to the flow of cases in order to produce the greatest possible speed and efficiency compatible with justice. Other functions that court administrators have undertaken include: budget preparation; the lobbying of legislative bodies; providing the public and the media with information; supervising court-support personnel; compiling and analyzing judicial statistics; and managing financial matters, juries and records. Formerly many of these duties were badly neglected, or were the province of both over-worked and often unprepared judges and of clerks of the court.

While professional administrators have been increasingly employed at the state and federal levels, there has been some resistance to their utilization in some of the trial courts.[18] However, professional managers are here to stay for the courts as well as for other institutions, such as hospitals and schools. This development is good news, not only for those who look for improved efficiency in the judicial branch, but also for those who aspire to careers within that branch. Professional training, which is becoming more widely available, offers a better defined and more rational career ladder for the court's non-judicial staff.

In addition to the use of computers and new managerial expertise, American courts are experimenting with videotape transcription, new budget systems, automated methods of processing traffic offenses, and more sophisticated records management. Because needed change is coming, the courts promise to be an exciting place to work in the foreseeable future.

COURT ENFORCEMENT OFFICERS

Of the many symbolic representations of justice, one of the most common is the statue of a blindfolded woman with scales in one hand and a sword in the other. The weapon she holds is a device to remind us that courts are arenas where the outcome of a case may involve the highest possible stakes. Without the power to protect its process in making decisions, a court would undoubtedly face the prospect of emotional outbursts, threats, and even violence. To prevent such disruptions, most American courtrooms are staffed with a uniformed bailiff. However, the armed bailiff is simply the most visible of the officers whose responsibility is the protection of the judicial process.

In addition to their protective function, court enforcement officers provide the judge with the power to compel certain actions. One of the most ancient tasks entrusted to officers of the court was to compel individuals to appear before the king's magistrate. This power can be used to enforce civil orders as well as criminal orders. For example, court enforcement officers can be called upon to physically evict a tenant who has been found illegally in possession of a rented property. Similarly, officers may be ordered to seize and sell property belonging to an adjudged debtor so that he cannot defy a court order by refusing to pay the judgment against him. Without such powers to enforce decisions, courts would be held in general contempt, and certainly could not perform their mission of peacefully resolving conflicts.

The term "court enforcement officer" is useful on three accounts. First, it identifies these officers as belonging to or acting on behalf of the judicial branch of government. Secondly, it separates officers of the court from individuals who have general enforcement duties, i. e., the policemen who are involved in the active search for violations of criminal law. Finally, it allows us to generalize about the activities of a number of organizations which utilize a great many different designations and titles.

Types of Officers

The most famous of these organizations is of course the Office of the United States Marshal. The federal judiciary obtains all of its supporting enforcement services from this organization. However, within the state courts, court enforcement services may be provided in many different ways. For example, in California, the rural justice courts are served by elected constables or by appointees of the county sheriff. The municipal courts have marshals appointed by judges, or deputies furnished by the county sheriff; the choice is up to each county. Finally, California law mandates that superior courts receive their enforcement services from the sheriff. California thus furnishes not only an example of the same general type of service provided by officers with three different titles, but of three separate means for allocating tasks: election, appointment, and legislative mandate upon a non-judicial elected official. Court reform may eventually simplify this not uncommon situation. There are strong reasons for allowing the judges to appoint the chief court enforcement officer for a particular district, and for keeping the court officers separate from individuals having general law enforcement duties. At the same time there are savings and other advantages that may be realized from consolidating court services with other sworn officer activities.[19]

Duties of Officers

What court enforcement officers do is best described by separating their activities according to location. Within the courthouse, security is the primary concern. In multi–judge courts, security is generally a matter of three or more layers of protection—consisting of courtroom bailiffs, area security for several or all courtrooms and adjacent areas, and, finally, overall protection for the building. This last may depend on contract guard services, or might involve a cooperative arrangement with other agencies housed in the facility, such as a police department. Security problems can range all the way from lone defendants who attempt to bolt from the courtroom, to unruly mobs or revenge-minded victims. In urban courts, the human protective elements are likely to be supplemented with closed circuit television, listening devices, sophisticated locks, and various kinds of alarms.[20]

In a criminal department the bailiff has a threefold security responsibility. During hearings he has custody of the accused, who may or may not be under restraint. Additionally, the bailiff must be prepared to deal with potentially disruptive or violent behavior on the part of spectators. Lastly, he is expected to maintain quiet and gain the cooperation of attorneys, probation officers, and others who are frequently trying to attend to their business in the courtroom. In short, the skillful bailiff must have the capacity to be alert to everyone in the room. At the same time he must be able to deal effectively with individuals who compose the entire spectrum of the human condition, many of them under pressure in one way or another. Hence, it is not surprising that many high volume courtrooms, such as arraignment court, may be staffed by more than one officer.

The bailiff in the criminal department will also attend to many of the same tasks as his or her counterpart in a civil department. Such tasks would include: preparing the courtroom for service; announcing the judge's arrival; seating witnesses; maintaining custody of a jury; assisting the clerk with exhibits; and generally managing the flow of traffic in the courtroom. Since the judge, the clerk, and the stenographer (if one is present) cannot divert their attention from the case immediately before them, the bailiff will frequently be called upon to hunt down witnesses, intercept telephone calls, obtain books from the law library, and perform other services involving mobility. [21]

All of these tasks show that the bailiff's role involves some ceremonial duties, some security duties, and a great many housekeeping duties that may, at first glance, appear trivial. Upon closer observation, however, it will be seen that all of the bailiff's activities are aimed at moving cases with expedition and dignity.

Court officers leave the halls of justice for three purposes: to compel some action relating to a civil judgment; to act as the court's emissary in serving some sort of official notice; or to perform tasks related to the criminal process. We have previously taken notice of such civil procedures as evictions and levies upon property. Functions relating to official notice involve the delivery of documents such as a subpoena, an injunction, or a summons. An individual who receives a summons or summons-complaint from the court's officer is thereby notified of a suit against him and of the time and place for hearing. Some civil notices are served by the officers for a fee paid by a party to the action, while others may be handled by private process servers.

Tasks that involve the criminal process include such undertakings as extraditing individuals from other jurisdictions and serving warrants of various types. Warrants are classified as misdemeanor, felony, search, or bench warrants. While the serving of warrants is not a very glamorous task, it is very important in that prompt service forces individuals to recognize the power of the court and to comply with their responsibilities. [22] Many urban courts have allowed huge backlogs of bench warrants to pile up for individuals who have failed to appear on traffic matters. Such a backlog is a drag upon record-keeping, and creates a poor image of the court's efficiency and financial situation. Some courts are very prompt in the service of warrants, while others attend to this matter in a very sporadic fashion.

Having considered the court officer's role, both in and out of the courthouse, some mention should be made of exceptional or highly specialized activity. Modern court security is a relatively new activity, a product of the last ten years. In part, this is due to the violent demands for social changes that have recently wracked American society. Many of these demands were dramatized through the trials of individuals who claimed that their activities had a social objective or a political motivation. In addition, the 1960s and 1970s witnessed a surprising number of trials involving exceptional crimes or criminals. The names of Charles Manson, Juan Corona, and David Berkowitz are just several that will come to mind in this connection.

As a consequence, many urban jurisdictions have found it necessary to design or redesign their court facilities to meet the challenge of sensitive trials involving massive publicity. Several such cases have involved the use of supersecure courtrooms equipped with the most modern security technology. [23]

Another task that has received increasing importance for court officers involves the protection of government witnesses. Since 1970, the United States Marshals have operated a program designed to provide ironclad protection to organized crime figures who testify on behalf of federal prosecutors. Though there has been intense (and justifiable) criticism of some aspects of the alias program, it seems likely to be continued in some form or another. [24] In the problems of highrisk trials and witness protection, court officers have shown that they can be responsive to changing needs. Doubtless, they will continue to add new techniques and responsibilities to their time-honored roles as protectors of the court's process, enforcers of the court's orders, and as emissaries of the judiciary.

SUMMARY

The complexity of the American court system is a product of two factors: the dual system of the federal and state courts, and the enormous variety within the state court systems. The concepts of jurisdiction and classification are the key to unraveling matters. As defined here, jurisdiction refers to the scope of matters allowed to the court for decision. Classification makes possible the fairly easy separation of courts into higher and lower appellate units, and into superior or inferior trial units. While the processes of judicial selection, discipline, and removal are simply described for the federal courts, the states have developed not only complex judicial systems, but a greater variety of methods for selecting and managing their judges. This diversity can be expected to persist in spite of outbursts of enthusiasm for various ways of doing things based on models developed by various states.

More than any other component in the criminal justice system, the court is evaluated on the performance of those occupying just one role—the judges. What judges do can be reduced to a simple formula, but, "rules times the facts equals the decision," only begins to express the complexity and the subtlety of the decision-making process. In the end, it is the caliber of the judges that makes the difference; this is why the process of judicial selection occupied such a prominent place in our study.

Because judges wouldn't accomplish much if it fell to them to type the minutes, calendar the cases, summon the jurors, and mark the exhibits, courts are furnished with clerks. In addition to the above tasks, the responsibilities of the court's support personnel include the preparation of case files, maintaining various records, handling bail, and such activities as scheduling pre-trial conferences. More and more, these operations are being automated or otherwise supported by new technology. Similarly, the management of the courts is receiving the attention of specially trained professional administrators, who bring into the courthouse skills in such diverse areas as caseflow management, budgeting, and planning.

Beside the bench stands the power of compulsion. Without it, every disgruntled litigant or reluctant defendant could turn the judicial process into a shambles. Court enforcement officers not only protect the court's proceedings, but also act as the bearers of official notice. They carry out levies, evictions, and attachments so that the court cannot be treated with contempt. Finally, they may be called upon to serve various kinds of warrants, provide special security measures for high-risk trials, and to protect witnesses.

Within the courts and in the larger political process, several trends or issues affecting the courts have been mentioned. The court administration movement, the contending proposals for merit selection of judges, schemes for the improvement of the country's lower courts, and the trend toward the limitation of judicial discretion in sentencing are several of the topics that promise to remain subjects of controversy for years to come. So long as Americans believe that institutions exist in order to be improved and constantly reformed, the courts will change. Consequently, the reader should take notice of such matters in the expectation that his or her voice may have a part to play in future adjustments that are certain to occur.

DISCUSSION QUESTIONS

1. Discuss the jurisdiction of each court on the federal and state levels. Is there any duplication of functions? If so, describe them.

2. Discuss the judicial process in terms of types of decisions made, rules, facts, and discretion. Are there any discrepancies?

3. What roles do the court support staff and court enforcement officers play in the judicial process? List each, and briefly describe their functions.

4. What is meant by the dual structure of the federal courts, superior courts, and inferior courts?

REFERENCES

1. Lewis Mayers, *The Machinery of Justice: An Introduction to Legal Structure and Process*, (Totowa, N.J.: Littlefield Adams & Co., 1973), pp.9-11.

2. Joseph F. Spaniol, Jr., *The United States Courts: Their Jurisdiction and Work*, (Washington: U.S. Government Printing Office, 1975).

3. Merlin Lewis, Warren Bundy and James L. Hagne, *An Introduction to the Courts and Judicial Process*, (Englewood Cliffs, N.J.: Prentice Hall, Inc., 1978), pp. 56-58.

4. Spaniol, *United States Courts*, pp. 4-7

5. Lewis, *Introduction to the Courts*, pp. 33-39.

6. Gordon v. Justice Court for Yuba Judicial Dist., 12 Cal. 3d 323, 115 Cal. Rptr. 632, 525 P. 2d 72, (1974).

7. Karen Markle Knab, *Courts of Limited Jurisdiction: A National Survey*, (Washington, D.C.: National Institute of Law Enforcement Assistance, 1977), pp. iii-xi, 30-36.

8. Mayers, *Machinery of Justice*, pp. 94-97.

9. Lewis, *Introduction to the Courts*, pp. 54-58.

10. Larry C. Berkson, Steven W. Hays and Susan J. Carbon (eds.), *Managing the State Courts*, (St. Paul, Minn.: West Publishing Co., 1977), pp. 134-139

11. Ibid., pp. 150-161.

12. Jill Hockenson, "Sillas' Plan to Take Traffic Tickets Out of the Courtrooms, "California Journal, Volume VIII, Number 8 (August, 1977) pp. 282-283.

13. Jerome Frank, *Courts on Trial*, (N.Y.: Atheum, 1970), pp. 14-21.

14. C. Gordon Post, *An Introduction to the Law*, (Englewood Cliffs, N.J.: Spectrum, 1963), p. 162.

15. Stephanie Schubert, et al., *Criminal Procedures*, (San Bruno, California: Court Support Personnel Project, n.d.).

16. Berkson, *Managing the State Courts*, pp. 286-287.

17. Ibid., p. 188.

18. Ibid., pp. 192-194.

19. Theani Lonskos, et al., *The Court Enforcement Officer*. (San Bruno California: Court Support Personnel Project, n.d.).

20. James L. McMahon, et al., *Court Security: A Manual of Guidelines and Procedures*, (Washington D.C.: National Sheriff's Association, 1978).

21. David R. Turner, *Court Officer*, (N.Y.: Arco Books, 1970), pp. 93-95.

22. Lonskos, *Court Enforcement*, pp. 6-10.

23. McMahon, *Court Security*. pp. 5. 26-29.

24. One example is Fred Graham, *The Alias Program*. (Boston: Little Brown, 1976).

8

Grand Juries/
Trial Jurors

CHAPTER OBJECTIVES

After reading this chapter the student will be able to:

1. Discuss the history of the grand jury from its early, English influence to the present.

2. List the qualifications and procedures for the selection of grand jurors and trial jurors.

3. List the responsibilities of the grand jury.

4. Define the concept of the right to jury trial.

5. Discuss the process for specific juror challenge.

The role juries have taken in the United States is extremely important to the criminal justice process. The two most common types of "juries" recognized in the U.S. today are grand juries and trial juries. The two "juries" are very different from each other and serve completely different roles.

In this chapter we will discuss in detail the history of the grand jury, the selection of jurors, and their required qualifications. The grand jury performs many functions for the citizens of the county which it serves. Many of these functions are mandatory, but are not commonly known. We will discuss each function and identify the responsibilities mandated to the grand jury.

The accused in any prosecution has the right to a trial by jury. This right is very fundamental to our legal process, and its significance will be discussed in detail in this chapter. How twelve impartial jurors are selected, and the importance of the selection process which they go through will be discussed. The method for challenging each specific juror will also be identified.

THE GRAND JURY

The History of the Grand Jury

The institution of the grand jury originated centuries ago in England as a protection for the citizens against suppression and arbitrary acts by the king. It was recognized in the *Magna Carta*, which was granted by King John upon the demand of the people in 1215. Originally, the grand jury was a body which not only accused, but also tried public offenders. The grand jury remained in full effect in England until 1933, when it was abolished. The institution of the grand jury was adopted in in this country at the time of its settlement, but at that time the grand jury had developed into an informing and accusing party only, without whose action no person charged with a felony could, except in certain special cases, be put upon trial.

Just as this country adopted the majority of the laws of England at the time of its founding, it adopted the concept of the grand jury as well. Grand juries are provided for by the statutes of all fifty states. Each of the judicial districts of the United States has a federal grand jury. There is a federal grand jury which sits in California, and which constitutes the districts of California as well as other parts of the western states. Its concern primarily involves the federal government's rules and regulations.

Even though the grand jury was abolished in England in 1933, it has remained in the United States as a regulatory function which oversees government agencies and departments. It also investigates specific types of criminal behavior in the state and counties whereby it has jurisdiction.

The California Constitution, in Article 1, Section 8, provides that "A grand jury shall be drawn and summoned at least once a year in each county." In addition, the California Penal Code Section 888, states "A grand jury is a body of the required number of persons returned from the citizens of the county before a court of competent jurisdiction, and sworn to inquire of public offenses committed or triable with the county."

Method of Selection

The superior court has the basic responsibility for the initiating the annual selection process. In addition to the superior court, however, there are city and county officials who are also involved in this process who, along with the court, have some latitude in the selection of the jurors. The grand jury is to consist of twenty-three members in a county having a population exceeding four million, and nineteen members in all other counties.[1]

The actual selection process of the members of the grand jury may vary from county to county, but normally occurs in a manner similar to the one described as follows: each year the judges of the superior court will nominate and summon five to fifteen members more than the number they will actually need for the actual swearing in as members of the grand jury. The names of potential grand jurors generally will come from the suggestions of prominent citizens in the community. In counties where there is more than one superior court judge, each magistrate will submit a series of names which are placed on one master list. Each magistrate will have the opportunity to review that list and eliminate those who they feel would be inappropriate nominees for a position on the grand jury. The law requires that nominees shall be persons: suitable and competent to serve as jurors; who are not exempt from serving; who are in possession of their natural faculties; who are not inept or decrepit; and who are of fair character and are of sound judgment. From this group, the names of twenty-three persons or nineteen, depending on the county, are selected by lot who will thereupon be sworn in as grand jurors.

The original panel of persons is selected in order to constitute as complete a cross section of the county as possible. The original nominees may be selected at a later time to fill vacancies that may occur on the grand jury. As previously stated, in those counties having an excess of four million people, the minimum number of grand jurors shall be twenty-three. There is only one county in the State of California that falls into this category—Los Angeles County. All other counties' grand juries consist of nineteen members.

Because of the responsibilities and duties of the grand jury, the members who are selected are normally citizens of the county who have some stature and are of some prominence, but who also consist of an adequate cross section of the county as is possible.   The nominees selected by the judges normally will have a wide variety of interests and come from various parts of the county.   The law does not require that members of the grand jury be of a specific social or economic group, but that they be of a cross section of the community.   Because of the time and effort involved in fulfilling the duties of the grand jury, usually only those people who have genuine interest and are willing to donate their services will be asked to participate.

Qualifications of Grand Jurors

The Code of Civil Procedures, section 198, identifies the qualifications of grand jurors:

1.   A person serving as a member of the grand jury must be a citizen of the United States.
2.   He must be at least 18 years of age.
3.   He must have been a resident of a county or a city for one year immediately before he is selected and returned as a member of the jury.
4.   He must be in possession of his natural faculties and of ordinary intelligence.
5.   He must not be decrepit.
6.   He must be able to speak and understand English.

Other sections of the Code of Civil Procedures further explain who is qualified to act as a member of the grand jury.   In addition to the requirements stated in Section 198 of the Code of Civil Procedures, the following are additional requirements:

1.   If a person has been convicted of malfeasance of office, he would be disqualified as a member of the grand jury.
2.   If a person has been convicted of any felony or any other high crime, he would be disqualified.
3.   Any person who has been discharged as a juror or grand juror by any court of record within this state within a period of a year would not be eligible until that year has expired.
4.   Any person who is currently serving as a grand juror or trial juror would be disqualified to serve as a grand juror.

Some of the traditional qualifications that have been utilized by superior court judges in selecting grand jurors bear examination.   The occupation of a prospective grand juror is certainly of some importance.

Normally, those people who are selected for grand jury duty are likely to be employed in some form of business as professionals or as managerial people. Because the grand jury will be investigating specific functions of government, a certain amount of expertise is desirable; therefore, those people who have the ability to establish their expertise would have a better opportunity to serve on the grand jury. Such things as race, sex, religion, political party preference, and past grand jury service are other important qualifications that judges would take into consideration. From a subjective point of view, the philosophy of prospective grand jurors is also considered.

Impanelment & Organization

Once the jury has been selected, its members are administered an oath which is intended to bind them to certain standards of conduct. To educate jurors in their indictment and regulatory activities, the court supplies them with certain data which apprises them of such things as their responsibilities and limitations. Upon impaneling the grand jury, the presiding judge will select one of its members to serve as foreman. The foreman presides over all meetings of the grand jury, and acts as its liaison with the judges, the district attorney, and the county counsel. Other officers are selected by members of the grand jury. The foreman pro tempore acts as a substitute when the foreman is not present. A clerk keeps the records, files, and minutes of all meetings of the grand jury, records the attendance of the members of the grand jury, and handles all correspondence. The sergeant of arms sits at the door of the grand jury room and allows only authorized persons into the meetings of the grand jury.

Grand Jury Committees

There are several elements that may determine the committee organization used by the jury to execute its responsibilities for overseeing the county which it serves:
1. *Experience/Interests of Jurors.* As previously stated, normally, the members of the grand jury will be selected from citizens of the county who have some expertise in business or professional organizations. Their experience and their interests will sometimes dictate the types of emphasis with which the grand jury will be involved. For example, in one county, the grand jury consisted of two public school teachers. Because of their interests, a careful examination was made into the county public schools office, with a lengthy report as to recommended changes in the operation of the County Superintendent ensuing.
2. *Suggestions From Previous Grand Juries.* At the end of the year,

the grand jury is responsible for submitting a final report outlining their accomplishments and making recommendations for county government improvements.   One of the recommendations that could be made by a grand jury would be a followup of a project that was initiated, a complaint that was made, or an idea that was established which could not be completed by the existing grand jury.

3. *Suggestions by Public Officials.* The grand jury receives many requests for investigative services by various public officials in the county in which they serve. For example, the district attorney, the welfare director, or other top government officials will have insight into problems in the county and can request grand jury members to investigate the causes and circumstances of those problems.

4. *Suggestions by Organized Groups of Private Citizens.* There are many organizations and groups in the community that have a genuine interest in the efficiency and effectiveness of county operations.

5. *Critical Community Problems.* One of the major responsibilities of the grand jury is that they are held accountable for the needs of, and must address themselves to, the specific county in which they are living and serving (for example, the need to determine a construction project for a new jail or a lack of certain recreation facilities in the community). The grand jury may initiate a lengthy investigation and make recommendations for solving the problems that exist in the county.

6. *Social Services.* Many of the committees are clearly identified with the social service aspects of community life: for example, education, welfare, health and sanitation, law enforcement, hospitals, jails, probation, recreation, juvenile and public safety. With this in mind, the grand jury will normally organize itself into committees that address the interests and needs of the community. Each committee will have a chairman who is appointed by the foreman.

Rules of Procedure

Grand juries have no staff to help them discharge their responsibilities. The ability of the grand jurors to compensate for this limitation is therefore a critical factor in producing a final report which is comprehensive and carefully documented, and not one that is shallow and general.

The law requires the concurrence of twelve grand jurors to return an indictment or an accusation. Beyond this, no rules of procedure are prescribed. In practice, procedure is usually developed by the grand jury itself.

Compensation

Each grand juror is normally compensated at the rate of $6 for each day's attendance at a grand jury meeting, and an appropriate amount for each mile necessarily traveled for such attendance. He is paid a like amount for attendance at the grand jury committee meetings of which he is a member. Each member is responsible for keeping accurate records of his meetings and mileage for which compensation is allowed. He files his claim for compensation to the county clerk for payment. Beyond this, the grand jury is a volunteer organization and is not compensated for services.

Duties

One of the most familiar responsibilities of the grand jury as we know it today is the investigation into public offenses committed or triable in the county within which the grand jury has jurisdiction. Penal Code Section 917 states that the grand jury may inquire into all public offenses committed or triable in a county, and may present them to the court by indictment. This is not a mandatory function, but rather is a permissive function; that is to say, the grand jury is not required by law to investigate into specific public offenses committed in the county. We will recognize that in certain other cases, the grand jury does have mandatory responsibilities, but this is not one of those cases. However, because of the emphasis and importance placed on the role of the grand jury in most counties, we will see that one of the grand jury's most important duties is that of inquiring into public offenses committed or triable in the county of jurisdiction. In the State of California, a felony may be prosecuted either through information filed by the district attorney or through an indictment found by the grand jury, but the district attorney prosecutes the majority of felonies through information, rather than indictment. Of note is the wording in the Penal Code section authorizing grand juries to investigate public offenses. From a practical point of view, the grand jury will be involved only in felony offenses, but because the wording does state "public offenses," it is permissable for the grand jury to investigate into lesser public offenses also. The only exception to this would be where such misdemeanors are breaches of public trust committed by public officials.

If a member of a grand jury knows or has reason to believe that a public offense triable within the county has been committed, it is his responsibility to declare it to his fellow jurors who will therefore be required to investigate it. [2]

Investigation of Public Officials

A required duty of the grand jury is to inquire into any possible willful or corrupt misconduct on the part of public officials in office. The grand jury *shall* inquire into the willful or corrupt misconduct in office of public officers of every description with the county.[3] Because of this responsibility, the grand jury has sometimes been dubbed as the watch-dog or overseer of public government. As the grand jury was developed in the United States, and as laws were established in California, the legislators wanted to ensure that this was one of the primary responsibilities of the grand jury. Our form of government does not have an actual person or organization that is responsible for this function. Therefore, the grand jury has the primary role of checking into the corruption or misconduct of public officials.

Any time a member of the grand jury has reason to believe that there is willful to corrupt misconduct in office on the part of a public official, the grand jury generally initiates a priority investigation to determine the authenticity of the complaint.

Investigation of County and District Affairs

The grand jury shall annually make a careful and complete examination of the accounts and records especially those pertaining to revenue of all officers of the county and report as to the facts it has found with such recommendations as may be deemed proper and fit.[4] This requires that the grand jury examine the accounts of all officers of the county, especially those pertaining to revenue, and that it report the facts, with such recommendations as they deem appropriate. The law permits, rather than requires, the grand jury to examine at any time the books and records for any special purpose of taxing a district wholly or partly in the county. After examination of such accounts and records, the grand jury may order the county counsel to initiate a suit to recover any monies that, in his judgment, are due the county.

The performance of the above duties may require the employment of an accountant or auditor. The law provides that the grand jury be able to select an independent auditor to be employed for the purpose of assisting the grand jury in conducting an audit.

Salary Investigation

The grand jury shall, in even-numbered years, investigate and report on the needs for increase or decrease in salaries of the County Supervisors, the   District Attorney and the Auditor.[5] From time to time, the persons mentioned above will request personal interviews with the grand jury so that they may state their needs and justify any increases in salaries. Upon reviewing the evidence, the grand jury will make recommendations on increases or decreases in salaries which must be transmitted to the Board of Supervisors.

Local county government has the option of supporting the recommendations of the grand jury, and are in no way accountable to instigate the recommendations of the grand jury.

County Agency Needs

The grand jury shall investigate and report upon the needs of all county officers in the county, including an abolition or creation of offices and the need for equipment.[6] One of the standing committees that grand juries establish is the committee to investigate the area described in the above section. The members of the committee will contact department heads in the county, and will conduct investigations and interviews to determine the needs of the county officials. Many times department heads will initiate contact with the grand jury so that the needs of that particular department will be publicly made. If the grand jury committee initiates the investigation, then it is a requirement of the department heads to cooperate with the grand jury, and to provide it with the information it needs.

County Jails

"The grand jury shall inquire into: The case of every person imprisoned in the jail of the county on a criminal charge and not indicted and the condition and management of public prisons within a county."[7] The above responsibility is an extremely important duty of the grand jury. The purpose of this requirement is to prevent public officials from incarcerating persons in county jails without appropriate due process. In addition it requires that the condition and the management of the public prisons be of such a nature that prisoners are not being treated unjustly or inhumanely. Grand jury members will determine that proper meals are being fed prisoners, that they are receiving needed medications, and that they are receiving adequate treatment in other aspects of their daily activities.

Sessions

Sessions of the grand jury must be held when the district attorney desires to present a criminal case, or when so ordered by the court. In all other instances, the grand jury will determine the time of such meetings. Normally, a regular hour and day for the general sessions is affixed by the grand jury foreman with the concurrence of the grand jury members. The frequency of the meetings will depend upon the activity that is being conducted by the grand jury. One meeting a month is usually enough. Experience has shown than more time is devoted to committee activities than to jury sessions.

As previously stated, a quorum for a meeting for the transaction of business consists of twelve jurors, where population of the county is less than four million. The grand jury may act only as a body. An individual grand juror has no more authority than any private citizen. The importance of grand jury work requires that each member be present at all sessions, excepting more cogent reasons not to attend.

When a criminal charge of misconduct in office is being considered by the grand jury, no person is permitted to be present except the members of the grand jury, witnesses actually under examination, the district attorney or his deputy, or, in some instances, the attorney general or his deputy, and the stenographic reporter. The judge may be present only when his advice is requested. No persons other than the grand jury may be present during deliberations. If the investigation involves the district attorney, any of his deputies, or like employees, none of them may be present unless called as witnesses. During such a preceeding, the foreman is empowered to employ special counsel and special investigators to investigate and present the evidence.

Return and Presentation of an Indictment or Accusation

An *indictment* is a written accusatory statement presented by the grand jury to the superior court, charging either a private citizen or a public official with a public offense. An *accusation* is a statement, presented by the grand jury, charging a public official with willful or corrupt misconduct in office. Conviction under any indictment may result in either incarceration or fine or both. Conviction under an accusation can result only in the defendant's removal from office.

The procedure for the finding of an indictment or accusation is substantially as follows: the foreman will describe the subject to be considered and the name of the person suspected of having committed the offense. He will then direct any member of the grand jury who is prejudiced regarding either the case or the person named to retire during the course of that investigation.

The witnesses are sworn in by the foreman to testify. The district attorney will examine witnesses. If a grand juror desires to ask a question, normally he will have the district attorney ask in his behalf. There may be legal reasons a question could not be asked, and since an indictment must be based on legal evidence, the district attorney would evaluate the question before asking it. The grand jury is empowered to compel by subpoena the attendance of witnesses, and to require the production of books, records, documents and other physical evidence. The grand jury itself cannot issue subpoenas. When the grand jury directs subpoenas to be issued, the foreman will notify the office of the district attorney, which will then be responsible for completing the subpoena request, and for seeing that they are issued. A stenographic reporter will be provided by the court and will be sworn in to perform his duties in reporting witnesses' testimony. In the event that an interpreter is necessary and is called, he too will be sworn in and be required to be present while functioning as such. No part of the proceeding other than the examination and testimony of witnesses should be reported.

While investigating an alleged public offense, the grand jury is to receive no evidence other than that given by witnesses produced and sworn, or received from legal documentary evidence.

The grand jury is not bound to hear evidence for an accused person. However, if desired, it may permit the accused person to appear and testify under oath.   Under no circumstances is an accused person permitted to be accompanied by his attorney, secretary, or other assistant in the grand jury room.

The grand jury is not expected to hear or observe all evidence that might be introduced in the trial. However, from a practical point of view, it is instructed to review only that type of evidence that will later be admissable in a court of law.

Rights and Duties of Witnesses Before a Grand Jury

A witness called upon to testify before a grand jury has certain rights and duties which should be understood and respected. The grand jury, like a court, normally asks only such questions as are pertinent to the matter under consideration.

The grand jury must at all times remember the constitutional privilege of every person against self-incrimination. That is, no person may be compelled to give evidence that is self-degrading or self-incriminating. In a criminal trial, the defendant cannot be compelled against his will to take the stand. This privilege does not extend to a prospective defendant in a matter under consideration by the grand jury. Nor may any person refuse to answer preliminary questions if the answers would not tend to incriminate him. However, every person may refuse to respond to a question if the answer would subject him to criminal prosecution.

Voting

The grand jury votes on the return of indictment in privacy, with all members of the public excluded. When grand jury voting is open, it is conducted by roll call and not by written or secret ballot.

Finding an Indictment or Accusation

An indictment or accusation requires the concurrence of at least twelve grand jurors, each of whom must have attended and heard all of the evidence.

When an indictment or accusation has been properly voted and found, a formal written indictment or accusation must be prepared. It must include, in appropriate form, the name of the defendant or accused and the charge made against him. The names of witnesses examined or those depositions which have been read must be placed upon the indictment or accusation. It must be endorsed "true bill," and signed by the foreman. Normally, the indictment or accusation will be prepared for the grand jury by the district attorney.

An indictment must be presented by the court in open session, and must be given by the foreman in the presence of the grand jury, or at least in the presence of all grand jurors who attended when the indictment or accusation was voted.

Civil Liability of a Grand Juror

A grand juror is not civilly liable for damage resulting to a person indicted or accused by the grand jury. However, any comments in its reports upon a private citizen or public official who is not indicted or not privileged could, if libelous, be the basis for a change of civil or criminal libel.

Final Report

At the end of the year of service, each grand jury is required by law to submit a final report to the court. This report normally contains a detailed account of the past year's activities, together with any suggestions and recommendations as may be indicated. The foreman will normally appoint a special committee to prepare the final report. The chairmen of the various committees submit their reports to this committee, which then consolidates and edits them, thus assuring a consistent style, and eliminating duplication. The presiding judge, in his charge to the grand jury, will set the date by which the preliminary report must be made to that court. This report must be submitted on or before December 31 of each year. No later than sixty days after the discharge of the grand jury, the board of supervisors must comment on the findings and recommendations, and elected county officers must report to the board on recommendations pertaining to them. All such comments and reports must be submitted to the presiding judge, and a copy must be filed with the county clerk.[8]

Rise and Decline of Grand Jury Indictments

In a case filed November 9, 1978, the Supreme Court of California for all intents and purposes eliminated the procedure of taking a criminal case to the grand jury for review and the issuance of an indictment. The case was James Hawkins et al v. The Superior Court of the City and County of San Francisco. Before we discuss the provisions of this case, let us first review the rationale for the grand jury indictments and some of the advantages for having the grand jury file indictments in criminal matters.

Since 1849, the California Constitution stated that "No person shall be held to answer for a capital or otherwise infamous crime, . . . unless on presentment or indictment of a grand jury; . . . ."[9] From the time the constitution was established, provisions were made for filing criminal complaints through the grand jury. In 1934 the people adopted an amendment to Section 8, Article 1, preserving the language of the original section and adding various specific provisions. The effect of this amendment was to further support the use of indictments for criminal offenses through the grand jury. In 1974, the voters approved a more simplified version of Section 8, renumbering the provisions as Section 14, which provides in part that: "Felonies shall be prosecuted as provided by law, either by indictment, or, after examination and commitment by a magistrate by information." This appeared to clearly define the functions of the grand jury and the procedures to follow upon filing indictments. Specifically, if a defendant was charged through a grand jury indictment, there would be no examination or review by a magistrate, such as is the case in a criminal offense being prosecuted by information.

Advantages of Grand Jury Indictments

Over the years, there have been several established reasons for prosecutors to utilize the services of the grand jury for filing indictments, rather than through the preliminary information process. By utilizing the grand jury procedure in filing criminal accusations, the prosecutor is able to maintain a certain amount of secrecy for a longer period of time. There are some valid reasons for this procedure.

First, in some cases, the prospective defendant cannot be located, and therefore the prosecutor is able to file his case to the grand jury. The grand jury is able to review the case and determine whether there is enough legal evidence to warrant prosecuting the individual in court. In this procedure, the defendant need not be present at any time during the procedure.

Second, there are some cases which are of a delicate nature, and hence witnesses may fear testifying in court. By utilizing the services of the grand jury, the secrecy factor could allow a witness to testify without fear of public concern or notoriety.

Third, in some cases there is a tremendous potential for prejudicial, pretrial publicity. If the prosecutor were to utilize the information in a preliminary hearing procedure, because of its advisory nature, the evidence which the prosecutor is going to use during the trial would be brought up at this time. Since it is public record, the news media would have access to the testimonial evidence for use in news articles. This could make it very difficult to obtain an impartial trial, thereby increasing the expense to the public.

In some cases where undercover investigators are utilized, the prosecutor will attempt to maintain the secrecy of that investigation. However, if he were to utilize the preliminary hearing route, the investigation could be jeopardized for the simple reason that the prosecutor would have to name witnesses, including undercover agents, as part of his case when requested by the defendant.

On some occasions, there could be an unnecessary or prolonged delay because of the number of defendants or the complexity of a case if the prosecutor is required to go through the preliminary examination process. This again would increase the costs of the prosecution and be a burden on the taxpayers.

The above are but a few reasons for prosecutors to desire to take cases before the grand jury rather than following the preliminary hearing procedure. Most prosecutors keep grand jury use at a minimum—only in those cases where they feel that it is absolutely crucial to maintain secrecy, or when they desire speed in bringing a person to trial.

Hawkins versus Superior Court City and County of San Francisco

The California Supreme Court, in November of 1978, for all intents and purposes eliminated the option which prosecutors have in utilizing the services of grand juries, or of filing indictments of accused persons charged with criminal offenses in the State of California. The Supreme Court ruled that the denial of a post—indictment preliminary hearing deprived defendants accused of criminal offenses equal protection under the laws guaranteed by Article 1, Section 7 of the California Constitution. The Supreme Court stated that if the prosecutor obtains an indictment through the grand jury, and if the defendant makes a timely request for a preliminary hearing, then the court, at its discretion, can require the prosecuting attorney to refile the indictment as a complaint, thereby initiating the preliminary hearing procedure. The case in detail is described as follows:

Defendants were charged, in a multiple count indictment returned by a San Francisco grand jury, with conspiracy and grand theft. The defendants were arraigned and each pleaded "not guilty" to all counts. Their motion for dismissal, or alternatively, for a post-indictment preliminary hearing was, in due course, denied. The defendants then requested a writ of mandamus, asserting their rights under the due process and equal protection clauses of the United States and the state constitution to a adversarial preliminary hearing.

The Supreme Court, in a split decision, agreed with the defendants. Justice Mosk wrote the majority opinion for the court:

It is undeniable that there is a considerable disparity in the procedural rights of the defendants charged by the prosecutor by means of information and defendants charged by the grand jury in an indictment. The defendant accused by information immediately becomes entitled to an impressive array of procedural rights, including a preliminary hearing before a neutral and legally knowledgable magistrate, representation by retained or appointed counsel, the confrontation and cross examination of hostile witnesses, and the opportunity to personally appear and affirmatively present exculpatory evidence.

In vivid contrast, the indictment procedure omits all the above safeguards; the defendant has no right to appear or to be represented by counsel, and consequently, he may not confront and cross examine the witness again; object to the evidence introduced by the prosecutor; make legal arguments; or present evidence to explain or contradict the charge. If he is called to testify, the defendant has no right to the presence of counsel, even though, because of the absolute secrecies surrounding grand jury procedures, he may be unaware of the subject of the inquiry or position as a target witness.

The prosecuting attorney is typically in complete control of the total process in a grand jury room; he calls the witnesses, interprets the evidence, states and applies the law and advises the grand jury on whether a crime has been committed.

The domination of grand jury proceedings by the prosecuting attorney no doubt derived at least in part from the grand jury's institutional schizophrenia. They are expected to serve two distinct and largely inconsistent functions; accuser and impartial fact finder.

The denial of the post indictment preliminary hearing deprives the defendant of "such fundamental rights as counsel, confrontation, the right to personally appear, the right to a hearing before a judicial officer, and the right to be free from unwanted prosecution."

"We conclude that the denial of a post indictment preliminary hearing deprives defendants herein of equal protection of the laws guaranteed by Article 1, Section 7 of the California Constitution. The remedy most consistent with the state constitution as a whole and least intrusive on the legislator's prerogative is simply to permit the indictment process to continue precisely as it has, but to recognize the right of indicated defendants to demand a post-indictment preliminary hearing prior to or at the time of entering a plea. If the defendant makes a timely request for such a preliminary hearing, at the discretion of the court, the prosecuting attorney shall refile the indictment as a complaint."

TRIAL JURORS

"In all criminal prosecutions, the accused shall enjoy the right to a speedy and public trial, by an impartial jury of the state and district wherein the crime shall have been committed . . ." (Amendment 6 of the United States Constitution).

"The right of a trial by jury shall be secured to all and remain inviolate; but in civil actions, three fourths of the jury may render a verdict. A trial by jury may be waived in all criminal cases, by the consent of both parties, expressed in open court by the defendant and his counsel, and in civil actions by the consent of the parties signified in such manner as may be prescribed by law. In civil actions and cases of misdemeanor, the jury may consist of twelve or of any number less than twelve upon which the parties may agree in open court" (California Constitution, Article 1, Section 7).

As can be seen by the Sixth Amendment of the United States Constitution, and by the California Constitution, Article 1, Section 7, a great deal of importance has been placed on the rights of an accused to have a trial by jury. The United States Constitution is not as specific as the California Constitution, inasmuch as it does not state the minimum number that must be involved in a jury, or does not state the manner in which the jury must be involved in deliberations. As we can see by analyzing Article 1, Section 7, the California Constitution is very explicit concerning the right of an accused to have a trial by jury. This is a protection that is secure to all, and cannot be violated except with the approval of the court and prosecutor at the request of the defendant. This extends the right of a jury trial to more than the wishes of the defendant. In other words, the defendant does not have the legal right to refuse to have a jury trial, but he cannot be refused a jury trial. In some cases, the defendant may not wish to have the jury decide his case because of such things as public concern or notoriety. The prosecutor, on the other hand, may feel it is the responsibility of the public to be involved in the rendering of the decision, so, in this situation, the prosecutor has the right to a jury trial. In this case, even over the objections of the defendant, a jury trial would be held.

The courts generally have been very flexible in allowing the defendant to waive his right to a jury trial. The prosecutor in almost all cases will go along with the request of the defendant. In fact, the time of the request is not an important issue. The defendant, in some cases, has actually changed his mind after the jury has already been selected and decided that he desires a court trial. In one case, People v. Medina[10], the court allowed the change of request by the defendant after the selection of the jury had already begun.

Number of Jurors

The California Constitution states that there must be a minimum of twelve jurors; however, there is a stipulation that with the consent of the defendant, a jury consisting of eleven or even fewer could be allowed to render a decision if, in fact, the defendant waives his right to the minimum of twelve jurors. From time to time, this will occur because of sudden illness on the part of a juror, etcetera.

Waiver of a Right to a Jury Trial

As previously discussed, it is allowable under the California Constitution that the defendant waive his right to a jury trial with the express consent of the prosecutor made in open court. In criminal cases, the waiver must be expressed in open court by the defendant, and in a case where the defendant is represented by counsel, along with his counsel. This provision has been strictly construed not only to require a waiver by the defendant himself, but also to require oral or written expression of the waiver.[11] There have been several cases dealing with the issue of the defendant waiving or apparently waiving his right to a jury in open court. As previously stated, the courts have been extremely restrictive in their interpretation of how a defendant can waive his right to a jury trial. For example, in the case People v. Pechar, the defense counsel answered "yes" to the judge's inquiry. The defendant moved his head in a downward motion as if nodding in agreement with the counsel. The case was reversed by the California Appellate Court. The court indicated that a great amount of uncertainty could arise in the form of gestures on the part of the accused; therefore it was necessary that unequivocal replies be given to the court in the form of written or verbal expression.

It has become the policy of most courts to specifically ask both the counsel and the defendant separately as to the interpretation or intentions of the defendant regarding this question. The court will require that the defendant specifically state whether he wishes to waive his right to a jury trial.

Before we leave the subject of waiver of the jury trial, one further point needs to be made with references to the defendant's right not to have a jury trial. In People v. Eubanks [12] the court stated, "while a defendant charged with a felony has a constitutional right to trial by jury, it does not follow that he has a constitutional right to be tried by the court without a jury. In the absence of authority to the contrary, we are of opinion that the provision of the constitution for waiver of jury trial does not take away from the trial courts power to require that the case be tried by jury." This decision clearly authorizes the court to overrule not only the defendant's wish for a court trial, but also both the defendant's and prosecutor's requests for a court trial.

Qualifications

At the beginning of this chapter we discussed the qualifications of grand jury members in the State of California. If the student reviews that section, he will understand the qualifications for trial jurors. The same qualifications hold in this case as in the case of grand jurors. The Code of Civil Procedures, Section 198 sets forth the specific qualifications as previously discussed. Please refer to the section on grand juries for review of those qualifications.

Selection of Jury

The Constitution assures that a defendant will receive a jury trial which will consist of an impartial jury from the district and county wherein the crimes were committed. The wording, "impartial jury," has had a tremendous significance in court decisions in the past several years dealing with what constitutes an impartial jury. Generally speaking, the jury is selected from a cross-section of the community within the judicial district of a given court. For example, if prospective citizens are being solicited for duty as jurors in a superior court, then the judicial district would include, normally, the entire county. Citizens from all areas of the county would be identified as potential jurors, providing they met the minimum qualifications as stated by law. Historically, the most fair and impartial method of selecting jurors is to draw names from the voter register list within the county of the court having jurisdiction. Common practice is to select names at random off the voter registration lists. For example, every third name, every fourth name, etcetera, on that list would be selected until a minimum of jurors had been obtained.

The above method is not required by law and there are other possibilities which courts could use in making a proper selection for jury duty. One suggested alternative would be to utilize the records from the Department of Motor Vehicles. That is to say, that the individuals having driver's licenses and/or identification from the Department of

Motor Vehicles could be identified and names placed in a lot from which they could be drawn. The only problem with this alternative is that there are many individuals who are between the ages of sixteen and eighteen years of age who would be ineligible to participate on the jury. The important thing to remember, with whatever alternative is used, is that it is absolutely necessary that a crosssection of the community be obtained. This means not only geographic, but economic, social and with no reference to sex, race, or other disqualifying factor not stated in the law.

Juror Discrimination

Several court decisions have encountered the issue of particular racial or group discrimination. If it appears that any method being utilized systematically excludes certain members of minority races or other groups in our society, then this would be considered a denial of protection under the United States Constitution and the California Constitution. Questions have arisen as to whether or not specific minorities must comprise a certain percentage of the jury in a case where a representative of that minority is the defendant in a criminal prosecution. In Adams v. Los Angeles Superior Court [13], the defendant appealed his case based on the fact that there was improper representation of his race on the jury. The case occurred in Los Angeles, where the superior court is presently divided into nine districts—a central district and eight others. Prospective jurors for criminal cases tried in the central district are selected on a county-wide basis, but a person tried in one of the other eight districts for precisely the same crime has a jury drawn exclusively from residents of that district. Although eleven percent of Los Angeles County's population is black, the central district, with twenty-two percent of the county's total population, is 31.5 percent black. A county-wide selection of jurors resulted in a black representation of eight percent. Defendant Adams was charged with several felonies, and his trial was being held in the central district. He argued that an equal percentage of members of his own race should be on the jury. The California Appellate Court denied his request, stating that the governing constitutional principle is that jury selection systems must draw jurors from a fair cross-section of the community. So long as there is a fair cross-section of the county's population, it is constitutionally permissible to enact provisions aimed at minimizing inconvenience to jurors and expense to the county, such as limiting geographical areas from which jurors are chosen for service in a particular district.

Social and Economic Selection

If a judicial district attempted to select members of the jury based on specific social or economic factors, this would obviously be a violation of a defendant's right to an impartial and fair trial. The so-called "Blue Ribbon" juries are extremely biased and would be improper in a California Court.

In People v. White [14] the selection of the jury was based primarily from membership lists of service clubs and similar organizations. There was an attempt to get as many businessmen as possible on the jury. The Supreme Court of California overruled the case, stating that this was an improper method of jury selection. The court stated that "The American system requires an impartial jury drawn from a cross-section of the entire community and recognition must be given to the fact that eligible jurors are to be found in every social strata of society."

Juror's Sex

On the federal level, if a judicial district were to systematically exclude women as members of the jury, it would be a violation of federal rules and regulations. In California, there is no violation of a defendant's rights if females are excluded from the jury. California Code of Civil Procedure Section 204 states that "selection of men and women is discretionary only."

Challenging the Jury

To this point, we have discussed only the method by which prospective jurors are summoned for court duty. We will now discuss how the specific number of jurors is selected and how they are rejected according to the law.

When individuals are selected for jury duty, they are placed in groups called jury panels. Penal Code Section 1046A provides that if a county has two or more superior court judges, that a separate panel of jurors may be draw, summoned, and impaneled for each judge. A panel consists of a number in excess of the minimum of twelve required in a criminal prosecution. The number impaneled will depend on the type of trial, and on the potential for disqualification of prospective jurors during the selection process. Normally, there would be from twenty to thirty members on the panel. The names for inclusion on the panel result from a lot that has been selected at random by the court clerk.

The law authorizes either party in a litigation to challenge the jury. "A challenge is an objection made to the trial jurors and is of two kinds:" 1. to the panel. 2. to an individual juror. [15]

Panel

"A panel is a list of jurors returned by a sheriff, marshal, constable, or other proper officer to serve at a particular court, or for the trial of a particular action." [16] A challenge to the panel is an objection made to all the jurors returned and may be taken by either party. Penal Code Section 1059 authorizes the challenge to a panel in one of two situations:

1. When there is a material departure from the forms prescribed in respect to the drawing and returning of a jury in civil actions.
2. The intentional omission by sheriffs, marshals, constables, or other officers to summon one or more of the jurors drawn.

It is rare when a successful challenge will occur regarding the entire panel. The present methods and procedures have pretty much eliminated the problem with respect to selecting a uniform cross-section of residents in the community. The procedure for challenging the panel would be done prior to the prospective jurors being sworn in by the judge, which occurs just prior to the commencement of the trial. [17]

Voir Dire Examination

Before we discuss the specific determination of qualifications for jurors in a criminal prosecution, we first must discuss the method by which prospective jurors are examined by the prospective attorneys represented at the trial. The term "voir dire" refers to the questioning of prospective jurors or witnesses concerning their competency and qualifications regarding the specific trial at hand. At the time the jury is selected, Voir Dire examination would occur.

This is an extremely important phase of a criminal prosecution. The prosecutor and defense attorney would naturally want an active role in determining the type of questions that are to be asked of prospective jurors. As can be recognized, lengthy Voir Dire by counsel could be a serious cause of delay in criminal trials.

In 1927, Section 1078 of the Penal Code was amended to state, "It shall be the duty of the trial court to examine the prospective jurors to select a fair and impartial jury." This eliminated most of the individual questions that would be asked by attorneys. The magistrate is given the primary responsibility to determine the specific qualifications of prospective jurors and to bring out those biases and prejudices that would make them unqualified for that particular trial.

The addition of the phase in Penal Code Section 1078 does not totally eliminate the guarantee of both counsels to examine jurors in terms of reasonable questions which may not have been covered by the court's examination. The magistrate in a criminal prosecution has a great deal of discretionary authority in determining to what extent each counsel will be allowed to ask questions of prospective jurors. Some magistrates will allow fairly extensive questioning, whereas other magistrates will not and will refuse to allow counsels or to ask any questions. [18]

Questions on voir dire may involve any issue dealing with the current action before the court. Some of the more popular questions that would be asked are in the following areas:

1. *Opinion on guilt.* This is the most serious kind of bias that could occur in a criminal prosecution. It is imperative that the court be satisfied that prospective jurors have not already become opinionated to the point where they could not render a fair and impartial verdict.

2. *Associations.* If a prospective juror is a member of any political, religious, social, industrial, fraternal, law enforcement, or other organization that would cause them to render a verdict in favor of that particular organization, then it would be unconstitutional for that individual to serve as a member of the jury. A series of questions will be asked to determine knowledge of, or activity or involvement in the types of organizations that apply to a given trial.

3. *Racial, Religious and Similar Prejudices.* If at any time there is any question regarding the prejudice of a prospective juror in relationship to the defendant, victims, witnesses or other persons participating in a trial, the judge has the duty to bring out those prejudices through Voir Dire examination.

4. *Prejudices from Nature of Crime Charged.* Because of the requirement that a cross-section of the community be obtained for jury duty, it is possible that a prospective juror could have been convicted of a crime similar to that with which the defendant is being charged. He could have very close friends or relatives who have been charged with the same type of offense, and for this reason would be considered biased and unable to render an impartial verdict. The judge will ask specific questions regarding the background of the individual to determine if this is in fact the case.

5. *Knowledge of Prior Convictions of the Defendant or Knowledge of Prior Trials of the Defendant.* In some instances, a defendant may have been tried on a previous occasion for the same offense he is being charged with at this time. The trial may have been continued or dismissed because of technical points of law. If the prospective jurors were aware of that trial, or were aware of prior convictions of the defendant, this certainly would raise questions regarding their prejudices and biases. This knowledge could disqualify a prospective juror from jury duty.

In addition to challenging the panel, the defendant or prosecutor may also challenge individual jurors.

Challenge for Cause

A challenge for cause may be made by either party and is an objection to a particular juror. Penal Code Section 1071 establishes two kinds of challenges for cause: that in general, the juror is disqualified from serving in an action on trial; or that, in particular, he is disqualified from serving in an action on trial.   A challenge for cause may be made only when the justification for the challenge is stated by law.   There are no limitations to the number of jurors who can be disqualified by this method.   As long as the attorneys making the challenges can justify them, based on existing statutory law, they could continue to exhaust the jury panel until they have eliminated all objections under this category.   General causes of challenge are stated in Penal Code Section 1072 and are:

1.   A conviction for a felony.

2.   A want of any of the qualifications prescribed by law to render a person a competent juror.

3.   Unsoundness of mind or such defect in the faculties of the mind or organs of the body as renders him incapable of performing the duties of a juror.

As can be seen, these disqualifications would render a prospective juror incapable of participating in any kind of criminal prosecution.

Particular Causes of Challenge

Particular causes of challenge are of two kinds:

1.   *Implied Bias* "For such a bias as. when the existence of the facts is ascertained, in judgment of law disqualifies the juror, in which is known in this code as implied bias."

2.   *Actual Bias*:   "For the existence of the state of mind on the part of the juror in reference to the case, or to either of the parties, which will prevent him from acting with entire impartiality and without prejudice to the substantial rights of either party, which is known in this code as actual bias" (Penal Code Section 1073).

Implied Bias

There are seven reasons stated in the Penal Code for eliminating a prospective juror under the category of implied bias:

1.   Blood relationship to the fourth degree with relationship to anyone injured by the offense charged, to the complaining witnesses, or to the defendant.

2.   Any relationship of the parties involved in the trial, including attorneys, members of the family of the defendant, victims, witnesses, etc.

3.   On being a party against the defendant in a civil action, or having complained against or been accused by him in a criminal prosecution.

4. Having served on the grand jury which found an indictment or on a coroner's jury which inquired into the death of a person whose death is the subject of indictment or information.

5. Having served on a trial jury which has tried another person for the offense charged.

6. Having been one of the jury formally sworn in to try the same charge, and whose verdict was set aside or which was discharged without a verdict after the case was submitted to it for deliberation.

7. Having served as a juror in a civil action brought against the defendant for an act as an offense.

Actual Bias

Actual bias deals with the state of mind of a prospective juror regarding the specific charge at hand or to either parties involved in the particular case. Actual bias would occur in the opinions of prospective jurors regarding the defendant's guilt, or in the opinions of prospective jurors on other material issues involving the defendant and the criminal prosecution. Many times the prospective juror will have inherent biases because of a particular offense with which the defendant is being charged. An example of this would be seen in an individual who does not consume any alcoholic beverages, and who is violently opposed to anyone else who does. This individual probably would be biased against the defendant in a case where he has been arrested for driving while under the influence of an alcoholic beverage. Another example would be in the case of a defendant who is a member of a radical organization. The prospective juror could be aware of the philosophies and attitudes of that association, and because of his prejudicial reaction to those philosophies, could be biased, and therefore affect the defendant's right to a fair and impartial trial.

Peremptory Challenge

The challenges to prospective jurors that have been discussed up to this point are contained in the Penal Code; in order to successfully make a challenge, the attorney's challenges must be justified through statutory provisions. Peremptory challenges, on the other hand, are not based on statutory provisions, but are a rejection of a juror without having to show any specific reasons. In other words, an attorney might want to eliminate a potential juror because of feelings or other unmeasurable types of attitudes. Because these are not statutory in nature, but rather subjective, the law provides for a limited number of challenges.

Penal Code Section 1070 authorizes the specific numbers of peremptory challenges. Once the defendant or prosecutor have exhausted their peremptory challenges, they must accept the prospective juror. If the offense charged is punishable with death, or with imprisonment in the state prison for life, a defendant and prosecutor are entitled to twenty-six peremptory challenges each. For any other offense, the defendant and prosecutor are entitled to thirteen peremptory challenges each. If the offense charged is punishable with a maximum term of imprisonment of ninety days or less, the defendant and prosecutor are entitled to six peremptory challenges each. When two or more defendants are jointly tried for any public offense, felony or misdemeanor, the state and the defendant shall be entitled to the number of challenges as stated above. The challenges must be shared by each defendant. Each defendant shall also be entitled to seven additional challenges, which may be exercised separately. The state shall also be entitled to additional challenges equal to the number of all the additional separate challenges allowed by the defendants. In the case where the two defendants are being tried for an offense where the maximum term of imprisonment is ninety days or less, then the defendant and prosecutor will be entitled to four additional challenges, rather than the seven, as previously stated.

The intent of the above provision is to limit the amount of peremptory challenges that may be made by either counsel. The more serious the offense, the more challenges the defendant and prosecutor will be granted. In the case of a capital offense, there are twice as many challeges granted as in the case of a minor felony. The counselors are in no way required to utilize all of their peremptory challenges. On some occasions, none of the peremptory challenges will be used. If the defense and prosecuting attorneys are satisfied with the selection of the jury after the challenges for cause have been conducted, then they would certainly be under no obligation to continue to disqualify jurors based on peremptory reasons. If, after the prosecuting attorney or defense attorney have utilized all of the peremptory challenges authorized by law, the court will certify the jury as competent and set the trial in action. Typically, counselors for the defendant or prosecution will use their best judgment in making a decision on whether or not disqualifying a prospective juror is for a peremptory reason. They usually have asked questions during Voir Dire Examination regarding the feelings of prospective jurors, and have sensed whether or not the juror is inclined to be defense oriented or prosecution oriented. As indicated previously, peremptory challenges are extremely subjective and in many cases, it is strictly the particular feeling of the attorney at hand as to whether or not he will challenge a juror under this category.

Before we leave the subject of peremptory challenges, it must be recognized that in the case of alternate jurors, the law provides for additional challenges to that alternate. In other words, if there is one alternate juror, then the attorneys will each receive one additional peremptory challenge.   If there were two, then there would be an additional two challenges.

SUMMARY

The California Constitution requires that each county summon and draw a grand jury each year. A total of nineteen members are chosen in all counties, except in Los Angeles where twenty-three members are chosen.   The law requires that grand jury members possess certain qualifications, which are basically the same as for trial jurors.

Since grand jurors are sworn to perform specific functions of overseeing the operation of local governments, usually citizens with special skills and interests are chosen to serve.

Duties which are mandatory on the part of the grand juries are as follows: 1. Investigation of Public Officials, 2. Investigation of County and District Affairs,   3. Certain Salary Investigations,   4. County Agency Needs, 5. County Jails.

The grand jury at its option receives evidence and determines if there is sufficient evidence to indict defendants for public offenses. As we saw in the *Hawkins* case, the post indictment procedure must be followed by a preliminary examination if the defendant so requests.

The right to a trial by jury has two distinct principles: 1. The defendant has the absolute right to trial by jury. 2. The public has the same absolute right to a trial by jury.

The law also requires that a unanimous decision be rendered by the jury for innocence or guilt.

Since the jurors are picked at random, the selection process is very important.   A cross-section of the community must be represented. Once the selection process begins, only the most qualified jurors will remain.   All others will be challenged and eliminated from jury duty. The selection process includes the following procedures: 1. Challenging the Panel. 2. Challenging an individual juror.

The method for examining prospective jurors for qualification is called voir dire. The judge, in cooperation with attorneys for both sides, will question jurors to determine their qualifications.

DISCUSSION QUESTIONS

1. The role of the grand jury has changed dramatically in recent times. Describe the process for utilizing the grand jury for criminal cases. Indicate the procedure before Hawkins et al v. Superior Court of the City and County of San Francisco. What changes have been made since the *Hawkins* case?

2. Briefly describe the functions which are mandatory on the part of the grand jury.

3. Discuss the concept of the right to a jury trial in California. What is the alternative to a jury trial? Indicate the advantages and disadvantages of each.

4. Describe the process for selecting members of a trial jury. What protections are there for eliminating potential biases and prejudices?

REFERENCES

1. California Penal Code, Sections 888 and 888.2

2. California Penal Code, Section 918.

3. California Penal Code, Section 919.

4. California Penal Code, Section 925a.

5. California Penal Code, Section 927.

6. California Penal Code, Section 928.

7. California Penal Code, Section 919(a & b).

8. California Penal Code, Section 933.

9. California Constitution (1849), Article 1, Section 8.

10. 9 Cal. App. 2d 259, 49 P. 2d 332 (1935).

11. People v. Holmes, 54 Cal. 2d 442, 5 Cal. Rptr. 871, 353 P. 2d 583 (1960).

12. 7 Cal. App. 2d 588, 46 P. 2d 789 (1935).

13. 27 Cal. App. 3d 719, 104 Cal. Rptr. 144 (1972).

14. 43 Cal. 2d 740, 278 P. 2d 9 (1954).

15. California Penal Code, Section 1055.

16. California Penal Code, Section 1057.

17. For details on the form and method of challenging a panel, refer to The California Penal Code, Sections 1060 thru 1065.

18. People v. Estorga, 206 Cal. 81, 273 P. 575 (1928), and People v. Barrett 207 Cal. 47, 276 P. 1003 (1929).

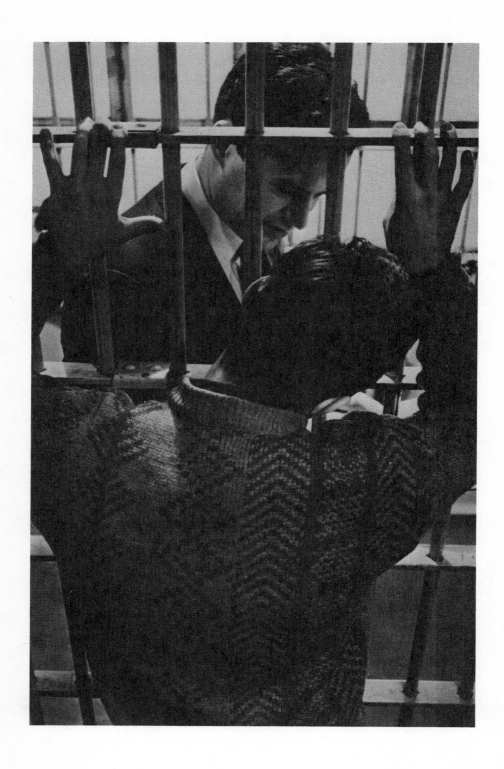

9

Initial Confinement

CHAPTER OBJECTIVES

Upon reading this chapter the student will be able to:

1. List the two basic purposes of initial confinement.
2. Identify the three categories of bail and describe their operation.
3. Recite the conditions and times for the granting of bail.
4. Define O.R., and list a minimum of six guidelines for developing an O.R. Program.
5. Describe the purpose of plea bargaining and list four types of plea bargaining.

This chapter will be devoted to the initial confinement and the surrounding activities that involve the defendant who has been charged with a criminal offense. It must be remembered that the person so charged, at this stage of the criminal justice process, is still considered innocent. If we analyze what takes place in and around the initial confinement process, we can see what would appear on the surface to be some conflicts between the concept of innocence and the necessity of maintaining security of the accused. The reason for initial confinement, the placing of a person in a detention facility, is to immediately protect society from this individual while he awaits final disposition by the courts. On the other hand, this must be balanced with the attitude that the accused is innocent until proven guilty. Therefore, provisions have to be established to grant the defendant as much of his freedom as is realistically possible. In this section we will discuss some of the alternatives for confinement—ways in which we can ensure that the defendant will take care of his responsibilities and yet be restricted to the minimum degree necessary. We will also examine the concept of plea bargaining and its effect in the criminal justice system in the United States, as well as in California, today.

INCARCERATION

An individual who has been formally arrested or charged with a criminal offense is going to be required to be placed in an institution for two reasons: to maintain the necessary protection that society demands from a person formally accused of committing a crime; and to maintain the identity and security of an individual for the purpose of prosecuting him in court.

Each of the counties of the state of California has a detention facility, normally operated by the sheriff of each county. The purpose of this facility is to house prisoners until such time as they have been adjudicated in court or have been released from custody after their appearance in court has been assured. The detention facility is also a post—trial facility where misdemeanor offenders are sentenced to serve time in conjunction with the crime they committed.

Because the defendant is considered innocent until proven otherwise, the purpose of housing the presentenced defendant is dramatically different from that of the postsentence offender. As we have discussed above, the defendant has the responsibility both to attend all court actions as ordered by the magistrate, and to ensure that his case is adjudicated in a court of law. If the individual so desires, he can be released after putting up sufficient bail monies or securities, or convincing the court that he should be released on his own recognizance. If the offense is so severe that the defendant would be a serious risk to society, then the magistrate will make it very difficult for him to be released. On the other hand, if the offense is less severe and is no threat to society, then the chances of being released are much greater. After the defendant has been identified conclusively, and there is no question as to who he is or what his intentions are, then he should be released as soon as possible. For further discussion of jails and other institutions see Chapter 13.

Bail

The Eighth Amendment of the United States Constitution states that, " . . . excessive bail shall not be required." The California Constitution, Article 1, Section 6, and California Penal Code Sections 1270 and 1271 are much more specific: "A defendant charged with an offense punishable with death cannot be admitted to bail, when the proof of his guilt is evident or the presumption thereof great . . . If the charge is for any other offense, he may be admitted to bail before conviction, as a matter of right." As can be seen in the wording of the state constitution and statutes, the defendant has the right to be admitted to bail in all criminal prosecutions, with the exception of capital offenses, and only when the evidence appears to be very strong against him.

Purpose of Bail

Before we can go any further, we must first define the purpose of bail. Bail has been part of our criminal justice system since the inception of criminal law in the English Common Law era. We have always recognized that a person formally charged with a criminal offense is not always necessarily guilty of that offense. Because of this, it is necessary to have provisions in our system to allow a person to remain free during the time that his case is being decided in a court of law. We know that the majority of persons that are subjected to arrest by law enforcement agencies will eventually be found guilty in the court system. However, there are certain percentages of individuals where this will not be the case.

The sole purpose of bail is to ensure the appearance of the defendant in court at the specific time and place as indicated. Bail is simply a security of some sort that is given by or for a person in custody and who is charged by formal complaint, indictment, or information. It would be idealistic to allow the defendant to remain free without any personal expense or limitation prior to the time that he is actually tried and convicted in court. Since he is legally innocent until that time, it would appear appropriate that he not be restricted in any way. From a practical point, we know that an accused, if he did not have a compelling reason for taking care of his responsibilities with the judicial system, might attempt to flee the jurisdiction of the court. Because of this common occurrence, it is necessary to have some type of procedure whereby the defendant will be less likely to flee the jurisdiction of the court.

In People v. Calvert [1] the court stated that the sole purpose of bail in criminal cases "is to insure personal attendance of the defendant in court at all times when his attendance may be lawfully required." From the above definition we can see that the purpose of bail is very explicit. The amount required for bail must be reasonable. The amount must be justified according to the charge and/or defendant. If it appears that the government is imposing a bail which is more severe than is reasonable, then it would be held unconstitutional, and the defendant would be released from custody with a more appropriate amount.

Normally a defendant is entitled to be released on bail any time after his arrest and before his conviction. Generally the greatest passage of time will occur between the arrest and the conviction, and therefore the defendant should be allowed his freedom whenever possible. As can be seen, a defendant could spend from five days to six months, or in some cases, an even longer period of time in jail waiting for his trial. If he were not able to be released after depositing some type of securities to establish that he would, in fact, take care of his responsibilities, he could lose his job, lose his standing in the community, and many other negative things could occur to him. On the other hand, if he is allowed to remain free he can continue working, and continue to meet his obligations as the head of a household, etcetera.

The term "bail" most accurately means the security, cash or bond, given for the appearance of a prisoner. In other words, we are simply talking about some form of security that is put up by the defendant, or by someone for the defendant, in order to assure his appearance in court for some part of a criminal proceeding. Bail normally falls into three categories: 1. Cash bail. 2. Evidence of equity in real property. 3. Written assurance of another person or persons.

Cash Bail. The defendant or any other person, in lieu of giving bail, may deposit with the clerk the sum mentioned in the order.[2] The proper time for depositing the cash bail would be any time after an order admits the defendant to bail, or at any time after the defendant has been arrested and booked for a misdemeanor offense. In those misdemeanor offenses where the arraignment has not been scheduled, or where the bail has not previously been fixed by a magistrate, then the standard bail schedule would apply for the determination of the amount necessary for the release of the defendant. The defendant then could put up the amount required in cash, and give it to the officer in whose custody the defendant is in. In the case where the defendant does provide cash for his release, then he must be discharged from custody.[3]

When money has beeen deposited, a receipt must be given to the person who has made the deposit. If the money remains on deposit at the time of the judgment, and if as part of the judgment there is a fine, the clerk will, at the direction of the court, apply the cash towards the amount of the fine. Of course, if there is any surplus, the amount must be returned to the defendant. It must be recognized that oftentimes the defendant will not be able to provide the cash necessary for his release, but has instead obtained the money through a friend or relative, which was then deposited through the court or the custodial officer. In this case the money, upon a final judgment, cannot be used towards the fine. Since it is the responsibility of the person receiving the money to issue a receipt in the name of the depositor at the time of judgment, it will be determined who actually made the deposit; at that time a decision is made as to whether or not the bail will apply towards the fine or not. If the person to whom the receipt for the deposit was issued is not the defendant, then the deposit after judgment must be returned to him within ten days after he requests that his money be returned. If a claim is not made by the depositor, the clerk has a responsibility to notify him of the exoneration of bail so that he may make a request for it and receive it.[4]

Equity and Real Property. In lieu of a monetary deposit, the defendant or any other person may deposit bonds of the United States or the state of California for the value of the cash deposit required; the defendant may also give as security any equity in real property which he owns. In order for the defendant to be released on bail when he chooses the latter, it is necessary that the equity in that property equal twice the amount which is required for bail. The magistrate may call a hearing and have witnesses testify or be examined in order to determine the true value of the real property, and the equity which the defendant has in that property.[5]   As can be seen, this is a rather cumbersome process for obtaining a release from custody. Because of the necessity of determining the correct value of the real estate, and the requirement that the equity be twice the amount of the actual bail, the defendant will rarely use this as an option for his release.

Written Assurance of Another Person (Bail Bond)

Bail can be posted as a written undertaking when executed by two sufficient sureties (with or without the defendant, in the discretion of the magistrate), when acknowledged before the court or magistrate.[6] Bail bond then is a written undertaking which is executed by two sufficient sureties who are acknowledged before the court or magistrate, admitting the defendant's bail.

The wording of the section, "must be executed by two sufficient sureties," requires some explanation. In California, if two individuals are residents of the county in which the defendant is being accused of a criminal offense, and each is worth the amount required for the bail, then the magistrate may accept the bond in lieu of cash from these individuals. The magistrate may accept the bail bond from individuals who reside outside of the county, as long as he is satisfied that they are legitimate individuals who have the necessary sureties in order to satisfy the law's provisions.[7] The bond must in all cases be justified by an affadavit that is taken before the magistrate, and which establishes the qualifications of the individual putting up the sureties. This affadavit is a rather lengthy statement requiring justification of the amount of bail that is required. The individuals putting up the bail must set forth their legal description of the real estate owned, the net worth etcetera, to the satisfaction of the court. Witnesses may be called in this case to determine the qualifications of these individuals to ensure that they accurately stated their net worth as required in the affadavit.

Upon the allowance of bail and the execution and approval of the undertaking, the magistrate must, if the defendant is in custody, make and sign an order for his discharge; upon its delivery to the proper officer, the defendant must be discharged.[8]

The bail bondsman is under no obligation to put up the bail for the defendant when the defendant so requests. The relationship between the bail bondsman and the defendant is very similar to the relationship an individual would have in applying for a loan with the bank. In other words, the bail bondsmen must be satisfied in his own mind that the defendant will, in fact, take care of his obligations, and will pay the amount of charges necessary to have the money, in effect, loaned to him. The application for bail, which is filled out by the defendant, requests very detailed information regarding the defendant's financial ability to pay, his past experiences with reference to loans and paying his debts, as well as his roots in the community. The less responsibility the defendant shows, the less likelihood there is of his release through the services of the bail bondsman.

The bail agreement between the defendant and the bail bondsman resembles a typical contract between two parties. In other words, the major portion of the bail bond is a statement of the contract. For exchange of the services provided by the bail bondsman, the defendant is required to pay a service charge according to the amount of bail required by the courts. In California, the cost of bail when the deposit is less than $500 is a fee of $10, plus 10 percent of the amount fixed on bail. If the cost of the bail is more than $500, then the fee is 10 percent of the amount of bail.

As can be seen, the most popular type of release would be under provisions of the bail bonds agreement. Due to the fact that most

Surety Insurance Company
of California
HOME OFFICE
Box 754
La Habra, California 90631

APPLICATION FOR BAIL

P A No. __80-4311__

Amt. of Bail $ __5,000.00__

Date of Exec. __2/21/80__

Agent __Root__

Booking Name __Brian Adams__   True Name __Brian Adams__

Date of Arrest __2/20/80__   Where Held __L.A. County__   Charge __211 P.C.__

Court __Superior__   Jud. Dist. __Hawthorne__   At _____   County __Los Angeles__

Date to appear __3/15/80__   Case No. __80-11153__   Time __1200 HRS__

Defendant's Address __3310 Argyle Rd.__ City __Redding__ How long? __3 years__ Phone __221-1151__

Employer __Self Employed__   How Long __2 years__   Address _____

Occupation __Laboror__   Soc. Sec. No. __551-54-5841__

Union __None__   Local _____ At _____

Sex __M__ Age __20__ Height __6-0__ Race __Cauc__ Nationality __Amer__ Married - Single __X__ Divorced - Separated _____

If Naturalized—Where _____ When _____ First Papers _____ Port of Entry _____

Spouse's Name _____ No. Children _____ Spouse Employed _____

Spouse's Employer _____ Address _____

If Divorced—Where _____ When _____ Child Support _____

Years in City _____ County _____ State _____ Where Born _____

Where Raised __Shasta County__   Previous Address __Unknown__

Lodge _____ Armed Service _____ Discharge _____

Serial No. _____ Disability _____ Pension _____ $ _____ /Mo.

Previous Arrests __1__ When __1/10/78__ Where __Sacramento__ Charge __211 P.C.__

Bonded Before __No__ By Whom _____ Where _____

General Comments _____

Relative or Reference __Unknown__   Address _____

Relative or Reference _____   Address _____

Defendant's Attorney __None__   Address _____

FINANCIAL STATEMENT OF: __Brian Adams__   Address __3310 Argyle Rd.__ Phone __221-1151__

Bus. or Employer __Self Employed__   Address _____ Phone _____

I have on deposit $__15.00__ Checking/Savings with __B. of A.__ Branch __Downtown__ Bank

I own the following real estate __None__

Value $_____ $ _____ Liens $_____ $ _____ To _____

Motor Vehicle __None__ Year _____ Type _____ License _____

Liens _____ Legal Owner _____ Operator License _____

I own the following personal assets __None__

AUTHORIZATION TO SOLICIT   __2/21__ 19__80__

I hereby authorize __J. Root__ , or your authorized agents, to solicit and negotiate for a Bail
(NAME OF BAIL AGENT)

Bond on my behalf with _____

You are also specifically and directly authorized to solicit the above named between the hours of 11:00 P.M. and 7:00 A.M.,
should you find it desirable.

Brian Adams
DEFENDANT

Statement of Information Required by Section 2100, Title 10, California Administrative Code

Brian Adams	J. Root	J. Root
Full name of person supplying information	Name of person negotiating bail	Name of person receiving information
3310 Argyle Rd.	1065 Old Oregon Tr.	2/21/80 1200 HRS
Address	Address	Date and time information received
	None	None
Connection or relationship to defendant	Connection or relationship to defendant	Manner in which information received
Telephone		
If same was defendant, how did he communicate?	Name of licensee who negotiated transaction	Name of other agent involved and commission paid
If writ _____ Name of Attorney	Was consideration other than money received? YES ☐ NO ☐ If yes, explain in and attach statement.	Name and sum paid unlicensed persons and service performed

304-01

defendants caught up in our judicial process are not able to provide the cash necessary for their release, they must turn to the services of a bail bondsman. Most bail bondsmen work in conjunction with large financial companies, such as the Surety Insurance Company of California, and other corporations which are in business for the sole purpose of loaning money to defendants so that they may be released pending the outcome of their trial.

Procedure for being Admitted to Bail

As previously discussed, the sole responsibility of granting bail falls upon a competent court or magistrate having jurisdiction in the matter. Upon being admitted to bail, the defendant is then discharged from actual custody. When the defendant, upon examination, has been held to answer for a public offense, the admission to bail may be granted by the magistrate who has jurisdiction in the case, or by any magistrate who has the power to issue a writ of habeas corpus in the state of California. In other words, any magistrate of competent jurisdiction may grant a defendant's request to be admitted to bail.

Nature of Bail

Penal Code Section 1273 sets the conditions for bail:

If the offense is bailable the defendant may be admitted to bail before conviction;

First for his appearance before the magistrate, on the examination of the charge, before being held to answer.

Second, to appear at the court to which the magistrate is required to return the depositions and statement upon the defendant being held to answer after examination.

Third, after indictment, either before the bench warrant is issued for his arrest, or after an order of the court committing him, or enlarging the amount of bail, or upon his being surrendered by his bail to answer the indictment in the court in which it is found, or to which it may be transferred for trial.

And after conviction, and upon an appeal;

First, if the appeal is from a judgment imposing a fine only, on the undertaking of bail that he will pay the same, or such part of it as the appellate court may direct, if the judgment is confirmed or modified, or the appeal is dismissed.

Second, if the judgment of imprisonment has been given, that he will surrender himself in execution of the judgment, upon its being affirmed or modified, or upon the appeal being dismissed, or that in case of the judgment be reversed, and that the cause be remanded for new trial, that he will appear in the court to which said cause has been remanded, and submit himself to the orders and process thereof."

As stated, there are three kinds of appearances before conviction after which a defendant may be released on bail: 1. Appearance at a preliminary examination before a magistrate. 2. Appearance at a trial after being held to answer. 3. Appearance at a trial after indictment. The provisions of Section 1273 of the Penal Code provide for the release of a defendant prior to conviction, as well as after conviction with certain conditions. We will now discuss the arrangements for bail being granted prior to and after the conviction stage.

On Arrest

At the time a warrant of arrest is issued, the magistrate has the responsibility of fixing the amount of bail which in his judgment is adequate to assure the attendance of the defendant in court following his arrest. Penal Code Section 815a provides that the magistrate shall endorse upon said warrant, the amount necessary and reasonable to assure the attendance of the defendant.

In the case where the defendant has been arrested without a warrant for a felony or a misdemeanor, provisions have been made by the various courts in the state of California to allow for the release of a defendant upon being arrested and booked into jail. A uniform bail schedule has been established which a custodial officer or court clerk may utilize in determining the proper amount of bail, without specifically contacting a magistrate. Penal Code Section 1269b provides that:

> an officer in charge of a jail where the defendant is being held or the clerk of appropriate court may approve and accept bail in the amount fixed by the bail schedule or order admitting to bail as follows:
>
> 1. *Misdemeanor Cases.* Any time the defendant is in custody of a jailor, clerk, or other appropriate person may accept bail in the amount specified in the schedule prior to a court appearance.
>
> 2. *Felony Cases.* If a formal complaint has been filed, the defendant, upon appearing before a judge on a charge, may be released on bail in the amount fixed by the judge, or in the case that has been indicated by the warrant.

In other words, for a felony offense, the only time that a defendant may be released on bail is in the case where he was arrested in obedience to a warrant (and the amount is indicated on the warrant), or in the case where the defendant has appeared before a judge as a result of a formal complaint being filed.

The custodial officer or other appropriate individual may accept cash or a security bond on behalf of the defendant and release him after setting a time and place for his appearance in court, according to the provisions and policies established by the particular courts of the county.

After Conviction

The defendant may be admitted to bail after conviction in specific cases. A defendant who has been convicted of an offense which is not punishable with death, and who requests probation or has appealed may be admitted to bail under the following circumstances:

> "As a matter of right, before judgment is pronounced pending application for probation in cases of misdemeanors, or when the appeal is from the judgment imposing a fine only.
>
> As a matter of right, before judgment is pronounced pending application for probation in cases of misdemeanors, or when the appeal is from the judgment imposing imprisonment in cases of misdemeanors.
>
> As a matter of discretion in all other cases."[9]

Penal Code Section 1272 therefore states that in the case of those offenses where the defendant will be sentenced by a fine only, or when the sentence is for a misdemeanor imprisonment, then the magistrate must grant the defendant's request for release on bail pending his application for probation, or upon his request for appeal. In all other cases the court has the discretion to release the defendant after he has been convicted.

Increase or Decrease of Original Bail Amount

The magistrate has the authority in any public offense where the defendant has been released on bail to increase or decrease the amount of the original bail that was set. Penal Code Section 1269c provides that if a person has been arrested for a felony without a warrant, and the officer believes that the defendant will not take care of his responsibilities by appearing in court, the officer may advise the court of this problem; if the court so desires it may increase the amount of bail appropriately to ensure the defendant's appearance. On the other hand, if it appears as though the defendant will take care of his obligations by appearing in court, then upon his or his attorney's application, the magistrate, upon being satisfied, may reduce the amount of bail to whatever amount he deems necessary to assure the defendant's appearance. The increase or decrease of the amount of bail are matters within the discretion of the trial court, to be exercised in the promotion of justice, and can be made only upon good cause shown. A court may not arbitrarily make an order increasing the amount of bail without showing justification for the increase.

Recommitment of the Defendant

The court having proper jurisdiction may direct the arrest of the defendant and may commit him to custody until legally discharged for the following cases:

1. When by reason of his failure to appear he has incurred a forefeiture of bail or money deposited thereof.

2. When it satisfactorily appears to the court that either of the acknowledged sureties are dead, have moved from the state, or when the bail is insufficient.
3. Upon an indictment being found or information filed whereby the bail is increased or the defendant is committed to custody.[10]

In addition to the magistrate having the authority to recommit the defendant to custody, a bail bondsman has a similar authority with relationship to the contract agreement between himself and the defendant. The bail bondsman may surrender the defendant to the officer in whose custody he was committed at the time of giving bail, and may nullify the bail bond obligation. For the purpose of such surrender, the bail bondsman may arrest the defendant, or may by written authority empower some other person to do so.[11]

Forfeiture of Bail

If without sufficient excuse the defendant neglects to appear for his arraignment, or for any portion of his trial when the court has ordered his appearance, the court must thereupon declare the bail forfeited.[12] The provisions of this section state that the defendant, due to his agreement with the court, is subject to losing whatever monies he has deposited for his release in the form of bail. In the case of the bail bondsman, the bondsman would lose the money due to the defendant's neglected appearance in court. It then becomes the responsibility of the bail bondsman to collect what money he can from the accused. The court does have the leeway to reinstate the original conditions of bail, providing the defendant makes a timely request, and can establish a justified reason for not satisfying the provisions of the court in appearing when so ordered. Generally speaking, if he makes the request within ninety days after the entry ordering the forfeit of bail, the defendant can have the order set aside. He must establish a legitimate reason for his failure to appear which must satisfy the court. Reasons for the court to grant his request would be because of physical inability, illness, insanity, or detention in another facility which prohibited him from appearing as ordered by the courts.

Personal Recognizance

In 1959 California made provisions for releasing defendants without a monetary or equitable deposit upon their written promise to appear. In other words, in conjunction with the themes that the defendant is assumed innocent until the contrary is proven, and that his right to freedom should be restricted only in the amount absolutely necessary to ensure the safety of society, the California legislators decided that under certain conditions a person could be released without having to deposit any cash, bail, or enter into an agreement with a bail bondsman to provide assurance that the defendant would take care of his obligations.   It is felt that an individual who can demonstrate to the court that he is responsible and that he will take care of his obligations therefore would not need to deposit any bail; the court could choose to release him on his own word. This is a discretionary authority, and the court is under no obligation whatsoever to release someone on his written promise to appear.

Penal Code Section 1318 states that "upon good cause being shown, any court or magistrate who could release a defendant from custody upon his giving bail including a defendant arrested upon an out-of-county warrant may release such defendant on his own recognizance if it appears to such court or magistrate that such defendant will surrender himself to custody as agreed." As we have seen in previous sections on bail, the maistrate is only one of several officials who may grant the release of a defendant prior to or during the court action. We found that the court clerk and jailors were individuals who had the authority to release individuals upon the deposit of sufficient amounts to be granted release.   The personal recognizance section authorizes the magistrate alone to allow an individual to be released on his own word.

Penal Code Section 1318.4 establishes the procedures for seeking the release on an "O.R." To be released on his own recognizance, the defendant is responsible for filing with the clerk of the court in which the magistrate presides an agreement in writing which he agrees to and signs. It stipulates that:

1. He will appear at all times and places as so ordered by the court or magistrate releasing him, and as is ordered by any court or magistrate before whom the charges are subsequently pending.
2. If he fails to appear as ordered and is apprehended outside of the state of California, he waives extradition.
3. Any court or magistrate having jurisdiction may revoke the order of release, and either return him to custody or require that he give bail or other assurances of his appearance as otherwise provided.

If at any time the court later chooses to require the defendant to provide bail, the court can revoke its own order of personal recognizance and stipulate that the defendant must give bail in the amount specified by the court. This will occur particularly in cases where the defendant has failed to appear, or has violated any conditions of the order releasing him or his own recognizance. The magistrate may also revoke the defendant's own recognizance order if there has been a change of circumstances which increase the risk of failure to appear, or if additional facts have been presented which were not known at the time of the original order. If the defendant is unable to give bail in the amount specified, then he would be committed to actual custody.[13]

In 1977 Penal Code Section 1319.4 was added to the Penal Code, which states that in addition to all other charges, if the defendant fails to appear as he has agreed after being released on his own recognizance then he is guilty of an additional felony; upon conviction he shall be punished by a fine not exceeding $5,000, or by imprisonment in the state prison or the county jail for not more than one year. If a defendant fails to appear on a misdemeanor charge after being released on his own recognizance, then he would additionally be charged with a misdemeanor for violating the O.R. agreement.

Vera Foundation Experiment

In 1961, the Vera Foundation in New York undertook a control group experiment to test the hypothesis that defendants identified as "good risks" could be released on their own recognizance without unduly increasing the rates of bail jumping or failure to appear at the trial. This experiment established that: 1. Defendants released on their own recognizance as good risks had a lower jump rate than the rate traditionally associated with money bail. 2. Defendants released and awaiting trial were less likely to be convicted than the defendants detained prior to trial.   3. If convicted, then the defendants released were likely to receive less severe sentences.

Other studies show that good risks, released on their own recognizance, often met the same standards used by bail bondsmen, and that "to an unknown extent, therefore, the impact of the release on own recognizances project is reduced financial hardship rather than recuded incarceration."   The office of Economic Opportunity stated that, "Although statistical data are not available, it is reasonably certain that the national population of pretrial detainees is greater today than when the Vera experiment began."[14] As a result of the Vera Foundation experiment, an application was developed to establish enough information to decide whether or not an individual should be released on his own recognizance.   The information contained in the application emphasizes several areas, which are as follows:

1. *The Crime.* The more serious the offense, the less likely that the defendant should be released on his own recognizance. The less serious the offense, the more likelihood that the defendant will remain in the area to take care of his responsibilities.

2. *Citizenship.* It was discovered in the Vera Foundation experiment that the more roots a person has in a community, the less likelihood there is that he will ignore his responsibilities and obligations. It is understandable that if a defendant has lived in a county for a long

period of time, and additionally owns his own residence or is purchasing his residence, that he is less likely to ignore his responsibilities than would a transient who is just passing through and staying in a local motel.

3. *His Dependents.* Conversely, if a defendant has a lot of responsibility in caring for dependents, then the chances of him leaving the area are less than if he is dependent only upon himself. Therefore if he has children, a wife, or if there are special circumstances regarding his dependents, then they can be considered as part of the criteria for releasing this individual on his good word.

4. *His Employment or Related Status.* As can be seen if a defendant is unemployed, then he has less reason to remain in the community where he is being charged with a crime. On the other hand, if he has been working at a job for a period of time and shows job stability, then this is an indication of his character. The longer an individual has been at his current job, the more chances that he will remain in the area and therefore would be considered for his own release without having to put up bail.

5. *Previous Record.* This section deals with the defendant's prior convictions. If the defendant has been convicted of several offenses or has been convicted of serious crimes such as felonies, then he would be less likely to be released on his own recognizance.

As a result of the above categories, the magistrate can review the past experience and background of an accused and make a decision as to whether or not that individual should be released on his own recognizance. The Vera Foundation study established a point system whereby the defendant would be released if a certain point value was reached. Points are assigned to the specific subject groups, as described above. The more signs of stability, the more points the defendant would receive, and the less trouble the defendant has been in, the more points he would receive. A minimum score would be required. If the person obtained the minimum, then he could be released based on the fact that he would be a "good risk."

In a guide book to improve the handling of misdemeanor offenders (printed by the U.S. Department of Justice Law Enforcement Assistance Administration and the National Institute of Law Enforcement Criminal Justice), certain guidelines were established that should be considered in developing or creating an 'own recognizance' program; they are as follows:

1. The program should be administered by an agency and staffed by personnel that are trusted and respected by the magistrates who will make the decision whether or not to release on OR or to reduce the defendant's bail.

2. The operating agency and staff should also be completely acceptable to law enforcement agencies, although the program should not be operated by them.

3. The pretrial release program, with the court prosecution's support, should have as its major goal the maximum and reasonably safe reduction of the number of persons in jail awaiting trial.

4. The program should be so organized as to reach its clients on the day of arrest or early the next morning, and should have twenty-four-hour-a-day access to a judge to ensure early and effective action.

5. The program should be staffed by people with sufficient knowledge of human behavior to pick up signs of personality stability or instability which is not always identified through the use of rating forms.

6. Special efforts should be made to remind those defendants of the time and place of their trial. In some cases escort measures should be arranged.

7. Program funding should permit the employment of a staff which is capable and not overburdened.

8. The program should have a built-in evaluative component of sufficient sophistication and provide the testing of valid release criteria, and an assessment of the general program consequences.

9. The rating forms used in the program should be subject to revision, based on valuative findings regarding their relevance and usefulness. [15]

There are no statutory guidelines as to what constitutes good cause for determining whether or not an individual should be released on his own recognizance; however, the studies have shown the relevance of the nature and extent of the defendant's ties to the community, which are determined by the following factors: whether the defendant is currently employed; whether he is residing with his family; the length of his residence at the same address; whether there are references who will vouch for him; whether he has had any previous convictions; whether he previously has been released on bail or on his own recognizance and, if so, whether he appeared as directed; the nature of the charge against him;   and whether he has any special local ties, such as receiving unemployment insurance or local medical care. The more information that can be gathered about the defendant, and the more that information is determined to be accurate seem to be the crucial factors in whether or not the OR program is a successful program or not. Legal scholars usually agree that, whenever possible, an individual should not be required to put up finances unless it is absolutely necessary. Many would agree that this is a form of punishment inasmuch they are being required to pay fees for bail bondsmen, or to come up with the money out of their own pocket, until such time as they can exonerate themselves in court.   On the other hand, society has to be protected and assured that the defendant is going to be responsible and take care of his obligations; there would appear to be a necessary balance to maintain between these two elements. With this in mind, own recognizance can be effective pretrial release procedure, providing that it is managed adequately.

PLEA BARGAINING

One of the most interesting strategies used by prosecutors in disposing of cases is that of plea bargaining. Its use is very controversial, and has generated much discussion. It is difficult to develop a policy which all prosecutors would agree to, or one that public defenders would feel is justified.

Plea bargaining refers to the policy established by prosecutors in a county to "deal with the defendant" regarding the disposition of his case. Plea bargaining can occur when the prosecutor is willing to reduce the charge to a lesser offense or degree, or is willing to stipulate that the defendant receive special sentencing as authorized by the law.

Types of Plea Bargaining Most Commonly Dealt With

In the process of determining the proper charge and sentence for a defendant, the prosecutor and the defendant will many times discuss the details of the case and then compromise on the specific crime and sentence that the accused will end up with in a court of law. Most often they are broken into four general areas:

1. *Plea Bargaining Concerning the Charge.* This type of plea bargaining deals with the specific charge with which the defendant has been accused. For example, in offenses which carry degrees, such as homicide, assaults, and sex offenses, the defendant is willing to plead guilty, for example, to second degree murder rather than first degree, etcetera. This type of plea bargaining is common, particularly when there is a great deal of evidence against the defendant and the defendant is concerned about a death penalty or extended time in jail.

2. *Plea Bargaining Concerning a Sentence.* California has several types of offenses which are called alternate sentence crimes, or "wobblers." Many times a defendant is willing to plead guilty if he is convinced that he will not have to go to prison. Alternate sentence crimes are those crimes which the magistrate will have the authority to either sentence the defendant to prison or to a county jail. If the prosecutor and magistrate agree, the defendant will plead guilty and be sentenced to the county jail rather than taking his chance on being sentenced to a state prison.   The other example where this type of

bargaining often occurs is in cases where the defendant wishes not to go to jail at all, but rather requests probation. The defendant will plead guilty to the offense as charged, knowing that the judge will suspend sentence and place him on some type of probation. This is usually the most frequent type of bargaining used in the criminal justice system in California.

3. *Plea Bargaining on Several Counts of the Same Charge.* This type of plea bargaining occurs when the defendant has been charged with multiple counts for the same offense; for example, the crime of burglary. Many times, upon arrest, an accused will admit to several other burglaries which he committed. The same occurs for the crime of robbery. The defendant is willing to plead guilty to one count if the remaining counts will be dropped. This method primarily concerns the length of the sentence that the defendant will receive.

4. *Plea Bargaining for the Elimination of Specific Charges.* This type of plea bargaining is very similar to the one just described. This type occurs when the defendant has been charged with several types of offenses arising out of the same incident. The defendant is willing to plead guilty to one of the charges specified in the accusatory pleading if the remaining charges will be dismissed, or if there is some combined dropping of charges, pleading guilty to what is left.

Arguments in Favor of Plea Bargaining

Most district attorneys in the state of California believe that plea bargaining should be an acceptable option to have at their disposal for dealing with criminal cases. There are several reasons for maintaining the plea bargaining policies that exist today.

One of the most obvious reasons for plea bargaining is to reduce the workload most district attorneys have in the state of California. By utilizing the plea negotiation policy, the prosecutor is able to dispose of cases much more easily without the necessity of taking the defendant to trial, which is very time consuming and expensive. If it were not for the plea bargaining policy, the defendant would have nothing to lose and would demand a court or jury trial much more often. By having the option of reducing charges or sentencing the accused is then much more willing to discuss the merits of his case with the prosecutor. Another justification for plea bargaining is the fact that in some cases the prosecutor is absolutely certain of the defendant's guilt; however, he is not so certain that he can prove it in a court of law. By offering the defendant an option to plead guilty to a lesser offense or receive a lesser sentence, the accused would be willing to negotiate that plea, rather than take the chance of going to trial and being found guilty of the more severe charge, being sentenced accordingly. Therefore, the prosecutor is satisfied that the defendant will be found guilty, rather than going free entirely.

In some cases there will be more than one defendant being charged with a crime arising out of the same incident. If the prosecutor has the option of talking to one of the co-defendants, allowing him to plead to a lesser offense or receive a suspended sentence, then this individual would be more willing to cooperate and testify against the other co-defendants in the trial. This may be the only way that a prosecutor could genuinely get a conviction for the other defendants in a trial. Without the testimony of one of the persons involved in the crime, all defendants could possibly go completely free, without any conviction whatsoever.

The above justifications for continuing the negotiated plea are but a few of those that have been disucssed by experts in the area of plea bargaining. They serve as an introduction so that the reader may more fully understand the rationale, behind the prosecutors' need to maintain the policy of plea bargaining.

Objections to Plea Bargaining Process

Most critics of the plea bargaining policies address their arguments to one area; most are concerned with the fear that a defendant is going to plead guilty to a crime which he did not commit. The classic example is where the defendant has been charged with a crime that will put him in prison if he is convicted. This individual may not be fully aware of the criminal justice system. The evidence can appear to be overwhelming against him; for example, there may be witnesses testifying regarding his involvement. The accused is innocent however, and is afraid that he will not be able to prove his innocence in a court of law. Because of this rationale he is willing to plead guilty to a lesser offense and spend perhaps thirty days in the county jail, rather than take the chance of going to trial and being found guilty by a jury after the evidence has been presented.

Another fundamental problem with plea bargaining is the fact that when a "deal" is offered to a defendant, the defendant, if he elects to go along with the deal, is surrendering his rights to a trial. Of course, the greatest danger involved in this type of bargaining or when the defendant is going to be given a "special deal" for a guilty plea, when he again could be innocent and might be willing to plead guilty rather than take his chance "at the trial."

The third area which seems to be of concern to most opponents of the plea bargaining system deals with the public defender and the prosecutor. Due to the workload of the public defender, and the fact that he is a public official, many scholars are concerned that an accused will not receive adequate representation, inasmuch as the public defender is unable to adequately prepare cases for trial, and is willing to negotiate pleas more often to reduce his workload. The other factor is that since the public defender is a public official, he maintains a dual role inasmuch as he is a representative of the county in which he is employed, as well as the defendant's representative. Some studies have indicated that the public defender maintains a close, harmonious role between the prosecutor, police, and himself. Because of this association, the public defender is more willing to convince his client that he should plead guilty to a lesser offense, or should negotiate a sentencing arrangement.

In conclusion, the National Advisory Commission on Criminal Justice Standards and Goals advocated the abolition of the plea negotiation. Part of the recommendations by the commission are quoted as follows:

> As soon as possible, but in no event later than 1978, negotiations between prosecutors and defendants, either personally or through their attorneys concerning concessions to be made in return for guilty pleas should be prohibited. In the event that the prosecution makes their recommendations as to sentence, it should not be effected by the willingness of the defendant to plead guilty to some or all of the offenses which he is charged. A plea of guilty should not be considered by the court in determining this sentence to be imposed.

> Until Plea Negotiations are eliminated as recommended in this standard, such negotiations in the entry of pleas pursuant to the resulting agreements should be permitted only under a procedure embodying the safeguards contained in the remaining standards in this chapter.16

SUMMARY

In this chapter we have identified the purposes for initial confinement; it is necessary for the protection of society, and to identify the accused for the purpose of disposition in court. The term "bail" was described as a means of ensuring a defendant's appearance in court. Since the defendant is presumed innocent until proven guilty in a court of law, he should remain free until such time as he is convicted.

Bail normally falls into three categories: 1. Cash Bail, 2. Evidence of equity in real property, 3. Written assurance of another person.

Also discussed was the fact that a defendant, in many cases, can be allowed to go free on bail until he has exhausted all court remedies, including appeal.

"Own recognizance" was defined as releasing a defendant on his good word pending the outcome of his case. In other words, no bail would be required; he need only show that he is a good risk and will take care of his obligations.

Plea bargaining was defined as the means of disposing of cases without going to trial by means of reducing the sentence or charge so that the defendant will agree to the charge and plead guilty. The four

204 Administration of Justice

most common types of plea bargaining were discussed. 1. Plea bargaining concerning the charge, 2. Plea bargaining concerning the sentence, 3. Plea bargaining on several counts of same charge, 4. Plea bargaining for elimination of a specific charge.

Finally the arguments for and against plea bargaining were discussed.

DISCUSSION QUESTIONS

1. Identify and discuss the two basic purposes of initial confinement. What are the alternatives to confinement? Does initial confinement conflict with the constitutions of California and of the United States? Justify your answer.

2. List and describe the three categories of bail.

3. Define "O.R." Explain the process of obtaining O.R. What are the strengths and weaknesses of an O.R. program?

4. Plea bargaining has been under attack for many years in the United States and in California. Indicate the advantages and disadvantages. Take a position and justify your decision.

REFERENCES

1. 129 Cal. App. 2d 693, 277 P. 2d 834 (1954).
2. Section 1295 of the California Penal Code.
3. California Penal Code, Section 1295.
4. California Penal Code, Section 1297.
5. California Penal Code, Section 1298.
6. California Penal Code, Section 1278.
7. California Penal Code, Section 1279.
8. California Penal Code, Section 1281.
9. California Penal Code, Section 1272.
10. California Penal Code, Section 1310.
11. California Penal Code, Section 1300 and 1302.
12. California Penal Code, Section 1305.
13. California Penal Code, Sections 1318.6 and 1318.8.
14. Office of Economic Opportunity (The OEO Release Program, Washington D.C. Office of Economic Opportunity 1972).
15. The Guide to Improved Handling of Misdemeanor Offenders sale by the Superteindent of Documents U.S. Government Printing Offices, Washington D.C. 20402 page no. 8 & 9.
16. See pages 46-49 of Commissions recommendations for further details.

10

Accusatory Pleadings

CHAPTER OBJECTIVES

Upon reading this chapter, the student will be able to:

1. Identify which pleadings will be filed by the prosecution in misdemeanor cases.

2. Identify which pleadings will be filed when a case is endorsed by a grand jury for prosecution.

3. Identify which pleadings will be filed when a prosecutor handles a felony case without using the grand jury.

4. Recognize items that must be included in accusatory pleadings.

5. Determine if multiple crimes and/or multiple defendants may be tried in one trial.

6. Understand that items of pleading can be added or changed by amendment without dismissing the case.

7. Discuss the specific alternatives that the defense may use to attack the pleadings.

The accusatory pleadings are those documents filed with a court which formally open the prosecution of a suspect. Once the case is filed, the suspect is referred to as the "defendant." If an arrest warrant is sought prior to arrest, the papers used to obtain the warrant serve as the pleadings. In the case of misdemeanors, a "complaint" will be filed in either a municipal court or a justice court. A complaint is also filed in these courts to initiate felony proceedings unless the prosecutor decides to take the case to the grand jury, or unless the grand jury begins the proceedings on their own initiative. In such a case, the complaint will govern the case through the preliminary hearing. If the defendant is held to answer at the preliminary hearing, the prosecutor will file an "information" in the superior court. When prosecution is begun by hearings before a grand jury, an "indictment" will be filed in superior court to officially start the prosecution if the grand jury concurs that the case should be prosecuted.

This chapter will discuss the content of complaints, indictments and informations. It will also cover citations that may be used in lieu of the complaint in the prosecution of misdemeanors or infractions. Problems relating to joint charges of several crimes in one pleading will be analyzed. The formal motions which attack accusatory pleadings will also be discussed.

This chapter will not be concerned with the accusatory pleading used in juvenile court, called a "petition." It also will not cover the "accusation," an accusatory pleading used in a civil proceeding to remove a public official for misconduct in office. The pleadings used in military cases involving the commission of crimes will also not be covered. While each of these pleadings is accusatory in nature, they are beyond the scope of an introductory text.

ACCUSATORY PLEADINGS

California Penal Code Section 691 (4) defines "accusatory pleadings" as:

> [A]n indictment, an information, an accusation, a complaint filed with a magis-
> trate charging a public offense of which the superior court has original trial juris-
> diction, and a complaint filed with an inferior court charging a public offense of
> which such inferior court has original trial jurisdiction.

While earlier Penal Code sections contained separate rules governing the indictment, information, and complaint, revisions of the code in 1951 attempted to establish uniform rules for most pleadings. This, along with other revisions at that time, greatly simplified the format of pleadings in criminal cases.

The primary purpose of accusatory pleadings is to inform the defendant of the nature of the proceedings and thus satisfy due process. This requires that the pleading clearly give notice of all charges being brought against the defendant so that he can prepare a defense. Current rules of pleading do not require strict adherence to precise wording, but it is still necessary for the pleading to give adequate notice of the charge so that the defendant will be able to assess the consequences of conviction and structure his defense accordingly. However, it is not necessary to identify a specific code section that has been violated.

COMPLAINT

A *complaint* is the initial pleading in an inferior court (justice court or municipal court). It must be in writing and signed under oath or penalty of perjury by the complainant.[1] Any person who has knowledge of the facts in the complaint may sign it. The complaint may be sworn on "information and belief." This permits a person not having firsthand knowledge to sign the complaint if he has sufficient basis to believe that the facts as stated are correct. Thus, officers may sign the complaint if they have information from other officers that they observed the events listed in the complaint,[2] received reliable information from a tested informant,[3] or received information from the crime victim or witness. Officers should familiarize themselves with the law of evidence in order to be able to judge whether or not there is sufficient information to support a complaint in the cases under investigation. It may be helpful to keep in mind that obtaining a complaint follows the same process as that for issuing arrest warrants when a suspect is not in custody.

The prosecutor has a great deal of discretion and may refuse to file complaints requested by law enforcement officers (See Chapter 6). He may consider factors other than whether or not each element of the crime can be proven as a basis for refusing to file the complaint.

The complaint is filed before a magistrate by the prosecutor. A magistrate may be a judge of either the California Supreme Court, the court of appeals, superior court, municipal court or justice court.[4] As a practical matter, the magistrate is usually the judge of the municipal court or the justice court.

When the word "prosecutor" is mentioned, most people in California think of the district attorney. In misdemeanor cases the prosecutor may be the city attorney or the district attorney, depending on the local system. In special cases the prosecutor may be the attorney general. This occurred recently in Los Angeles County when a member of a law firm representing criminal defendants became an assistant district attorney, creating a conflict of interests.

Felonies

Although felonies are within the jurisdiction of the superior court, proceedings up to and including preliminary hearings are handled in inferior courts. Slight differences in procedure between justice courts and municipal courts exist, but this chapter will deal with the proce-

IN THE

JUSTICE COURT OF   JUDICIAL DISTRICT

County of Shasta, State of California

The People of the State of California,

Plaintiff,

vs.

Josephine Doe

Defendant

COMPLAINT---CRIMINAL

Roger Roe _____ of __City of Anywhere_____

in the County of Shasta, being first duly sworn, on information and belief,

complains and accuses defendant(s) of the crime of Burglary in the second degree in violation of California Penal Code Section 459.

committed as follows:

Defendant(s) on or about __February 10_____, 19 __80__, at __Cedar and 31st Street_____ Judicial District, County of Shasta, State of California, did unlawfully enter complainant's home by forcing open a locked window at approximately 3 a.m. Complainant observed defendant enter through the window and proceed to dismantle complainant's stereo set. Complainant cried out whereupon defendant attempted to leave through the open window. Complainant stopped defendant and he and his wife thereupon held defendant until the police arrived to take her into custody.

Complainant therefore prays that a warrant may be issued for the arrest of such defendant(s) and that __she__ be dealt with according to law.

_____

Subscribed and sworn to before me

this ___11___ day of February_____, 19 80 .

_Janice K. Upright_____

Janice K. Upright, Deputy District Attorney

dures generally followed. Each officer should familiarize himself with the procedure in the court where his cases will be filed.

Unless a case is taken to a grand jury, the complaint initiates felony prosecutions and will control the proceedings until the defendant is arraigned in superior court. If a defendant is not in custody, an arrest warrant may be issued when a complaint is filed. During proceedings in inferior court, a complaint must satisfy all due process requirements. Since an "information" supersedes a complaint, challenges to a complaint, must be made before an "information" is filed.

The complaint's sufficiency will be judged on common sense reading of the allegations; no technical language is required. Facts which make a misdemeanor into a felony, such as petty theft with a prior conviction,[5] or facts which will permit enhancement of a sentence, such as the use of a deadly weapon,[6] should be stated in the complaint. If necessary, these facts may be added at a later time by amendment before trial, but the defendant must be arraigned on the amended complaint.

Misdemeanors and Infractions

Misdemeanors and infractions are prosecuted in inferior courts and are started by the filing of a complaint. In most respects this process closely resembles that of the felony process, with the key exception that cases are prosecuted to judgment in the inferior courts.

Technically, traffic violations result in an arrest. Rather than taking the violator into custody, many traffic violation cases result in the issuance of a citation. The citation procedure for no-felonious vehicle code violations is set out in the Vehicle Code.[7] The *Notice to appear*, commonly referred to as a citation, must contain the following information in vehicle code cases: name and address of arrested person; license number of vehicle, if any; name and address of registered owner or lessee of vehicle (where available); offense charged; and time and place to appear in court. All information to be filed with the magistrate must be on copy of the notice to appear given to a defendant. No police report may be filed to supplement the notice to appear. If one of the forms designated by the judicial council is used, it will serve as a complaint. If any other form is used for the notice to appear, the notice will serve as a complaint if the defendant enters pleas of guilty or *nolo contendere*, but a complaint will have to be filed in all other circumstances. Since the vast majority of traffic violations go no further than posting bail, which is forfeited when no appearance is made (commonly thought of as paying a fine), an enormous amount of paperwork and time is saved by not requiring complaints to be filed.

The Vehicle Code also provides for the issuance of a *notice of violation* in cases involving traffic accidents. An officer with specified

[Form for Uniform Misdemeanor and Traffic Citation]   CR-130.0

FACE SIDE OF THE FORM

CITY OF

NOTICE TO APPEAR

NO. 0001

DATE	TIME	DAY OF WEEK
19		M

NAME (FIRST, MIDDLE, LAST)

RESIDENCE ADDRESS   CITY

BUSINESS ADDRESS   CITY

| DRIVERS LICENSE NO. | STATE | CLASS | BIRTHDATE |

| SEX
M F | HAIR | EYES | HEIGHT | WEIGHT | OTHER DES. |

| VEHICLE LICENSE NO. | STATE | PASSENGERS
M F |

| YEAR OF VEH. | MAKE | MODEL | BODY STYLE | COLOR |

REGISTERED OWNER OR LESSEE

ADDRESS OF OWNER OR LESSEE

VIOLATION(S)	CODE	SECTION	DESCRIPTION	☐ INFRACTION
				☐ BOOKING REQUIRED

| APPROX. SPEED | PF/MAX SPD. | VEH SPD LMT | SAFE SPD | CITY OF OCCUR |

LOCATION OF VIOLATION(S)
ON

COMMENTS: (WEATHER, ROAD & TRAFFIC CONDITIONS)

☐ OFFENSE(S) NOT COMMITTED IN MY PRESENCE. CERTIFIED ON INFORMATION AND BELIEF.
I CERTIFY UNDER PENALTY OF PERJURY THAT THE FOREGOING IS TRUE AND CORRECT.
EXECUTED ON THE DATE SHOWN ABOVE AT

ISSUING OFFICER   SERIAL NO.
_____ CALIF.
                    (PLACE)

| NAME OF ARRESTING OFFICER. IF DIFFERENT FROM ABOVE | SERIAL NO. | VACATION DATES
TO |

WITHOUT ADMITTING GUILT, I PROMISE TO APPEAR AT THE TIME AND PLACE CHECKED BELOW.

X SIGNATURE

BEFORE A JUDGE OR A CLERK OF THE MUNICIPAL OR JUSTICE COURT
   TELEPHONE: ADDRESS
☐ JUVENILE COURT, TRAFFIC DIVISION

☐ DATE	TIME		☐ WITHIN
19		M	15 DAYS

☐ OR YOU MAY APPEAR
  ON THE NIGHT(S) OF   AT   P.M.

FORM APPROVED BY THE JUDICIAL COUNCIL OF CALIFORNIA.
REV. 1-1-76 V.C. 40500(B) 40513(B) P.C. 853.9   **SEE REVERSE SIDE**

▨▨Grey areas indicate spaces subject to local or agency requirements.   [B2812] training in traffic accident investigation may issue a notice of violation if he has reasonable cause to believe a person involved in a traffic accident violated non-felony sections of the Vehicle Code or local ordinances. He must also believe that the violation was a factor in the accident.[8] Unlike other citations, this is not technically an arrest. The content of the notice of violation closely resembles that of the notice to appear, but the notice of violation will only serve in lieu of a complaint if a violator enters pleas of guilty or *nolo contendere*. In all other cases a complaint must be prepared and filed.

The Penal Code also permits persons arrested for infractions or misdemeanors to be released on a Notice to Appear if they do not demand to be taken immediately before a magistrate. This includes persons taken into custody pursuant to a "citizen's arrest."[9] If forms approved by the Judicial Council are used, no complaint will be filed. If other forms are used for this purpose, a complaint must be filed unless the defendant enters pleas of guilty or *nolo contendere*.

Except for a few specified charges, if a person otherwise eligible for release under Penal Code Section 853.6 is not released, an arresting officer must complete an appropriate form indicating the reason or reasons the person was not released. The reasons for nonrelease may include that the:

1. Person arrested was so intoxicated that he could have been a danger to himself or to others.
2. Person arrested required medical examination or medical care or was otherwise unable to care for his own safety.
3. Person arrested for one or more of the offenses listed in Vehicle Code Section 40302.
4. One or more outstanding arrest warrants for the person arrested.
5. Person arrested could not provide satisfactory evidence of personal identity.
6. Prosecution of offense or offenses for which the person was arrested, or the prosecution of any other offense or offenses would be jeopardized by the immediate release of the person arrested.
7. Reasonable likelihood that the offense or offenses would continue or resume, or that the safety of persons or property would be imminently endangered by the release of the person arrested.
8. Person arrested demanded to be taken before a magistrate, or refused to sign a notice ot appear.[10]

INFORMATION

If a defendant is held to answer at the preliminary hearing, it is the duty of the district attorney to file an *information* within fifteen days. Since some of the original charges may have been dismissed and new

In the
Superior Court of the State of California
in and for the County of Shasta

THE PEOPLE OF THE STATE OF
CALIFORNIA,

                           Plaintiff,

             vs.

John I. Doe

                    Defendant..... .

ARRAIGNMENT: January 20, 1980

No.

INFORMATION

The District Attorney of the County of Shasta, State of California, hereby accuses

John I. Doe

of the crime   of FELONY, IN ONE COUNT, to wit: COUNT I: ASSAULT
AND WITH DEADLY WEAPON, in violation of Section 245(a), California
Penal Code

in that on or about the   10th   **day of**   January   19 80, **in the
County of Shasta,** California   **said** John I. Doe

did willfully and unlawfully commit an assault upon Tom Jones with a
deadly weapon, to wit, .22 calibre RIFLE, and by means of force likely
to produce great bodily injury.

Dated, January 18, 1980

Janice Upright   District Attorney

charges added, the information must give adequate notice of all charges. The transcript of the preliminary hearing is considered to give additional notice of the nature of charges against a defendant. Due to the fact that the testimony at the preliminary hearing is considered in deciding whether due process is satisfied, the prosecutor may file charges not originally in the complaint or the inferior court order, holding a defendant to answer if evidence of such charges was introduced at the preliminary hearing. The information may not include charges which the magistrate dismissed at the preliminary hearing unless the information contains charges arising out of the same transaction as the dismissed charge.

If a defendant waives the preliminary hearing, it is the duty of the prosecutor to file an information within fifteen days of such a waiver. In this case, the information must follow the order holding the defendant to answer, unless testimony was taken in court. If a defendant pleads guilty to felony charges before a magistrate in the inferior court, proceedings will be certified to the superior court and the complaint will have the legal effect of an information.

The format for an information is specified in Penal Code Section 951. The information must be signed by a district attorney, or a designated assistant or deputy district attorney. There is no provision for the complainant to sign the information.

INDICTMENT

Indictments are returned by the grand jury (see Chapter 8). The proceedings before the grand jury are either initiated by the district attorney or by the grand jurors themselves. If the district attorney has filed a complaint in an inferior court prior to seeking an indictment on the same charges, it will be necessary to dismiss the complaint after the indictment is returned.

The *indictment* is defined as an accusation in writing, presented by the grand jury to a competent court, charging a person with a public offense.[11] The concurrence of twelve members of the grand jury (fourteen in Los Angeles County) is sufficient.[12] The basic format of an indictment is prescribed in Penal Code Section 951. The indictment must conform to all current rules of pleading. However, there are two requirements unique to indictments:

1. It must be endorsed as a "true bill." The endorsement must be signed by the foreman of the grand jury.[13]
2. Names of witnesses examined, or whose depositions were read to the grand jury, must be inserted at the bottom of the indictment.[14]

Similar to an information, the transcript of testimony before the grand

SUPERIOR COURT ·OF THE STATE OF ANYSTATE

FOR THE COUNTY OF MYCOUNTY

The People of the State of Anystate)
)
                 Plaintiff,)   NO.
)
        vs.   )   INDICTMENT
)
Bill Blaylock   )
_____)
             Defendant.)

DA File # 80 F 257
SO #80–9118B, 80–9118C

      The Grand Jury of the County of Mycounty hereby accuses

Bill Blaylock   of the crime of FELONY, IN TWO COUNTS,   to-wit:

SALE OF HEROIN,   in violation of §11352, Anystate Health and
Safety Code,
committed as follows:

      COUNT I: Defendant on or about the _7th_ day of __March__ ,
19 _80_ , in the County of Mycounty, State of Anystate, did willfully and
unlawfully furnish and sell and offer to furnish and sell a controlled
substance, to-wit: heroin.

      COUNT II: Defendant on or about the _9th_ day of __March__ ,
19 _80_ , in the County of Mycounty, State of Anystate, did willfully and
unlawfully furnish and sell and offer to furnish and sell a controlled
substance, to-wit: heroin.

Dated   ___April 15___   _1980_   A TRUE BILL

                                     Van Hardy
                                  Van Hardy, Foreman
The following witnesses were examined before the Grand Jury in its
consideration of the foregoing Indictment:

jury is considered with the indictment when assessing whether a defendant has adequate notice to satisfy due process.

PRINCIPLES OF PLEADING

Alleging the Crime.

Although pleading rules are quite liberal and specific language is not required, certain rules govern the content of the accusatory pleading. The contents must specify the title of the action, the name of the court in which it is filed, and the names of the parties. The following would satisfy these requirements.

SUPERIOR COURT OF THE STATE OF CALIFORNIA

COUNTY OF SANTA BARBARA

THE PEOPLE OF THE STATE OF CALIFORNIA,)		
)
Plaintiff,)	Case No. xx xx xx
)
vs.)	INFORMATION
)
JOHN JONES,)
)
Defendant.)
)

The pleading must give a statement of the public offense or offenses charged. Each crime is charged separately. If there are multiple charges, each must appear in a separate paragraph (see Illustration IV). Each charge is referred to as a "count." A later section of this chapter will explain what charges may be combined in one pleading.

To be sufficient, the pleading must satisfy the requirements of Penal Code Section 959 by showing the following:

1. That it was filed in a court having authority to receive it.
2. If an indictment, that it was found by a grand jury of the county in which the court was held.
3. If an information, that it was subscribed and presented to the court by the district attorney of the county in which the court was held.
4. If a complaint, that it was made and signed by a person who was placed under oath before an officer entitled to administer oaths.
5. That the defendant is named, or if his name is unknown, that he is described by a fictitious name.
6. That the offense charged therein is triable in the court in which it is filed, except in the case of a complaint filed with a magistrate for the purpose of a preliminary examination.

7. That the offense was committed at some time prior to the filing of the accusatory pleading.

The crime may be described in either the language of the statute, or in clear and concise non-technical language. The crucial question is whether or not a defendant is given adequate notice of the crime being prosecuted. Thus, in a murder case, it could be alleged that "John Jones did willfully, unlawfully and feloniously, and with malice afore-thought, kill Jane Doe." It could also be alleged that "John Jones murdered Jane Doe." The use of statutory language is probably the most common method of alleging the crime.

The precise time of the offense is usually not relevant and need not be stated in the pleading. To avoid later problems, but to still give notice, pleadings are frequently worded, "on or about" a given date. At a minimum, the pleading must allege that the crime was committed before the date the pleading was filed, and is within the statute of limitations. If the date stated is wrong and a defendant claims to be prejudiced thereby, he may be entitled to a continuance to enable him to prepare his case. This would occur when the pleading alleged that a crime occurred on one date, and the defendant prepared an alibi defense for that date. If it later appears that the date of the crime is different, the defense would have to be substantially altered and the defendant should be granted a continuance, if necessary.

The name of the victim of a violent crime is not an essential element of the pleading if the defendant has adequate notice of the crime. If the name of the victim is unknown, the pleading will usually contain a fictitious name, such as "John Doe" or "Jane Doe." Once the true name is known, or an error in naming someone is discovered, the pleading should be amended to indicate the true name.

Naming the defendant has been simplified. Older rules required that all aliases of a defendant be listed along with his true name. It is now permissible to list only the name used at the time of arrest. This may cause problems if prior convictions are alleged and the defendant was using a different name at the time of the prior conviction.

A mistake in alleging the location of the crime, or of the property involved will not usually be fatal. An exception to this would arise when the mistake makes it appear that the court has no jurisdiction over the crime. These errors can be corrected by amendment.

The Penal Code specifies items that do not need to be included in pleadings. [15] Presumptions or items which the court may take judicial notice of do not need to be alleged. The manner in which the crime was committed need not be alleged. Thus, in an armed robbery case, it would not be necessary to specify the weapon used, even though it will be necessary to prove the fact that a weapon was used at the trial.

Where a specific mental state, such as premeditation, is an element of the crime, it must be alleged in the pleadings. Many felonies do not have mental states specified in the code, and the addition of the terms "feloniously," "willfully," or "intentionally" are not needed. The Penal Code specifies special rules of pleading in cases of libel, slander, perjury (or subordination of perjury), and obscenity.

While it is desirable to allege the degree of the crime in the pleading, it is not mandatory. Neither is it necessary to allege facts that would indicate the degree of the crime. Thus, a charge that, "AB did willfully and unlawfully enter the dwelling house of CD with intent to commit larceny," could result in conviction for either first degree burglary or second degree burglary.

The California Penal Code no longer distinguishes between principals and accessories before the fact. All participants in a crime are simply designated as principals. The allegations in the pleading for any principal may be the same, even though their actions were considerably different.

Multiple Offense.

Penal Code Section 954 sets standards for joining multiple counts in the same accusatory pleading or joining counts originally alleged in separate pleadings:

> An accusatory pleading may charge two or more different offenses connected together in their commission, or different statements of the same offense or two or more different offenses of the same class of crimes or offenses, under separate counts . . . .

This process is referred to as "joinder." The pleading should contain facts sufficient to show the counts were properly joined. If properly joined with a felony charge, a misdemeanor may be tried in superior court.

Crimes Connected in Their Commission. Case law interpreting "connected in their commission," has permitted broad interpretation, and has found that a common element of substantial importance in the commission of the crimes to be sufficient. Thus, crimes by the defendant involving the use of the same weapon have been properly joined under this rule.

Penal Code Section 54 has been held to compel a joinder of offenses arising out of one transaction in most cases. As stated in Kellett v. Superior Court[16]: "When . . . the prosecution is or should be aware of more than one offense in which the same act or course of conduct plays a significant part, all such offenses must be prosecuted in a single proceeding unless joinder is prohibited or severance permitted for good cause. Failure to unite all such offenses will result in a bar to subsequent prosecutions of any offense omitted if the initial proceedings culminate in either acquittal or conviction and sentence." The court went on to list exceptions to the rule:

1. When a different prosecutor handled the cases and the first prosecutor does not seek the more serious charge; or
2. When the defendant quickly enters a guilty plea to the less serious charge; or
3. When the prosecutor is justifiably ignorant of the more serious charge. [17]

For example, assume a defendant is first tried for armed robbery and is acquitted. He is next tried for possession of a firearm, based on the fact that he carried a firearm during the robbery already charged. If convicted on this second charge he would be able to have the conviction reversed.

The defendant is not entitled to this defense if the multiple prosecutions were the result of his own trial tactics. Neither would this rule prevent the filing of charges for murder or manslaughter in a case where the first charge of battery on the victim was brought to trial and judgment before the victim died.

Crimes of the Same Class.   Crimes may be joined if they are the same offense, or have similar characteristics. Thus, multiple rape count counts against one defendant may be tried together even though they involve different victims and occurred on different dates. This would be considered the "same offense."   A variety of sex offenses or a variety of theft offenses charged against one defendant may be tried together because they have similar characteristics. Quite a bit of discretion is permitted in determining what constitutes similar characteristics.

Different Statement of Same Offense.   This is not a true joinder, but it permits the same offense to be plead in more than one form. For example, a defendant may be charged with being a principal to embezzlement in one count, and of being an accessory after the fact to the embezzlement in another count, based upon the same actions. The defendant may only be convicted for one such offense, but the jury may be appropriately instructed in that regard at the time of the trial. The practice of stating the offense in more than one way is called "pleading in the alternative." It permits the prosecutor to satisfy due process without bearing the burden of accurately guessing what further investigation, and what testimony at the trial, may reveal. The strict time constraints in filing a complaint after arrest frequently make this a necessary procedure. Counts that later appear to be without sufficient foundation may be dismissed before trial either on the prosecutor's motion or on a defense motion. It may also be necessary to dismiss counts during the trial if prosecution witnesses do not testify to all of the necessary elements of the charged crimes.

Multiple Defendants.

The joinder of multiple defendants is also governed by Penal Code Section 954. Defendants who jointly commit crimes may normally be tried together. A defendant is entitled to reversal for improper joinder only if he can show actual prejudice in his case.

The United States Supreme Court, in Bruton v. United States,[18] held that separate trials may be necessary if one defendant has confessed, implicated another defendant, but at trial refuses to take the witness stand. Due to the privilege against self incrimination, the defendant who confessed cannot be forced to testify. If he refuses to testify, the other defendant is denied his right to cross examine those who accuse him. The court found that merely instructing the jury on the matter was an inadequate substitute for cross examination. This leaves the prosecutor with two choices in multiple defendant cases, where one defendant has made statements that implicate other defendants; he may either keep the confession out as evidence, or provide the defendants with separate trials. After a defendant has been convicted or acquitted, the privilege against self incrimination will not permit that defendant to refuse to testify. Thus, the prosecutor, at a later trial of the codefendant, may call the defendant who made the statement to take the stand so that cross examination may take place. However, this may cause problems in relation to a defendant's right to a speedy trial.

The California Supreme Court set forth a similar rule in People v. Aranda[19] and specified one additional alternative: the prosecutor may delete all parts of the statement that are prejudicial to defendants not making such statements. This can only be done when the remaining portions of the statement effectively protect the rights of both defendants.

AMENDMENT

An accusatory pleading may be amended to correct errors in the original pleading or to add charges. Once the pleading is changed by amendment, the defendant must again be arraigned on the pleading.

If the defendant has not entered a plea or demurrer to the accusatory pleading, the prosecutor is free to amend without seeking permission from the court. At stages of the proceeding after the plea or demurrer is entered, the prosecutor must obtain permission from the court to amend the pleading. The court has broad discretion in granting permission to amend, and normally grants permission if the change relates to the crime already charged.

Amendment can be used to correct errors in dates, names of victims, addresses, and descriptions of property. It can also be used to correct the allegation of crimes committed if the wrong code section is alleged, as long as sufficient facts were alleged to give notice. This type of correction can be made even after the statute of limitations has run out if it is clear that the same facts are the basis for the charge. This is probably more useful in felony cases because the transcripts of testimony at the preliminary hearing or before the grand jury are considered to determine if the defendant had adequate notice. In the case of misdemeanors the complaint alone must give notice.

The pleading can be amended to add essential elements of charges that were omitted, or charge additional offenses arising out of the same transcaction already alleged. This can be done up to the beginning of the trial. Allegations that the defendant has previously been convicted of one or more felonies may also be added by amendment.

If the amendment will alter the defense, the court shouid grant a continuance, if necessary, to allow the defendant and his attorney to prepare the case. This may arise where dates and names are corrected, as well as new charges are added. The granting of a continuance, and the length of the continuance are within the discretion of the court. To have a conviction reversed for failure to grant an adequate continuance, the defendant must show that he was actually treated with prejudice by the denial of the continuance.

Since indictments are made by a grand jury and not the prosecutor, the prosecutor may not alter the crimes charged in the indictment. Corrections of names, dates, and other clerical errors can be made if the correction arises from evidence in the transcript of testimony before the grand jury. The prosecutor has the authority to add charges to the information by amendment if the transcript of the preliminary hearing gives notice of facts behind the new charges.

ATTACKS ON PLEADINGS

The pleading may be challenged on procedural grounds by either a motion to set aside, or a demurrer. These procedures challenge the content of the pleading, procedures at the preliminary hearing or before the grand jury, or sufficiency of the evidence presented to the grand jury or at the preliminary hearing. Neither is a test of guilt or innocence. A successful challenge has the effect of dismissing the action, but does not bar a refiling of the charges if there is sufficient admissable evidence, and if the statute of limitations has not run out.

Motion to Set Aside.

The *motion to set aside* attacks either an indictment or an information and is authorized by Section 995 of the Penal Code. The indictment can be attacked on the basis that there was no reasonable or probable cause shown in testimony before the grand jury that would justify an indictment.   In a similar manner, the information can be attacked for failure to show reasonable or probable cause at the preliminary hearing. If there are multiple counts, any one or all counts may be challenged. When the challenge is on these grounds, the court determines "whether the magistrate [or grand jury], acting as a man of ordinary caution or prudence, could conscientiously entertain a reasonable suspicion that a public offense has been committed in which the defendant has participated."[20] Note that the standard is "reasonable suspicion," and not 'beyond a reasonable doubt'.   If the credibility of a witness is in question, great deference is given to the opinion of the magistrate or of the grand jury, who had an opportunity to observe the demeanor of a witness while testifying.   Normally, their decision will not be overruled unless the testimony is inherently improbable.

The evidence used to support an indictment or an information may be attacked, even though it is sufficient to raise a reasonable suspicion, if the evidence is inadmissible.   Since evidence obtained by illegal search and seizure is inadmissible, an indictment or information based upon it will be set aside, even though the evidence showed a crime had been committed, unless there is sufficient other admissible evidence to establish the crime.   Hearings on whether or not confessions and searches are legal frequently occur in felony cases after the case is in the superior court.   If the defense successfully obtains a ruling that evidence was illegally obtained, a motion to set aside will follow if the admissible evidence remaining is thought to be insufficient to establish probable cause.   For example, if the marijuana seized is ruled inadmissible in a case charging possession of marijuana, there normally will not be enough evidence remaining to establish the charge, and the motion to set aside will be granted.   A motion to determine whether or not evidence is legally obtained is made under Penal Code Section 1538.5, and may be accompanied by a motion to set aside under Penal Code 995. Many practitioners in the field refer to these motions simply as "995 motions," and "1538.5 motions."

The motion to set aside may also be made on the basis of procedural defects in obtaining the indictment.   In the case of an indictment, such errors include too few grand jurors present when evidence was presented (the Penal Code requires twelve in all counties except Los Angeles County, where fourteen are required), and gross errors in formation of a grand jury.   The indictment must be properly signed by the foreman of the grand jury, but failure to do so is easily corrected by amendment.

The information can also be set aside for procedural defects.   However this will not be done for minor errors.   Procedural defects that will justify setting aside an information include failure of the magistrate to advise a defendant of his right to counsel, or failure to advise him of the charges against him.[21]   Undue delay may also be grounds for granting the motion. If the identity of an informer is important for cross examination on the legality of an arrest or a search, failure to disclose this may also be grounds for setting aside.

Writ of Prohibition.

The *writ of prohibition* acts as an appeal in felony cases when there is a denial of a motion to set aside. It may be applied for on the grounds that pleadings fail to state an offense within the language of the criminal statute, or that no admissible evidence before the grand jury or at the preliminary hearing supports the charged offense. The procedure for obtaining such a writ is set out in Penal Code Section 999a.

Demurrer.

Demurrers are permitted in both misdemeanor and felony cases. They must be in writing, and must be signed by the defendant or his attorney. The function of a demurrer is to challenge defects that appear on the face of the pleading. Neither the sufficiency of evidence presented at the preliminary hearing, nor defects in obtaining an indictment may be raised by demurrer. Failure to state a crime, either by leaving out an element of the crime, or by interchanging elements of two different crimes, can be challenged by demurrer. The demurrer may be to the complaint, indictment or information.

The demurrer must be made before a plea is entered, and must be based on one of the following grounds: lack of jurisdiction in the court where filed; uncertainty as to charges, judged by the language of the pleading; improper joinder of offenses; the facts as stated do not constitute an offense; or the prosecution is barred (for example, by statute of limitations or double jeopardy). The demurrer must clearly specify which ground is relied upon.

The judge must hear the demurrer and make an order sustaining or denying it. If there are multiple counts, any one or more count can be challenged. If the defect in the pleading can be repaired by amendment, the court must grant leave to amend. This gives the prosecutor a time period, set by the judge, to refile a corrected pleading. If there does not appear to be a way to correct the defect, or if the prosecutor does not refile within the specified time limits, the case will be dismissed.

SUMMARY

Accusatory pleadings are filed at the beginning of the court case against the criminal defendant. The pleadings must show sufficient facts to give the defendant adequate notice of the charges against him. This is a requirement based upon the due process of law.

The complaint is the pleading filed in an inferior court. In the case of misdemeanors, it will be the only pleading filed. For felonies, it will be followed by an information when the case reaches superior court. The complaint must be based upon the sworn statement of a person who has sufficient knowledge of the facts of the case. It will be filed by the prosecutor. In some cases the complaint will be replaced by a notice to appear or a notice of violation.

The indictment is the accusatory pleading filed at the end of a grand jury investigation. It must be signed by the foreman of the grand jury and must list the names of the witnesses before the grand jury. The information is the pleading filed by the district attorney in superior court after the defendant has been held to answer for a felony at the end of the preliminary hearing.

All pleadings must give the name of the court, the parties, and the nature of the pleading. The crime may be alleged in any language sufficient to give the defendant notice of what is being charged. Multiple offenses may be joined in one pleading if they are of the same class, connected in their commission, or are a different statement of a crime already charged in that pleading.

The pleading may be changed by amendment. This may be simply the correction of clerical errors, or may go to the substance of the pleading. In some circumstances, additional crimes may be added to the pleading by amendment.

The pleading may be attacked by a motion to set aside. This challenges the procedures used in obtaining the indictment or information, and the sufficiency of the legally admissible evidence presented to the grand jury or the judge at the preliminary hearing. The defense may appeal the denial of the motion by seeking a writ of prohibition. Errors on the face of the pleading may be attacked by demurrer.

DISCUSSION QUESTIONS

1. Identify all accusatory pleadings that could be filed for: petty theft, speeding, a violation of the vehicle code that resulted in a traffic accident, robbery, murder.

2. List what should be included in an information charging: burglary, robbery, kidnap, murder. What changes would be made in the pleading if an indictment was filed, instead of an information?

3. D stole a car on the first day of the month. On the second, D burglarized A's house and took $500 cash. On the third, D got mad at his wife and kicked and hit her. On the fourth, D robbed a liquor store and kicked and hit the clerk. On the fifth, D's wife died from injuries suffered on the third. Which crimes can be combined in one pleading? Why?

4. An information was filed charging D with one count of robbery and

224 Administration of Justice

one count of burglary. Which of the following errors could be corrected by amendment?: date of robbery was wrong; address of burglarized building was wrong; D's name was incorrectly stated; the wrong Penal Code sections were listed; the robbery actually occurred in a different county.

5. What procedures could be used to attack the pleadings in a petty theft (misdemeanor) case? ... grand theft (felony) case? What reasons could be used for each attack?

REFERENCES

1. California Penal Code, sections 740, 806.

2. U.S. v. Ventresca 380 U.S. 102, 85 S.Ct. 741, 13 L.Ed. 2d 684, 1965.

3. Aguilar v. Texas 378 U.S. 108, 84 S.Ct. 1509, 12 L.Ed. 2d 723,1964.

4. California Penal Code, section 808.

5. California Penal Code, section 666.

6. California Penal Code, section 12022.

7. Vehicle Code, section 405000 et. seq.

8. Vehicle Code, section 40600 (a).

9. California Penal Code, sections 853.6 (h), 853.9.

10. California Penal Code, sections 853.7, 853.8.

11. California Penal Code, section 889.

12. California Penal Code, section 940.

13. Ibid.

14. California Penal Code, section 943.

15. See California Penal Code, sections 961 to 969e.

16. 63 Cal. 2d 822, 827, 48 Ca. Rptr. 366, 370, 409 P. 2d 206, 210, (1966).

17. 63 Cal. 2d 827-828, 48 Cal. Rptr. 370, 371, 409 P. 2d 210, 211.

18. 391 U.S. 123, 88 S.Ct. 1620, 20 L.Ed. 2d 476 (1968).

19. 63 Cal. 2d 518, 47 Cal. Rptr. 353, 407 P. 2d 265 (1965).

20. People v. Jablon 153 Cal. App. 2d 456, 458, 314 P. 2d 824 (1957).

21. California Penal Code, section 858.

11

Arraignments, Pleas and Preliminary Hearings

CHAPTER OBJECTIVES

Upon reading this chapter the student will be able to:

1. List the four major purposes of an arraignment and their significance.

2. Give a step–by–step accounting of the arraignment as described in this chapter.

3. List the six authorized pleas.

4. Describe the effects of each plea when entered.

5. Describe the procedure for entering a demurrer.

6. List and explain five purposes served by the preliminary hearing.

7. Identify the types of crimes which allow for allow for a preliminary hearing.

8. Chart the criminal justice process from the arraignment through to the preliminary hearing.

Once an arrest has been made, the officer has the responsibility to immediately bring the accused before a magistrate to answer the charge in an *arraignment*.   Of all the court appearances that an accused will make, the arraignment is probably the most important.   This court appearance is usually the first formal contact that an accused will have with a magistrate and the judicial system.

The general purpose of the arraignment is to give the accused the opportunity to determine the specific charges against him, to be informed of his constitutional protections, and to answer the charges brought against him.

People from all social and economic environments have always had a fear of the legal process.   Much of the fear stems from the fact that most people do not know what to expect once they have been arrested and charged with a criminal offense.   The purpose of the arraignment is to establish specifically what is in store for them as their case works its way through the legal process.

This chapter will discuss the specific purpose and responsibilities of an arraignment.   Also covered will be a step by step procedure of what takes place in the arraignment.

The six specific pleas an accused may make in California will be explained in detail, along with a description of their significance and what effects a plea has on the defendant and the procedures in the criminal justice system.   The demurrer, which is entered in place of a plea, will be identified along with its effect in a criminal prosecution.

Lastly we will be discussing the purpose of preliminary hearings in the overall process of administration of justice.   We will see that the preliminary hearing serves as a checkpoint to ensure that there is sufficient cause to proceed to a formal trial.   We will see that there are several important purposes of a preliminary hearing including allowing a magistrate to determine whether a suspect should be held for trial; to preserve evidence; to determine bail; and to determine if evidence obtained is legal.

THE ARRAIGNMENT

When an accusatory pleading is filed, the law requires that an accused be arraigned by the court which filed the accusatory pleading. [1] The accusatory pleading may be in the form of a criminal complaint, an information, or an indictment.   For the majority of criminal offenses, the first arraignment will occur as the result of a criminal complaint. The initial arraignment will generally take place in an inferior court which has jurisdiction in the offense charged.   If the defendant is in custody, the arraignment will normally take place within the county and jurisdiction where the defendant is being held.   If the defendant is not in custody, the arraignment will occur within the jurisdiction of the area where the offense occurred.

Since this is the accused's first confrontation with the judicial process, the arraignment must be conducted promptly and without delay. Any time a person is in custody, charged with a criminal offense, his case must be brought before a magistrate as quickly as possible. If the accused is on bail, urgency is not as important. We must remember that the accused at this point has not been convicted of any wrongdoing; therefore, the government cannot restrict his right to freedom any more than is necessary.

State law requires the accused, when in custody, to be brought before a magistrate in the county in which the offense is triable without any unnecessary delay. Unnecessary delay, as stated by the law, mandates that this period be no longer than two days after arrest, excluding Sunday and holidays.[2] From a practical point of view, the arraignment occurs within the next 'judicial' day when the accused is booked into jail.

Appearance of the Accused

Since this is the first official confrontation of the accused with the judicial system, the arraignment is a most important hearing. The law requires that the defendant, in all felonies, or his counsel, in misdemeanor offenses, must appear. The arraignment cannot be waived. Penal Code Section 977 states that in all cases in which the accused is charged with a misdemeanor, he may be represented by his counsel. In all felonies, the accused must be present.

Purpose of the Arraignment

As previously stated, most persons who appear before the court are confused and somewhat ignorant regarding the criminal justice process. The purpose of the arraignment is to clarify any confusion which an accused might have, and to educate him of the essentials with respect to the crime(s) with which he has been charged. The arraignment must be made by the court, the clerk, or by the prosecuting attorney under the court's direction. Prior to the arraignment, an accusatory pleading, in the form of a criminal complaint, will have been completed by the prosecuting attorney, and filed with the court. The complaint will be read by the court to the accused, who will be given a copy. The complaint specifically states the criminal activity, including a statement of the public offense or offenses charged, and the title of the action. The name of the court and the names of the parties involved must also be included. With this accomplished, the accused should now understand exactly what he is being criminally charged with. If the public offense

is a misdemeanor, the accused need not be given a copy of the complaint unless he so requests.

The court determines that the accused, as stated on the criminal
complaint, is the same person before the court. If there is an error, he
must declare his true name or waive any further objections to the name
error. The court also has the responsibility of determining if the accused
fully understands the nature of the allegations. If there is any question
regarding his ability to understand, the magistrate will fully explain the
charge to him.   If the accused is unable to comprehend because of
insanity or other causes of incompetency, the magistrate must continue
the proceedings until such time as the accused does understand. Normally the judge will set the arraignment over for twenty-four hours.

Rights Guaranteed Under the Constitution.

Before an accused can proceed with his case any further, he must be
informed specifically of his rights. One of the primary functions of the
arraignment is to inform the accused of these specific rights. We learned
in detail what they were in chapters one and two. At this point in the
process, the accused must fully be aware of them and understand them.
The following statement is typical of that which a magistrate would
deliver to an accused standing before him. This statement is for misdemeanor offenses. Felony arraignments would be slightly different.

> Each of you present today as a defendant has been charged with some violation
> of law, and this is the time fixed for your arraignment. This means that you will
> be told the charge or charges made against you, and you will be asked to plead
> or answer "guilty" or "not guilty" or "nolo contendere" (additional pleas
> available by law are "prior conviction or acquittal for the same offense," "once
> in jeopardy," and "not guilty by reason of insanity") to that charge or charges.
> It is also the time to tell you of certain rights guaranteed to you by our laws, and
> if you do not understand any procedure of this court please ask for an explana-
> tion.
>
> At the time your case is called, I will tell you the code sections that you are
> charged with violating and give you a brief description of each charge. If you
> would like the entire complaint read, do not hesitate to ask for this to be done.
>
> Under the law you have all of the following rights: you are entitled to a speedy
> and public trial within the judicial district wherein the alleged offense was
> committed, within thirty days of this arraignment, if you are now in custody,
> and within forty-five days of this arraignment, if you are not in custody at this
> time. The thirtieth day expires on _____ and the forty-fifth day expires
> on _____ . What this means is that you are entitled to a dismissal of
> your case if you are not brought to trial within these days, unless you have asked
> for or consented to a later date, or there is good cause shown for setting a later
> trial date. If you waive time by requesting or consenting to a trial beyond the
> thirty or forty-five day period, you are entitled to have your case dismissed if
> you are not tried on the date set or within ten days thereafter, unless there is
> good cause shown for a further delay. Your trial may be by court, which means

by a judge alone, or by jury, which means by a judge and twelve jurors. You have the right to be released on reasonable bail while waiting for your trial. The purpose of bail is to ensure your return to court as ordered. You are entitled to the process of this court to subpoena witnesses on your behalf, and to be confronted by and to cross examine witnesses who testify against you. You are entitled to have your correct name used in these proceedings; kindly tell me your true name if I call you by another name. You are further entitled to the services of an attorney of your own choice at all stages of these proceedings, including this arraignment, and if you want time to talk to an attorney before entering your plea, please tell me and I will continue your matter for that purpose. If you desire an attorney and the court finds that you are financially unable to employ one, you may be represented without charge by the public defender. Mr. _____ , standing before you, is a deputy public defender, and you may talk to him if you cannot afford your own attorney. Those of you under eighteen years of age must speak with the public defender and must tell the court your correct age before entering your plea.

If you plead "not guilty," a time will be set for your trial and each of you so pleading hereby ordered to personally appear—ready for trial, with witnesses and lawyer, if any—in division _____ of this court at the time set for your trial, and at any sentencing or other hearing hereafter.

If you are released on your own recognizance without posting bail, you should be warned that a failure to appear as you promise will be a second violation of the law.

If you plead "guilty" or "nolo contende," you have the right to postpone sentencing to a period of from six hours to five days after plea.

After a "guilty" or "nolo contende" plea, the court may sentence you to formal probation, where you must report to a probation officer, or, by suspending part or all of your sentence, to summary probation, where you do not have to report to a probation officer but may be required to report to the court. In either case you should understand that on a violation of a condition of your probation or any law during your probationary period, you will also be in violation of your probation and may be penialized under the present charge. Each of you receiving summary probation will receive a written memorandum of the terms of your probation and the date you shall return and report to this court, if ordered.

If you are fined or post bail, a penalty assessment of $5 for each $20 of your fine or bail will be charged, but I will announce only the amount of the fine or bail. This penalty assessment is required by law, and the money so collected by the clerk is placed in a special fund used for peace officer education.

Now, do any of you have any questions concerning your rights or any of the procedures we will follow here today?

After his rights have been explained, the accused must enter a plea. He will be asked to plead one or more of six specific pleas as authorized by California law. The second half of the chapter will discuss the specific pleas authorized.

If the accused pleads guilty, the judge will undertake the process of determining the proper jurisdiction for sentencing and/or the proper sentence that should be executed. If the accused pleads not guilty, then the magistrate sets a date for a preliminary hearing for felonies, or a trial date for misdemeanors. At this time the judge will ask the accused if he desires a jury trial.

If for some reason the defendant needs time to answer the charges specified on the accusatory pleading, the court must grant him a reasonable amount of time to answer, which shall not be less than one day for an offense originally triable in the superior court, and not more than seven days for an offense originally triable in an inferior court.

If for some reason the defendant fails to appear for an arraignment, the court has the authority to issue a bench warrant. The court bailiff or marshal will then arrest the defendant and forthwith bring him before the magistrate.

Arraignment for a Felony Offense

When a defendant is charged with the commission of a felony by a written complaint subscribed under oath and on file in a court within the county in which the felony is triable, he shall without unnecessary delay be taken before a magistrate of such court. The responsibility for the above requirement is usually placed with the court having the original complaint on file, normally the inferior court. Even though the inferior court does not have trial jurisdiction for felony cases, it will usually be responsible for the original arraignment.

Felony Accusatory Pleading by Information

The discussion to this point has centered around the original arraignment. If the offense charged is a misdemeanor this arraignment will satisfy all requirements for informing the accused of his constitutional rights, the charges against him, and the determination of his plea.

In the case of a felony which has not been initiated by grand jury indictment, the defendant must have a preliminary examination (see Chapter 10 for details).

As the result of the preliminary hearing, a new accusatory pleading will be filed, called an information (see Chapter 10). This will necessitate a second arraignment. The purpose of this arraignment is exactly the same as the original arraignment. The defendant will be given a copy of the information, the charges will be read to him, he will be re—advised of his constitutional rights, and will be given the opportunity to plead. If he pleads guilty, a sentencing hearing will be scheduled at a later date. If he pleads not guilty, the magistrate will set the date for the trial and determine if the accused wishes a jury trial.

PLEAS

Following the reading of the accusatory pleading and the determination that the accused is represented by counsel or has effectively waived counsel, the accused is asked if he is ready to plead. Penal Code Section 1002 states that the only pleading on the part of the defendant is either a plea or a demurrer. There are six possible pleas allowed for indictments, information, or criminal complaints:

1. Guilty
2. Not guilty
3. Former judgment of conviction or acquittal
4. Once in jeopardy
5. Not guilty by reason of insanity
6. Nolo Contendere

If a defendant refuses to answer when asked for his plea, the court will automatically enter a plea for him. A defendant who does not plead guilty may enter one or more of the other pleas. Every plea must be made in open court. The plea may be oral or in writing.

Procedure for Entering Plea

The court must keep accurate records of the plea. The plea, whether oral or written, must be recorded in substantially the following form.

1. If the defendant pleads guilty: "The defendant pleads that he is guilty of the offense charged."
2. If he pleads not guilty: "The defendant pleads that he is not guilty of the offense charged."
3. If he pleads a former conviction of acquittal: "The defendant pleads that he has already been convicted (or acquitted) of the offense charged, by the judgment of the court of _____ (naming it), rendered at _____ (naming the place) on the _____ day of _____ ."
4. If he pleads once in jeopardy: "The defendant pleads that he had been once in jeopardy the offense charged" (specifying the time, place, and court).
5. If he pleads not guilty by reason of insanity: "The defendant pleads that he is not guilty of the offense charged because he was insane at the time he is alleged to have committed the unlawful act."[3]

In the case of a misdemeanor offense, a plea may be made by the defendant, or by his counsel in the absence of the defendant.[4] This would include any pleas enumerated in Section 1016 of the Penal Code. However, in a felony case, the defendant must personally enter the plea in open court. The time and place for entering the plea to be entered at the time of the arraignment, or at such time as may be allowed to the defendant for that purpose. We saw in Penal Code section 990 that no more than the maximum of seven days would be allowed. The plea must also be made in open court. The only exception to this rule is in the case of not guilty pleas. The courts have allowed more flexibility in this area. Taking not guilty pleas in chambers was no problem in one case. Also pleas for traffic violations, particulary when the accused is out of the county, may be accepted through the mail.

In the case of guilty pleas by the defendant for a felony offense, the courts have been very strict of their interpretation of requiring the defendant to enter the plea himself. Particular problems have occurred in the past where the defendant does not speak English. In People v. Manriquez, the defendant's counsel entered the guilty plea for his client. Manriquez was standing next to him at the time. The Supreme Court of California reversed the case, stating that the plea had to be made by the defendant himself.[5]

In most cases if there is any doubt, the judge will quiz the defendant personally. Once the court has shown diligence in establishing the intent of the accused, the higher court will not interject. One other point must be covered before we move on. On some occasions even a plea made personally by the defendant may be held improper. There are two situations:

1. The defendant is insane at the time of the plea. A person cannot be held to answer, tried, or punished while he is insane.[6]
2. In the case of some felonies where the defendant is not represented by counsel.

The statutes and case law have unequivocally stated that a defendant must at least discuss his case with an attorney prior to pleading guilty, even if he has no intentions of requesting an attorney. "No plea of guilty of a felony for which the maximum punishment is death, or life imprisonment without possibility of parole, shall be received from a defendant who does not appear with counsel, nor shall any such plea be received without the consent of the defendant's counsel"[7] (This section was amended in 1977). In other felony cases the court must carefully examine the defendant to ensure that he fully understands his right to an attorney and that he does not want an attorney. The defendant will be required to expressly state in open court, to the court, that he does not wish to be represented by counsel.

Conditional Pleas

Crimes which are divided into degrees which call for different punishments (murder, burglary, etc.,) call for special attention when the defendant is pleading.

Normally the degree is not established until the defendant is found guilty or pleads guilty. Therefore it is essential that the plea specifically state the degree for which the offense is charged, particularly when the defendant is pleading to one or more offenses or lesser offenses. In 1957, the legislature authorized conditional pleas to be entered by the defendant with the approval of the prosecutor. The plea again must be made in open court, and the court must approve the plea. If approved, the defendant will be allowed to plea to a specific degree or lesser offense. If accepted, the defendant cannot be tried or punished for a higher offense.

From time to time a defendant will attempt to change his plea. For example, a person who failed to plead not guilty by reason of insanity is conclusively presumed to be sane at the time he committed the offense. Penal Code section 1016 authorizes the court, "for good cause shown," to allow the defendant to change a plea to not guilty by reason of insanity any time prior to commencement of the trial. A defendant may also seek to withdraw a not guilty plea for other pleas, such as insanity, jeopardy, etcetera, or to change a not guilty plea for a guilty plea for lesser offense(s). There is no implicit right to change a plea, however, when the court feels that the change is legitimate, the request may be granted. One last comment is necessary in regard to changing a guilty plea; the rights and condition of this request appear in Penal Code section 1018: "On application of the defendant at any time before judgement the court *may*, and in the case of a defendant who appeared without counsel at the time of the plea *must*, for good cause shown, permit a plea of guilty be withdrawn and a plea of not guilty substituted." According to this section, the court is directed to allow the change where no counsel is involved. In other cases, the court will require a very good reason before the change will be granted.

Specific Pleas

We will discuss in detail the meaning and consequences of each of these specific pleas: guilty; not guilty; nolo contendere; not guilty by reason of insanity; former judgment of conviction or acquittal; and once in jeopardy.

Guilty. "The defendant pleads that he is guilty of the offense charged" (P.C. 1017). Upon entering this plea the accused is simply stating that he agrees with the charge, and admits that a crime did in fact occur, and that he committed it. Specifically the plea has the following effects:

1. The defendant admits to every element of the offense charged. No other proof of the corpus delicti is necessary.[8]
2. The defendant agrees that there are no problems with the accusatory pleading. Legally, if there are technical problems with the wording of the pleading, or even substantial problems such as a wrong date for the crime, or incorrect pleading (etc.), the defendant cannot

later change his mind and file a motion for demurrer.[9]

3. Of course, when the defendant pleads guilty, he also waives his right to a jury trial. But, of significance is the fact that the court is not required to obtain an expressed waiver.

4. The guilty plea has the same effects as a conviction after a completed trial. Guilty pleas and convictions carry the exact same meaning.

5. A plea of guilty also waives the defendant's privilege against self–incrimination. The court may ask any questions regarding the offense charged, and may compel the accused to answer or be held in contempt of court.

6. The accused waives any and all other constitutional rights previously discussed, such as the right to call witnesses in his behalf, or to be confronted with the witnesses against him.[10]

Due to the seriousness of the plea of guilty, the accused must fully understand the consequences. Before a magistrate will allow the plea, he will inquire whether the defendant has a full understanding of the plea and its consequences.

The plea of guilty is valid only if it is voluntarily and intelligently made. This places a burden of responsibility on the court to determine this. The defendant must understand the nature of the charge, the seriousness of the offense, and the penalty which can be imposed. The court must be assured that the defendant is aware of specific defenses which are available to him.

In summary, the guilty plea terminates the defendant's objections to the charges made against him. The court will strive to protect itself and the defendant from making an ineffective plea.

Not Guilty. "The defendant pleads not guilty of the offense charged. The plea of not guilty puts in issue every material allegation of the accusatory pleading." [11] Upon making the plea of not guilty, the defendant places the duty and responsibility of the state of California to prove beyond a reasonable doubt that a crime was committed and that the defendant committed it. The accused is innocent until proven guilty. Because of the legal presumption, the burden on the state is not a light one. The defendant will automatically have a public trial by the court or his peers. He will have all the legal protections included in the constitutions and statutes of the United States and the State of California. By pleading not guilty, the defendant is setting the judicial machinery in operation. In the case of a felony not reviewed by a grand jury, a preliminary examination will be ordered. In the case of misdemeanors and indictments, trial dates will be set. In summary, the defendant need not exert any energy until such time as the people have established their case.

Nolo Contendere. Nolo Contendere is a latin word meaning "I will not contest it." As can be seen, the plea has the same effect as a guilty plea, but only for the particular offense charged. This plea has a special advantage to the defendant which a straight guilty plea does not. The plea cannot be used in a subsequent civil suit arising out of the same incident which caused the commission of the criminal charge.

A plea of nolo contendere is subject to the approval of the court. In addition, the prosecutor must give his approval. The court is required to determine whether the defendant completely understands that a plea of nolo contendere shall be considered the same as a guilty plea with the above exception. Therefore, the same requirements of the guilty plea must be adhered to by the judge in this case. One other protection afforded by the defendant upon being granted permission to plead nolo contendere is that any "admissions required by the court during inquiry it makes as to the voluntariness of and factual basis for the plea may not be used against the defendant as an admission in any civil action based the same incident."[12]

In many cases a defendant is not concerned with the fine and/or imprisonment of the offense for which he is pleading "guilty." His concern is with a subsequent civil suit arising out of the same incident. His intent is to take care of the criminal case as quickly as possible, and to pay his fine or spend some time in jail. He knows that a civil suit is

pending which could bankrupt him. If he were to plead guilty, the plaintiff would be allowed to use the plea as evidence against him. This could be very damaging to his defense. The effect of the nolo contendere plea prevents the plaintiff from introducing any admissions or statements of guilt made by the defendant during criminal proceedings.

This plea is used very often in traffic accidents where the accused is found in violation of a traffic violation. For example, the defendant runs a red light, and hits another car, which causes severe injury to an occupant of the vehicle. This injury could be a loss of both eyes, complete paraylization, or severe scarring. Criminally, the penalty would probably amount to a moderate fine and nothing more. The defendant is guilty, and is willing to admit it, pay his fine and forget it. The problem is that he knows that he faces a lawsuit. By pleading nolo contendere he is able to protect himself from any admission made in criminal court. The plaintiff in the civil suit then must prove his case in a manner which is completely independent of the criminal case.

A Former Judgement of Acquittal or Conviction. "The defendant pleads that he has already been convicted or acquitted." There are several Penal Code sections dealing with this plea. It prevents a defendant from being tried twice for the same offense if it has already been adjudicated, or from a case when the action is being prosecuted in "different ways" or by "different provisions."[13] If the accused has been convicted or acquitted for the same offense in another state, government, or county, he cannot be charged for the same offense in this state.

From time to time the prosecution for a crime will be within the jurisdiction of more than one judicial district. Penal Code section 794 prevents both jurisdictions from prosecuting for the same offense.[14]

The doctrine preventing the state from prosecuting an accused more than once is extremely important to our legal system. The government has a great deal of resources and power at its disposal. If it were allowed to continue prosecuting for the same offense, sooner or later it would get a conviction. At the very least the accused would be subject to extreme financial strains, extreme embarrassment, and total deterioration of his peace of mind.

The law simply states that the people of the state of California better have their case prepared as best they can the first time, because they are only going to have one chance.

Once in Jeopardy. "The defendant pleads that he has been once in jeopardy for the offense charged." Both the U.S. Constitution and the California Constitution have accentuated the importance of not holding a person responsible for a crime more than once. The Fifth Amendment of the United States Constitution states in part that, "nor shall any person be subject for the same offense to be twice put in jeopardy of life or limb." The California Constitution, Article 1, Section 13, states that, "No person shall be twice put in jeopardy for the same offense."

At first appearance it would seem to the reader that "once in jeopardy" and a former conviction or acquittal for the same offense are the same. Actually they are not; jeopardy generally applies to those cases where there has not been a disposition in the matter. Former conviction or acquittal means that the plea would be proper where the trial or judicial process has actually been completed. During the trial jeopardy "attaches"; at that point and until the case comes to a normal completion, jeopardy will apply. We will see that often a trial will not ever be completed. It is for these situations that jeopardy will be considered. We will discuss the point and time when jeopardy "attaches" in more detail later in this section.

A simple statement as to what jeopardy means and what effect it has on a criminal trial would say that a person in a criminal trial cannot be *tried* twice for the same offense. In other words, once the trial has begun, the state of California, unless there is a statutory exception, must present its case in the best manner possible, because they can only do it once. The law was established to prevent the state from a "continual effort to prosecute an individual who they wanted to convict."

The responsibility is on the state. Because of these two pleas— jeopardy, and former conviction or acquittal—the prosecutor and police must have exhausted all possible leads and examined all of the evidence. If at some time after the trial new evidence is uncovered which conclusively establishes the guilt of an accused, nothing can be done. The accused could not be retried. In fact, the accused, after acquittal or once jeopardy has attached, could call a press conference, including the police and the prosecutor, and shout to the world that he in fact committed the crime for which he was just tried. The state could do nothing. They had their chance. This protection requires the police and prosecutor to conduct a professional and diligent investigation of the offense and present their case with the knowledge that they only have one chance.

The jeopardy plea has extended implications of which one must be aware. The Penal Code has several sections which deal with jeopardy. The reader would be well advised to read these sections in detail. These sections will be mentioned in part for consideration. Penal Code section 1023 covers closely the same provisions as stated in the federal and state constitutions. penal Code sections 1101, 1188, and 1387 discuss dismissals, the discharge of criminal prosecutions, and the times when jeopardy attaches. The pleas—once in jeopardy, and former conviction or acquittal of the offense charged—are sometimes not thought of as actual pleas. However, the law specifically mandates them. Instead of pleading not guilty because one has already been charged, convicted, or acquitted, one actually declares that the state has no business holding a person for the offense charged. These pleas are not used very often in modern law because of the efficient electronic record keeping systems. However, if for some reason the offense charged was in fact already dealt with, these pleas would be in order.

Not Guilty by Reason of Insanity. "The defendant pleads that he is not guilty of the offense charged because he was insane at the time he committed the offense."   Before the reader goes any further it is extremely important to realize one fact in dealing with this plea. If a defendant pleads *"not guilty by reason of insanity"* he is first agreeing that he committed the offense charged. That is, even though there is not a guilty plea involved, he is saying that he did not commit the offense. He is stating, however, that he cannot be convicted of the offense, and that he committed it because at the time the crime was committed he was *insane.* One of the few conclusive presumptions our statutes carry provides that if a defendant merely pleads not guilty, then he is conclusively presumed to be sane at the time that he committed the offense. Thus, if he does not utilize this plea, he cannot then bring up the issue of insanity later.

If a defendant enters a single plea of not guilty by reason of insanity, then the sole issue before the court is whether or not he can be held responsible for his criminal act, because he declares that at the time he committed it he was *legally* insane. In other words, the issue centers around the mental condition of the accused at the time of the commission of the offense. The author has emphasized the issue of insanity at the time of the offense for a reason; the issue is what condition the defendant was in specifically *during* the offense, not before or after. In other words, the accused could have been sane just prior to committing the offense, and sane after he committed it. If he can show, and convince the court or trier of fact, that he was insane during the time he committed the offense, then he cannot be punished for it. This, as one could imagine, takes some doing.

The M'Naghten Test. What constitutes insanity for the purpose of this plea? Some confusion could occur because of the varied definitions of insanity. In 1843 the *M'Naghten* case was decided by the House of Lords in England. Lord Chief Justice Tindal stated the rule for the court which has endured until 1978. The rule was as follows: "We are of the opinion that, not withstanding the party accused did not act complained of with a view, under the influence of insane delusions, or redressing or revenging some supposed grievance or injury, or of producing some public benefit, he is never the less punishable according to the nature of the crime committed, if he knew at the time of committing such crime that he was acting contrary to law . . . ."

The justice simply stated that as long as a person could distinguish between right and wrong he was legally sane. This is in sharp contrast to mental insanity. The doctrine requires that if a person cannot control his actions to some degree, then he is insane.

Until 1978 the M'Naghten test for insanity controlled the issue in criminal courts. People versus Drew changed drastically the insanity rule.

People v. Drew [15]. The defendant was found guilty of battery on a police officer. During the insanity trial, two court appointed psychiatrists described the defendant's condition. He had a past record of state hospital commitment. One psychiatrist opined that, if left untreated, the defendant's state would deteriorate to paranoid schzophrenia. He then concluded that he was unable to appreciate the difference between right and wrong at the time of his attack upon the police officer. He was found sane and appealed his case to the Supreme Court of California.

The court reversed the case and stated the following: "The court concludes that it should discard M'Naghten language, and update the California list of mental incapacity as a criminal defense by adopting the test proposed by the American Law Institute and followed by most of the federal judiciary, and the courts of other states. Therefore, the M'Naghten Rule is terminated . . . The *definition* of *mental incapacitation* in the American Law Institutes model Penal Code (Section 4.01) specified that a person is not responsible for criminal conduct if at the time of such conduct as a result of mental disease or defect he lacks substantial capacity with which to appreciate the criminality (wrongfulness) of his conduct or to conform his conduct to the requirements."

The effect of this case is that a defendant may know the difference between right and wrong, but because of his mental condition is unable to control himself. The words "cannot appreciate" or cannot "conform his conduct to the requirements of law" add a new dimension to the rule.

Dual Plea

Before we leave this section we must discuss the dual plea regarding insanity. As previously discussed, a single plea of not guilty by reason of insanity admits guilt. Many times a defense counsel will enter two pleas. Not guilty, and not guilty by reason of insanity. This seems at first glance contradictory, or at least a duplication of pleas. Actually, it is not. The defendant is saying, "I did not do it, but if I did, I am not responsible for my actions." Because of the implications of insanity, the defendant may not know what he did. He is using his best judgment, based on his personality, reputation, character, past experiences, etcetera, to come to the conclusion that he could not have done what he is being charged with. Entering a double plea places two major issues before the court: the issue of innocence, and the issue of insanity. Because of the importance of these issues, the court must consider each separately. Thus the court separates the pleas and sets up two trials. This procedure is called a *bifurcated trial*. Penal Code section 1026 states: "When a defendant pleads not guilty by reason of insanity, and also joins with it another plea or pleas, he shall first be tried as if he had entered such other plea or pleas only . . . ."

In other words, the main issue in any criminal prosecution is the issue of guilt or innocence. There will be two trials, one to determine guilt, and the other to determine legal insanity. The question of guilt will be decided first, then the question of insanity. If the court finds the defendant innocent, then there is no need to determine his insanity. However, if the defendant is found guilty, then the question of sanity is important. If he is found insane at the time he committed the offense, he will then be adjudicated as such, and sent to a mental hospital, or in the case of complete recovery, will be released as a free man. The second "trial" can occur before the same jury (if the first trial had a jury), or before a new jury at the discretion of the judge. Unless the court finds that the defendant has completely recovered, it will order him to a state hospital for a minimum of ninety days before he can be released.[16]

DEMURRER

At the beginning of this chapter we said that the defendant could answer an accusatory pleading by one of six pleas or by a *demurrer*. This section will discuss the purpose of the demurrer. A demurrer is a statement by the defendant that he cannot plead to one or more of the six statutory pleas because of errors in the accusatory pleading. In other words, he cannot do anything because of problems with the charges, etcetera. A demurrer raises the issue of the accuracy of the accusatory pleading and it concerns mistakes which appear in the charges against the defendant.

Penal Code section 1004 establishes the grounds for a demurrer and states the following:

"1. If an indictment, that the grand jury by which it was found had no legal authority to inquire into the offense charged, or, if an information or complaint that the court has no jurisdiction of the offense charged therein;

2. That it does not substantially conform to the provisions of Sections 950 and 952, and also Section 951 in case of an indictment of information;

3. That more than one offense is charged, except as provided in Section 954;

4. That the facts stated do not constitute a public offense;
5. That it contains a matter which, if true, would constitute a legal justification or excuse of the offense charged, or other legal bar to the prosecution."

Lack of Jurisdiction

The defendant may object to charges on the grounds that the court does not have jurisdiction to try the case. For example, there would be jurisdictional problems if the crime occurred outside of the jurisdiction of the court, or if the time in which the case had to come to trial expired. This section also deals with grand juries. If they did not have legal authority to issue an indictment, then the defendant could raise the issue by demurrer.

Uncertainity

This portion of the section deals with the specific provisions contained in the charge stated in the accusatory pleading. The constitutions of the United States and of California specifically require that the defendant be informed of the nature and circumstance of the charge against him. These charges must be specifically stated. The language of the statute must be clear. The accused must understand what he is being charged with. The specific elements of the offense must be stated. For example, failure to specify that the defendant entered a specific structure to constitute burglary could create uncertainty. Filing a demurrer under this category is quite rare due to the simple format required in filing accusatory pleadings.

Misjoinder

Misjoinder applies to accusatory pleadings where two or more offenses have been wrongly joined. A person can only be charged for one offense arising out of the same incident when the offense charged is exactly the same.[17]

Procedure

A demurrer must be in writing, signed by the defendant or his counsel, and must be filed with the court. It must specifically state the objections to the accusatory pleadings. A special hearing before the magistrate will be held to determine the validity of the complaint. Arguments by both parties will be heard by the magistrate, and he will state the reasons for granting or denying the demurrer. If the demurrer is overruled, the court will then require the defendant to plead. If the demurrer is substained, the accusatory pleading will be corrected, if possible. If the accusatory pleading cannot be remedied, a new accusatory pleading will be ordered.

In summary, a demurrer is offered by the defendant when there is an error in the accusatory pleading. If the court grants the demurrer, then the prosecution is ordered to correct the error. The demurrer has nothing to do with the issue of guilt or innocence, but deals generally with the language or lack of language contained in the accusatory pleading. If for some reason the pleading cannot be corrected, the case stops and does not go any further. The defendant is released from further responsibilities required by the legal system.

PRELIMINARY HEARINGS

The criminal justice process is sometimes seen as a confusing maze of procedures which tend to provide more protection to the criminal suspect than to the victim or public. Most Americans support a justice procedure which is swift and sure. Despite considerable sentiment for "swift" justice in the United States, few have been willing to sacrifice sureness for speed alone. An example of the extent to which our system attempts to be "sure" in its judicial dealings is the preliminary hearing or preliminary examination. Despite the call for speed, the preliminary hearing is an important stopping and checking point designed to contribute to the surety of a judicial outcome.

A typical criminal case begins with a citizen report or police observation of a crime. Investigations may be conducted, clues developed and suspects identified. Information may be submitted to substantiate probable cause for arrest or search warrants. The prosecuting or district attorney may present a bill of information to the grand jury, leading to an indictment. Each of these operations or procedures requires a degree of sureness to prevent indiscriminate accusations being made against innocent citizens.

The police cross—check the citizen's report of the crime as much to gain the facts as to determine that the complaint is bona fide, and not a false report for revenge, insurance fraud, or for other self—serving purposes. A judge will crosscheck the information gathered by the police in determining the need for warrants, since the police may be adversely influenced in making arrests or searches due to pressure, such as a war on crime, or, as Justice Black phrased it, "the highly competitive enterprises of ferreting out of crime."

In major cases, primarily involving felony crimes, the decision to initiate a criminal prosecution is cross—checked by a select citizens' panel, the grand jury. However, the preliminary hearing is an alternative checking mechanism to the grand jury in determining the advisibility of initiating a major criminal trial.

General Considerations

The preliminary hearing serves as a checkpoint to ensure that there is sufficient cause to proceed to a formal trial. At this point in the criminal justice process, the victim of the crime usually has a substantial basis for believing that the suspect is guilty of the crime. The police are convinced as a result of observation, investigation, and supporting evidence that the suspect is guilty. The district or prosecuting attorney has reviewed the case, including the citizen's report of the crime, subsequent police activity, the evidence available, and applicable statute and case laws. With this information at hand, the district attorney may elect to present the case to the grand jury or to hold a preliminary hearing. The preliminary hearing procedure is used in certain federal cases, and is used in over half of the states.

General Purpose

The purpose of preliminary hearings may vary from jurisdiction to jurisdiction; however, the most important and consistent purpose is to allow a magistrate to determine whether a suspect should be held for trial. Other purposes are:
1. To preserve evidence and keep witnesses within control of the state.
2. To determine bail.
3. To allow the defendant to discover some of the prosecution's evidence.
4. To determine the legality of police arrest or search procedures.
5. To allow for the entering of an early guilty plea.

In some states the preliminary hearing is an alternative to presenting the case to the grand jury. However, in some jurisdictions, the preliminary hearing is a prelude to the presentation of a case to the grand jury.

Federal Procedures

A preliminary hearing was unknown as a procedure in English Common Law, and a careful reading of the United States Constitution reveals no mention of preliminary hearings. Any right to a preliminary hearing in federal cases is based solely upon statutory law enacted by Congress.[18]

State Procedures

Preliminary hearing procedures vary considerably in fifty states. Some states do not use the procedure at all, while others provide for a fairly detailed process. California law provides an example of the preliminary hearing process at the state level. Prosecution for felony crimes punishable by death or imprisonment in state prison can be initiated by grand jury indictment or an information. A preliminary hearing is required before the filing of formal charges, using an information.

682. Prosecution by indictment or information; exceptions

Every public offense must be prosecuted by indictment or information except:
1. Where proceedings are had for the removal of civil officers of the State;
2. Offenses arising in the militia when in actual service, and in the land and naval forces in the time of war, or which the State may keep, with the consent of Congress, in time of peace;
3. Offenses tried in municipal and justice courts;
4. All misdemeanors of which jurisdiction has been conferred upon superior courts sitting as juvenile courts;
5. A felony to which the defendant has pleaded guilty to the complaint before a magistrate, where permitted by law.

738. Offenses triable in superior court; preliminary examination; order holding to answer; commencement by complaint

Before an information is filed there must be a preliminary examination of the case against the defendant and an order holding him to answer made under Section 872. The proceeding for a preliminary examination must be commenced by written complaint, as provided elsewhere in this code.

Neither an indictment nor an information is needed in misdemeanor offenses.

The decision to initiate prosecution by indictment or information rested with the prosecuting attorney until the Calfornia Supreme Court issued a major decision in the case of Hawkins v. Superior Court.[19] The case was based upon a challenge of the constitutionality of the grand jury indictment procedure in comparison to using the preliminary hearing for initiating a criminal prosecution. [20]

The Preliminary Hearing Within the Criminal Justice Process

At this point it may be helpful to place the preliminary hearing within the criminal justice process so that you may understand how it relates to other elements of criminal prosecution.

In most felony cases a defendant is arrested and taken before a magistrate. This initial appearance is known as the arraignment. During the initial arraignment the defendant may decide to enter a plea of guilty. If a not guilty plea is entered, the magistrate must set the time for the preliminary hearing, allowing at least two days for preparation, but limiting the scheduled time to within ten days if the defendant remains in custody. The actual preliminary hearing may be postponed to allow the defendant to secure counsel.

860. Time to obtain counsel; examination of case; waiver of examination; order holding defendant to answer; time for filing information; juvenile court jurisdiction and procedure unaffected

At the time set for the examination of the case, if the public offense is
1. Not a felony, but within the jurisdiction of the superior court, or is
2. A felony which is punishable with death, or is

3. A felony to which the defendant has not pleaded guilty in accordance with Section 859a of this code, then, if the defendant requires the aid of counsel, the magistrate must allow the defendant a reasonable time to send for counsel, and may postpone the examination for not less than two nor more than five days for that purpose. The magistrate must, immediately after the appearance of counsel, or if, after waiting a reasonable time therefor, none appears, proceed to examine the case; provided, however, that a defendant represented by counsel may when brought before the magistrate as provided in Section 858 or at any time subsequent thereto, waive his right to an examination before such magistrate, and thereupon it shall be the duty of the magistrate to make an order holding the defendant to answer, and it shall be the duty of the district attorney within 15 days thereafter, to file in the superior court of the county in which the offense is triable the information; provided, further, however, that nothing contained herein shall prevent the district attorney nor the magistrate from requiring that an examination be held as provided in this chapter. Nothing contained in this section shall affect the jurisdiction or procedure of the superior court sitting as a juvenile court.

The examination is normally completed within a single session.

861. Duration of examination; postponements

When To Be Completed. Postponement. The examination must be completed at one session, unless the magistrate, for good cause shown by affidavit, postpone it. The postponement cannot be for more than two days at each time, nor more than six days in all, unless by consent or on motion of the defendant.

Additional statute law provides for: judicial direction for discharging the defendant on bail (Penal Code section 862); committing the defendant to the custody of a peace officer (Penal Code section 863); reading depositions into the preliminary hearing record (Penal Code section 864); examining witnesses in the presence of the defendant (Penal Code section 865); the examination of defense witnesses (Penal Code section 866); the right to counsel during the examination (Penal Code section 866.5); excluding and separating witnesses (Penal Code section 867); excluding the public, except for the attendance of a person of her own sex for female prosecuting witnesses (Penal Code section 868); directions for reporting and recording testimony (Penal Code section 869); and for matters pertaining to commitment formats and the treatment of witnesses (Penal Code sections 870-883).

The details of the preliminary hearing process in California are illustrated in the following flow chart. While the chart indicates several decision points where the defendant may waive the preliminary hearing, it is important to understand that this waiver may be made at any time the defendant is before the magistrate after being arraigned. In some serious cases, of course, the court may ignore the waiver and proceed with the preliminary hearing in the interest of ensuring justice. You may wish to review this section of the chapter and identify the specific sections of statute law which relate to the decision points illustrated on the flow chart.

Arrest resulting from police observation,
warrant supported by information, or
grand jury indictment

certain felonies

arraignment

right to counsel

Prosecution makes police arrest and
crime reports available

Defendant pleads guilty

Defendant pleads not guilty

certified to trial court

Date is set for preliminary hearing — a
minimum of two days from arraignment or
within ten days if defendant is in custody

right to counsel if not already obtained — two
to five day delay allowed if time to obtain
counsel is needed

Defendant may be released on bail

Defendant waives right to preliminary hearing

preliminary hearing

Defendant certified to trial court

reading of depositions made in the information

examination of witnesses

hearing transcribed

Defendant discharged

Defendant held to answer and
certified to trial court

The Preliminary Hearing In Practice

While the preliminary hearing process implies a long and drawn out procedure (which may contribute to the often lamented backlog of court cases), in practice the hearings are generally very brief. While definite research data are scarce, most preliminary hearings last only ten to twenty minutes. Observation of a few hearings within your own jurisdiction may be helpful in assessing the time consumed by the process. While clear research is also weak on the number of hearings which result in certification for trial, it is estimated that 90-95 percent result in certification and/or a reduced charge or plea bargain. Your local court clerk or magistrate may be able to provide you with information on the experience in your area.

Preliminary Hearing Recommendations of The National Advisory Commission On Criminal Justice Standards and Goals

The National Commission report on the courts proposed the following standard for criminal preliminary hearings and arraignments:

> If a preliminary hearing is held, it should be held within 2 weeks following arrest. Evidence received at the preliminary hearing should be limited to that which is relevant to a determination that there is probable cause to believe that a crime was committed and that the defendant committed it.
>
> Arraignment should be eliminated as a formal step in a criminal prosecution. The initial charging document, as amended at the preliminary hearing, should serve as the formal charging document for trial.
>
> If a defendant intends to waive his right to a preliminary hearing, he should file a notice to this effect at least 24 hours prior to the time set for the hearing.
>
> Commentary
>
> Where a preliminary hearing is held, the standard requires that it be held within 2 weeks of arrest. This will provide sufficient time for both sides to conduct the investigation necessary for a reliable determination of the limited matters at issue at the preliminary hearing.
>
> This standard proposes that care be taken to avoid unnecessary introduction of irrelevant evidence at the preliminary hearing. Extended and time-consuming preliminary hearings are carried primarily by the desire to use these proceedings as discovery devices. The provision for expanded discovery in Standard 4.9 would eliminate the necessity of using the preliminary hearing for this purpose. Thus the preliminary hearing could be held more expeditiously without sacrificing a defendant's tactical advantage.
>
> Efficient scheduling requires that if a defendant waives his right to a preliminary hearing, he give notice to this effect at least a day before the time scheduled for the hearing. This is of special importance, in view of the fact that other standards in this chapter establish time limits for discovery and pretrial motions based upon the time of the preliminary hearing or its waiver.
>
> The arraignment, under present practice, theoretically serves the function of informing the defendant of the precise nature of the charges against him and of

providing an opportunity for entry of a plea. As a practical matter it serves no useful purpose. The defendant already is aware of the charges and a plea can be entered without a formal appearance of all parties before the court. Therefore, the standard recommends abolishing the arraignment as a formal step.

SUMMARY

In this chapter the four major purposes of the arraignment were discussed. We found that the arraignment is the first experience a defendant will have before the court. Of paramount importance is the necessity to educate the defendant to his legal and constitutional rights. He will be informed of his right to counsel, right to have witnesses on his behalf and other rights necessary to afford the defendant a fair and impartial trial. Another important purpose of the arraignment is to inform the defendant of the specific charges against him. Before he can plead he must know exactly what he is being charged with. The third major purpose of the arraignment is to give the defendant the opportunity to plead one or more of the six pleas allowed. Finally the accused is scheduled for the next step in the criminal justice process. If he plead guilty, he must be sentenced. If a not guilty plea was entered then the preliminary hearing or trial date is set.

The six specific pleas were listed and defined. The six possible pleas allowed for indictments, informations, and criminal complaints are: guilty, not guilty, former jeopardy, not guilty by reason of insanity, former judgment of conviction or acquittal, and nolo contendere. We stated that the court is very careful to ensure that the defendant fully understands the significance of the offense charged, etc., before pleading guilty, because when making that plea he is admitting to all parts of the crime. The not guilty plea is a denial of the charges against him and requires formal proof by the prosecutor. Former judgment of conviction or acquittal and once in jeopardy basically prevent the defendant from being tried, or retried for the same offense. Not guilty by reason of insanity is an admission as to committing the act but is saying that the accused cannot be held accountable. The defendant must prove this state of mind. The nolo contendere has the same affect as a guilty plea in criminal cases, but has a special meaning for subsequent civil cases.

The preliminary hearing is only a small part of the total processing of a criminal case; however it serves the important function of providing a judicial review and screening of the case. It helps address the element of sureness, which is a part of the "swift and sure" philosophy of justice. It is frequently the proving ground for testing the skill of law enforcement agencies. It is the preliminary step in meeting the demanding requirements of "probable cause" and "beyond a reasonable doubt."

DISCUSSION QUESTIONS

1. Identify the four major purposes of an arraignment. Discuss each, its function, and indicate why it is necessary.

2. How many pleas are available to a defendant charged with a criminal offense? What effect does each plea have?

3. Discuss the following terms:
   a. Dual Plea
   b. Bifurcated Trial
   c. Demurrer

4. Describe the five specific purposes of a preliminary hearing. What types of crimes would require a preliminary hearing if the defendant so chose?

5. Chart the criminal justice process from the arraignment through to the preliminary hearing.

REFERENCES

1. Penal Code section 976.
2. This process is generally referred to as the original arraignment.
3. Penal Code section 1017.
4. In Re Tahl, 1 Cal. 3d 122, 81 Cal. Rptr. 577, 460 P. 2d 449.
5. People v. Manriques, 188 Cal. 602, 206 P. 63.
6. Penal Code Section 1367; People v. Gallantier, 47 Cal. 2d 148, 117 P. 2d 431.
7. Penal Code Section 1018.
8. People v. Jones, 52 Cal. 2d 636, 343 P. 2d 577.
9. People v. Beesly, 119 Cal. 82, 6 P. 2d 114.
10. Boykin v. Alabama, 395 U.S. 238, 89 S. Ct. 1709, 23 L. Ed. 2d 274.
11. Penal Code Section 1019.
12. Penal Code 1016.
13. See Section 656 for details.
14. See Sections 687, 1023, 1101, 1188, & 1387.
15. 22 Cal. 3d 333, 149 Cal. Rptr. 275, 583 P. 2d 1318.
16. The statement applies for serious felonies. See Penal Code Section 1026.
17. Read Section 954 for types of offenses which could be charged and not violate the misjoiner section.
18. For specific information regarding federal procedures refer to Rule 5 and 5.1, 18 USCA of the Federal Rules of Criminal Procedure.
19. James Hawkins v. Superior Court of San Francisco, 150 Cal. Rptr. 435, 586 P. 2d 916.
20. For a detailed discussion of the *Hawkins* case refer to Chapt. 8, Grand Jury Indictments.

12

Trial Procedure

CHAPTER OBJECTIVES

Upon reading this chapter, the student will be able to:

1. Describe how a jury is selected.
2. Identify and differentiate between the procedures by which the prosecution and the defense present evidence at trial.
3. List the specific jury functions.
4. Explain the sentencing process currently used in California.
5. Describe the specific methods used to determine the length of parole.

The right to a jury trial is a fundamental right guaranteed by the Sixth Amendment to the United States Constitution. The traditional concept is that a jury was to consist of twelve persons who must reach a unanimous verdict. Recent United States Supreme Court decisions indicate that a state legislature may authorize smaller juries, with six the apparent minimum size, and may authorize less than unanimous verdicts. California has retained the traditional size of juries and unanimity requirements for verdicts.

Yet, with this strong heritage which favors jury trials, few cases actually result in jury trials. Plea bargaining and other dispositions without trial account for as much as ninety percent of the cases filed in some courts. Additionally, many cases that do go to trial are heard by a judge without a jury present. Many tactical decisions are made between arrest and trial that cause the criminal defendant to waive what the founding fathers felt was a fundamental right. In order to keep the options open to the defendant, courts have ruled that harsher sentences may not be given to those who demand a trial than to those similarly situated who are willing to plead guilty.

Television and movies are fond of portraying the trial as a scene of tense, fast—moving drama and intriguing dialogue. While each person on trial may feel a dramatic emotional impact from the trial, few trials live up to the image portrayed by the media and in literature. For the officer who investigated the crime and who will testify at the trial, a trial usually represents a great deal of time spent merely waiting for his brief turn on the witness stand. In fact, he may not even be permitted to be inside the courtroom at other times.

After the verdict has been returned, the court will focus its attention on the sentencing process. California has recently adopted "determinant" sentencing. While this takes a great deal of guesswork out of calculating the length of time to be served, it does not foreclose the non-custodial alternatives open to the judge. A wide variety of sentences, in addition to state prison, are available in the average case. The sentencing report prepared by the probation department is crucial in assisting the judge in deciding which avenue will be used. Strangely, this aspect of the trial process is virtually unknown to the public and rarely mentioned in the media.

PROCEDURES AT TRIAL

Pre-Trial Conference

Once the case has been assigned to the courtroom where it will be heard, and any necessary waiting for other cases to be completed has passed, the judge will frequently hold a pre-trial conference. The purpose of the conference is to establish procedures to be followed in the trial, and to settle as many problems as possible before the trial begins. Since the conference is not part of the trial, it may be held in the judge's chambers and will not be part of the official record. Both prosecuting and defense attorneys will be present and the defendant may also be allowed to attend.

Last minute plea bargaining may be done at the pre-trial conference. Rules regarding discussion of the case with the news media may be set if there were no previous orders on the subject. The length of trial will be estimated. Necessary facts to enable the judge to examine jurors will be compiled. Motions in limine, a procedure to secure rulings in advance that no reference may be made to certain types of prejudicial evidence, may be heard. It will be determined if the defendant will admit or deny prior offenses, if any were charged in the pleadings. Special rules regarding conduct of the trial, such as whether or not attorneys may approach the witness stand without specific consent from the judge, will be established. If there are multiple defendants, the judge will establish rules regulating the order of proceedings among the various defense attorneys.

Selection of Jury

The process of selecting a jury begins by requesting that a group of jurors be sent to the courtroom from the jury assembly room. The number requested is based on a rough guess of how many will be needed. The court clerk will normally telephone the request to the jury clerk, who will randomly select prospective jurors from those present in the jury assembly room. These prospective jurors will be sworn to tell the truth in answering questions on voir dire.

Twelve of the prospective jurors will be seated in the jury box. The judge will announce the title of the case and the charges. He may explain what an indictment, an information or a complaint is, and emphasize that the jury is not to presume guilt from the fact that the defendant is now on trial. The judge may also give the jury explanations of the presumption of innocence and proof beyond a reasonable doubt. The judge will introduce each attorney, the defendant, and any witnesses present. These introductions are designed to assist jurors in determining whether they know any of the trial participants. Jurors will be asked if they are willing to decide the case solely on the evidence before them, and based on the law that the court will tell them is applicable.

While procedure varies on who will ask jurors questions (called voir dire of the jury), probably the most common procedure is for the judge to ask standard questions from a list, followed by both attorneys asking questions more specifically related to the case. The purpose of questioning the jury is to reveal biases of individual jurors. For instance, the judge may ask jurors questions relating to business or occupation, prior experience in serving on any jury, involvement of relatives or close friends of the juror in the case, or any law enforcement or legal training. The attorneys have the right to reasonably question the jurors. During this phase, jurors whose prior answers indicate that they are not legally qualified, or are biased in regard to the case, will be dismissed. This is referred to as challenge "for cause." Their place in the jury box will be filled with new jurors who will go through the same questioning. There are no limits on the number of jurors who may be dismissed for cause.

After both the prosecution and defense have completed questioning jurors, and there are twelve jurors in the jury box who have not been removed "for cause," attorneys will begin use of "peremptory" challenges. A peremptory challenge permits an attorney to dismiss a juror for subjective reasons that the attorney believes may influence the verdict. No reason is stated at the time the juror is dismissed. The number of peremptory challenges is governed by Penal Code Section 1070. For cases where only one defendant is on trial, each side has twenty-six peremptory challenges if the death penalty or life imprisonment could result from the charges, six challenges if the maximum imprisonment is ninety days, and thirteen challenges in all other cases. The number of challenges available is increased when there are multiple

The subpoena ordering President Nixon to appear and testify at the trial of his former aides. UPI photo

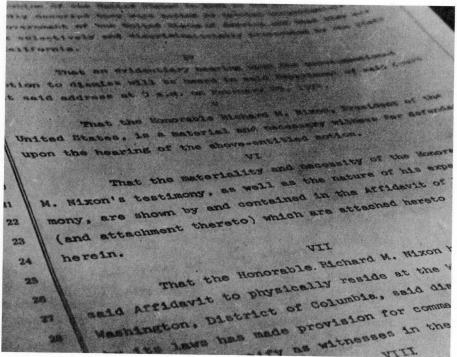

defendants (see Penal Code section 1070.5).

The prosecution is first asked if it will exercise a peremptory challenge. If it does, the juror will be excused and the seat filled by someone else from the jury panel. The new juror will be questioned in the same manner as previous jurors, and both sides will be given a chance to challenge the new juror "for cause." If he is challenged "for cause," the replacement process will be repeated until a juror is accepted. It will then be the defense's turn to exercise a peremptory challenge. Either prosecution or defense may pass a turn without using a peremptory challenge. The challenge and replacement process will continue until either both sides have exhausted their peremptory challenges, or both sides are satisfied with the jurors seated in the jury box.

Once twelve jurors have been selected, the alternate jurors will be selected. The purpose of having alternate jurors is to provide for the chance that one or more of the twelve jurors will have to be excused during the trial for illness or other causes. The number of alternate jurors varies with the time estimated for trial and other circumstances. Alternates will be questioned in the same manner as other jurors. There will be as many peremptory challenges as there are alternate jurors. Unused peremptory challenges after the selection of the twelve jurors may not be used to exclude alternate jurors. Once all jurors and alternates have been selected, the clerk will swear the jury to try the case.

Reading the Accusatory Pleading

Penal Code section 1093 (1) makes the reading of the accusatory pleading mandatory in the case of a felony, and permits the formality to be dispensed with in all other cases. If the pleading includes allegations of prior convictions, all reference to the convictions must be deleted if the defendant has confessed to the prior convictions.

The reading is usually done by the clerk. The defendant has the right to waive a reading of the charges. The jury should be instructed that the pleading does not constitute proof of the crime, and that no inferences of guilt are to be drawn from the pleadings.

People's Opening Statement

The purpose of an opening statement is to introduce the jury to the case and inform the jury what will be proved by the testimony that they are about to hear. It serves as a guide for the jurors as they try to piece together the facts each witness adds to the case. It is especially helpful in long or complex cases, and in cases where it becomes necessary to call witnesses to testify out of sequence.

The opening statement is not evidence in the case. Jurors may not rely on these statements in deciding guilt or innocence. While the statement is used to inform jurors what evidence they are to receive, it is not an error if it subsequently develops that not all pieces of evidence or testimony are produced during trial. Claims that highly prejudicial evidence will be produced, if made in bad faith, may cause reversal. Such cases are rare and hard to prove. It is not mandatory that either the prosecution or the defense make opening statements. The prosecution infrequently waives the right to make an opening statement. The defense has three options: make an opening statement immediately after the prosecution's opening statement, delay its opening statement until after the prosecution rests its case, or waive the right entirely. The second option is probably the most commonly used.

People's Introduction of Evidence

Following the opening statement, the prosecution must produce sufficient admissible evidence to establish the defendant's guilt beyond a reasonable doubt. The prosecution has the burden to prove every element of the crime.

The prosecution will call the witnesses it believes are necessary to prove the case to the jury's satisfaction. This may mean that several witnesses will testify to the same event. While the order in which witnesses are called is usually at the discretion of the individual attorney, the normal procedure is to call witnesses in a sequence that will allow their testimony to proceed in a logical order. When an item of physical evidence is to be introduced, the judge frequently requires all necessary testimony to support the admissibility of the item to be produced before the item can be accepted into evidence, although the judge may accept the attorney's statement that a later witness will provide the necessary testimony. Should the testimony not be introduced, the opposing side must make appropriate requests to exclude evidence and to have the judge properly instruct the jury.

When the prosecution calls a witness, the prosecutor must ask that witness specific questions designed to elicit answers that are relevant to the case. This is called direct examination. For example, the prosecutor might ask an eyewitness the following questions on direct examination: "Where were you on the night of July 3, 1978? Who else was at the liquor store? What was Mr. Jones wearing? What did Mr. Jones have in his hand?" Background information may be necessary to demonstrate to the jury that the witness is competent to testify about the subject involved. This information must also be sought by specific questions. With a few exceptions, the direct examination may not be in narrative form because this is likely to produce rambling testimony and irrelevant information. Leading questions may not be used on direct examination.

However, the court may relax these rules at its discretion. When children or feeble—minded persons are called as witnesses, it is not uncommon to allow them to give narrative responses, provided they stay on the subject. If a witness is called as an adverse or hostile witness, he may be questioned by the side calling him in much the same manner as if he were being cross—examined.

The trial judge has a great deal of discretion in procedural matters during a trial, and may permit or restrict the taking of evidence out of order, introduction of evidence that is merely cumulative, the amount of rebuttal evidence, and views of the scene of the crime. The court may also exclude evidence and questions, even though no objections were made by either counsel. The court may order protection for witnesses who have been threatened, exclude witnesses from the court-room when not testifying, appoint expert witnesses, and question witnesses. These acts can be done on the judge's own initiative or in response to a request by counsel.

Once the prosecution has completed questioning a witness, the defense has the right to cross—examine. Leading questions may be used for cross—examination. For example, the defense attorney might ask an eyewitness the following questions of cross—examination: "Wasn't Mr. Jones wearing a blue shirt? Wasn't there another man in the liquor store wearing a green shirt? Don't you normally wear glasses? Didn't you tell the police on the night of July 3, 1978, that the man who robbed the liquor store had brown hair?" Cross—examination can be

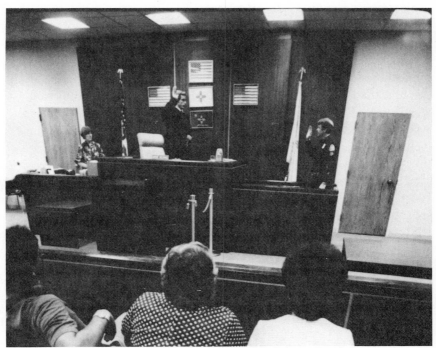

used to fill in details left out on direct examination, show facts that indicate the witnesses are not well qualified to make statements that are now on the record, and attack the credibility of the witness. For example, it may be brought out that an eyewitness was too far away to get a good look at the robber's face, has poor eyesight, or has a previous conviction for a crime involving dishonesty. Cross—examination is a fundamental right and the judge may not unduly restrict it. The questioning on cross—examination, except for attacks on credibility and qualifications of the witness, must be within the subject matter covered by that witness on direct examination.

When items of physical evidence are to be introduced, they will be marked (such as, Defense Exhibit 1, or People's Exhibit 1) and shown to the opposing counsel before they are entered into evidence. Any objection must be made prior to their being admitted. The "chain of custody" must be established to show that there has been no tampering with the evidence.

When an item is challenged as a product of illegal search and seizure or a confession as illegally obtained, the jury will be sent out of the courtroom while the court hears testimony on the illegality, unless the testimony was taken before trial. The jury will be given the item or confession only if the court rules it to be admissible. It is desirable to raise the illegality issue before trial by making a motion under Penal Code section 1538.5, and hence avoid the confusion during trial.

As testimony is being taken, the opposing attorney must enter objections as soon as possible. If he believes the questions asked are improper, the objection should be made before the witness answers. The reason for the objection must be given. For example, counsel might say, "Objection, hearsay," or "Objection, calls for a conclusion."

Either side has the right to request that persons who are anticipated to be called as witnesses be excluded from the courtroom except when testifying. The defendant will be allowed to remain at the counsel table with his attorney, and the investigating officer may be permitted to remain at the counsel table of the prosecution. The purpose of excluding witnesses is to prevent the witnesses from listening to each other and trying to "get their stories straight," instead of testifying about what actually happened. This should not be confused with permitting a witness to refresh his memory, which is proper. It may also be possible to introduce documents into evidence that were made by witnesses near the time of an occurrence to record the event if attempts to refresh the memory are to no avail.

After the prosecution has called all of its witnesses and the defense has completed cross examination, the prosecution rests. It is common for the defense to move for acquittal at this point. If the prosecution has failed to prove a necessary element of the crime, the judge will stop the trial and ask the jury to acquit the defendant. Due to the defendant's Sixth Amendment right to a jury trial, there is no corresponding motion in a criminal trial for the judge to direct a guilty verdict.

Defendant's Opening Statement

The defense's opening statement is normally given after the prosecution rests. While the defense does not have to disprove the crime, and may choose not to introduce any evidence, the defense will usually call witnesses. The opening statement will try to inform the jury what the defense is attempting to show by the witnesses to be called. Arguments on the prosecution's case do not belong in the opening statement, and should be reserved until all witnesses have been called.

Defense Introduces Evidence

The defense may call witnesses and introduce physical evidence about the crime. It may also produce evidence to impeach prosecution witnesses, or vouch for the defendant's character on relevant traits. The witnesses will be examined directly by the defense, and prosecution will be entitled to cross–examination. Redirect and re-cross–examination may follow.

The defendant may exercise his Fifth Amendment right against self–incrimination and not take the witness stand. If the defendant does testify, he must submit to cross–examination regarding matters within his testimony on direct and appropriate methods of impeachment may be used. At completion of direct and cross–examination of all defense witnesses, the defense rests.

Re-Opening and Rebuttal

With the permission of the court, the prosecution may call witnesses to introduce evidence not previously admitted. This is relatively rare. More commonly, the prosecution will call witnesses to refute testimony of one or more defense witnesses. This is called rebuttal. Cross examination provides the opportunity to question a witness and to clarify facts or show bias. The defense can call witnesses to show these weaknesses in the prosecution's case. The rebuttal permits the prosecution to attack the defense case by the use of witnesses other than those called by the defense. Witnesses called by the prosecution during its case in chief may be recalled to the witness stand. Rebuttal is not properly used merely to introduce new evidence of the crime. Surrebuttal may follow the rebuttal if the defense wishes to rebut testimony of the prosecution's rebuttal witnesses.

Closing Arguments

The closing argument permits the attorney to summarize his case and appeal to the jury. It may include discussion of individual facts and of law. It should be confined to facts actually introduced during trial. Motives of the defendant and witnesses may be questioned. Statements of personal opinions of the attorney on the case, and derogatory remarks about the defendant or attorneys not reasonably related to the case are improper. The prosecutor may not comment on the defendant's exercise of his Fifth Amendment rights by refusing to take the witness stand. Failure to call any other material witness may be mentioned. Since there is no duty to produce witnesses to testify to a defendant's good character, it is improper to argue to the jury that failure to call character witnesses is an inference of bad character. References to evidence that was not produced at trial, or evidence ruled inadmissible are also forms of misconduct. Unless there is an exception to the rule prohibiting introduction of prior crimes, reference to past criminal activities of the defendant is not permitted in argument.

In cases where a jury has discretion in determining the sentence, the prosecutor may tell the jury of possibilities for early parole. In most cases, penalty is fixed by law without recommendation from the jury, and it is improper to discuss sentencing in arguing the case to the jury.

The prosecutor may not allude to facts not in evidence, or argue his personal belief that the defendant is guilty. Similarly, the prosecutor may not state personal beliefs that the witnesses are truthful or untruthful. However, the prosecutor may argue that legally permissible inferences will, in his personal belief, lead to the correct conclusion. Both sides may refer to items of common knowledge even though such items were not introduced into evidence.

Appeals to the prejudices or passions of the jury are improper. These include racial slurs, falsely raising issues of political beliefs, references to wealth, and the type of crime committed. It is also improper to attack the court as lenient or "bleeding heart" in regard to admissibility of evidence or sentencing practices.

The defense has a broad scope of permissible argument, but law may not be inaccurately stated to the jury. Neither the prosecution nor the defense may make unsubstantiated statements on the effectiveness or ineffectiveness of the death penalty. The defense also has no right to bring in facts not in evidence or common knowledge.

The prosecution will offer their argument first. Defense will argue next, and prosecution will make the closing argument. Length of each of these statements is within the discretion of the trial judge.

Jury Instructions

The purpose of jury instructions is to state the applicable law to the jury. The jury is to use only the law as contained within the instructions to arrive at a decision on the defendant's guilt or innocence.

A large quantity of approved jury instructions are collected in the book *California Approved Jury Instructions, Criminal* (frequently referred to as CALJIC). Each instruction is a summary of a relevant point of law. The summaries are frequently composed of quotations from court decisions on point. As the law is changed by legislation or court decision, the standard instructions are revised. Each attorney will go over the case and decide which instructions will be necessary. A memo will be presented to the court listing the desired instructions. These are frequently listed by their catalog number only. If there is not a standard jury instruction on a point of law in the case, or if an attorney believes the standard instruction is inappropriate for his case, he will prepare his own instruction and attach it to the memo. These instructions which are not taken from CALJIC are referred to as Special Jury Instructions.

SAMPLE JURY INSTRUCTIONS

CALJIC 2.90   PRESUMPTION OF INNOCENCE–REASONABLE DOUBT–BURDEN OF PROOF

A defendant in a criminal action is presumed to be innocent until the contrary is proved, and in case of a reasonable doubt whether his guilt is satisfactorily shown, he is entitled to an acquittal. This presumption places upon the state the burden of proving him guilty beyond a reasonable doubt. Reasonable doubt is defined as follows: It is not a mere possible doubt, because everything relating to human affairs, and depending on moral evidence, is open to some possible or imaginary doubt. It is that state of the case which, after the entire comparison and consideration of all the evidence, leaves the minds of the jurors in that condition that they cannot say they feel an abiding conviction, to a moral certainty, of the truth of the charge.

CALJIC 8.48   INVOLUNTARY MANSLAUGHTER–ABSENCE OF INTENT TO KILL DUE TO DIMINISHED CAPACITY

Involuntary manslaughter is the unlawful killing of a human being without malice aforethought and without an intent to kill.

A killing is unlawful within the meaning of this instruction if it occurred:

(1) During the commission of a misdemeanor which is inherently dangerous to human life; or

(2) In the commission of an act ordinarily lawful which involves a high degree of risk of death or great bodily harm, without due caution and circumspection.

There is no malice aforethought and intent to kill if by reason of diminished capacity caused by mental illness, mental defect, or intoxication, the defendant did not have the mental capacity to harbor malice aforethought and to form an intent to kill.

The judge will meet with the attorneys near the end of the case to discuss jury instructions. Only instructions related to evidence in the case will be given. The instructions requested by both sides will be given. The judge will hear discussion from both sides on the applicability of other instructions that have been requested by only one side. He will rule whether or not each instruction will be given to the jury. Counsel opposing this ruling will be given a chance to formally state the objection on the record. It is not uncommon for the defense to request instructions on particular elements of the crime and leave the requests for general instructions, such as defining beyond a reasonable doubt, or the duty of jurors to deliberate as a body, to the prosecution. The judge has a duty to add necessary jury instructions if neither side has requested them. This duty extends to elements of crimes, included offenses, and defenses that are apparent from the record. It does not extend to every conceivable defense in a case.

Charging the Jury

The instructions will be read to the jury after the final arguments by counsel. Printed copies of jury instruction can be taken into the jury room for use during deliberations.

The judge has authority to make some comments to the jury about the case. The scope of comment is "such comment on the evidence and the testimony and the credibility of any witness as in its opinion is necessary for the proper determination of the case and in any criminal case, whether the defendant testifies or not, his failure to explain or to deny by his testimony any evidence or facts in the case against him may be commented upon by the court. The court shall inform the jury in all cases that the jurors are the exclusive judges of all questions of fact submitted to them and of the credibility of the witnesses" (Penal Code section 1127). While the last sentence quoted is the only statutory restriction on judicial comment, the courts also require the judge to remain impartial. Comments must be fair. No partisan attacks on the counsel, the defendant, or witnesses are allowed. The judge may comment on any portion of the evidence or on the total evidence admitted at trial, but he may not comment on the failure of the defendant to take the witness stand.

Jury Deliberations

After the charge by the judge, the bailiff will be sworn. He escorts the jurors to the jury room. The first order of business is to elect a foreman who will preside over deliberations. The jurors must discuss the evidence as a group, and attempt to reach unanimous verdict. All deliberations must be conducted in the jury room, with all jurors present. If the verdict has not been reached at the end of the day, the judge will decide whether to send the jurors home. or to have them confined in a hotel under the supervision of court personnel. Such confinement is referred to as being sequestered.

The jury will have access to the jury instructions, all items introduced into evidence as exhibits, and notes that each juror made during trial. Should the jury have questions on law they may send a note to the judge. He will have them return to the courtroom and hear the question. The attorneys and the defendant have the right to be present, and may confer with the judge on whether the jury should be given additional instructions. If the jury wishes to have the testimony of a witness read to them, they notify the judge in a similar manner. The judge will have the court reporter review her notes to find the testimony requested, and then read it to the jury. The testimony will be read in open court with the defendant and the attorneys present.

Should the jury deadlock, the judge may inquire to determine if additional time for deliberation would be beneficial. If the judge feels there is a chance for agreement, he may send the jury back for further deliberations. The judge may not exert undue pressures on the jury to reach a unanimous verdict. Use of the "Allen charge" (a jury instruction which instructs jurors in the minority to consider the fact that the majority do not agree with them) has been discontinued in California. If, after appropriate consideration, no unanimity is possible, the judge will dismiss the jury. The procedure is commonly referred to as a "hung jury." Normally, it will be possible for the prosecutor to request a new trial in these cases.

Verdict

If the jury reaches a unanimous decision, the foreman must sign the appropriate verdict. A packet of verdicts, consisting of a one page form for each possible verdict on each charged offense, is given to the jury when they first retire to begin deliberations. For example, in a case charging kidnap with intent to rob, under Penal Code section 209, the verdicts might be guilty of kidnap with intent to rob, guilty of simple kidnap (Penal Code section 207), and not guilty. The foreman signs the appropriate verdict and leaves the others blank. The verdicts are "returned," read in open court, with all jurors, attorneys, and the defendant present. Either the judge or the clerk will formally ask whether a verdict has been reached. The verdict will then be read. Upon request of one or more of the attorneys, the clerk will "poll the jury." This process requires the clerk to ask each individual juror "Is this your verdict?," or an equivalent question. If there are multiple charges, the clerk will ask about each charge separately.

Occasionally the jury will be instructed to return "special verdicts." In these cases the jury will be instructed to reach a verdict on specific facts—for instance, if the defendant was armed with a deadly weapon at the time of the crime, or whether the victim received great bodily injury. This is done in cases involving special circumstances, most commonly for acts for which an additional sentence may be imposed.

The jury specifies whether or not it found the situation to be factual and present. The judge renders judgment according to the findings.

Findings in Trial by Court

If the jury was waived, the trial is heard by a judge. No jury instructions are necessary. At the close of the case the judge will announce his findings on the facts. The format for these findings is basically the same as that for a jury verdict.

POST CONVICTION MOTIONS

California now permits challenges to jury verdicts based on affidavits of jurors that state facts showing misconduct of jurors during deliberations. Challenge to the verdict is also possible if jurors lied during voir dire to conceal their biases and the truth was not learned until after the verdict was returned.

The defense may move for a new trial. If granted, this motion results in the setting aside of the verdict, and the case being set for a new trial in the same court. If it was a jury trial, a new jury will be selected. The

Stages of Trial

Jury Impanelled (If Jury Trial)	Introduction of Evidence by Prosecution (Defense Has Opportunity to Cross-Examine Prosecution Witnesses)	Judge Instructs Jury on Law Applicable to the Case (If Jury Trial)
Accusatory Pleading Read by Clerk (Mandatory for Felonies, Optional for Misdemeanors)	Introduction of Evidence by Defense Counsel (Prosecution Has Opportunity to Cross-Examine Defense Witnesses)	Deliberation by Jury, if Jury Trial, or by Judge, if no Jury
Prosecutor May Make Opening Statement	Both Prosecution and Defense May Offer Rebutting Testimony	Verdict
Defense Counsel May Make Opening Statement (Defense May Also Wait Until After Prosecution Completes Case)	Closing Arguments by: 1. Prosecutor 2. Defense Counsel 3. Prosecutor	Sentencing

evidence will have to be presented at the new trial. The only grounds for granting a new trial are listed in Penal Code section 1181: absence of defendant during trial; jury received evidence out of court; jurors improperly separated during deliberations; verdict decided by lottery; verdict contrary to law or evidence; material evidence discovered that was not introduced at trial even though the defendant used due diligence to locate the evidence before trial; denial of the right to a transcript due to the loss of destruction of the reporter's notes, or the death or disability of the reporter.

The motion should be made in writing, specifying the grounds relied upon, and should be accompanied by a memorandum of points of law which support the motion. The prosecution will have the right to enter affidavits and points of law in opposition to the motion. Normally the motion must be made before the court pronounces judgment in the case. The judge who heard the case will hear arguments from both and make a ruling. He has a great deal of discretion in granting or denying the motion. If there were multiple charges, the motion may be granted for one or more charge. The judge may also alter the verdict by reducing the conviction to a lesser included offense.

ENTRY OF JUDGMENT PROBATION AND SENTENCING HEARING

After the return of a jury verdict, or the entry of findings by the judge sitting without a jury, the proceedings are usually recessed to permit a motion for a new trial and the preparation of a probation report. The defendant has a right to waive the probation report and demand to be sentenced immediately. The length of time allowed to obtain the probation report is generally twenty-one days in municipal court, and twenty-eight days in superior court (See Penal Code sections 1191 and 1449). Extension may be granted to enable probation officers to complete the reports, if necessary.

The defendant has the right to counsel at the sentencing hearing. At this hearing the defendant may make a motion in arrest of judgment. At the hearing, before judgment is entered, the court must ask the defendant if there is a legal reason why judgment should not be pronounced. Present insanity of the defendant is a ground for not entering judgment. The motion also may be based on the court's lack of jurisdiction. If a demurrer for failure to state a public offense was previously overruled, it may be renewed at this time. Motions can also be made at this time to remove allegations in the complaint that the defendant has prior convictions.

In the absence of a motion being granted in arrest of judgment, the hearing will proceed and judgment will be entered. In felony cases, the defendant must be present at the hearing, unless he is out on bail and cannot be found after a diligent search, or unless other special circumstances exist (See Penal Code sections 1043, 1193, 1203a, 1381). In misdemeanor cases the defendant need not be present at sentencing.

The common law "right of allocution" has been retained in California. This procedure requires that the defendant be permitted to make a personal statement to the court regarding his case, and why he feels judgment should be lenient or not even entered. The defendant's attorney may make this statement for the defendant. The defendant's also has a right not to make a statement. The speech may be used to rebut the probation report, or to introduce an equivalent report prepared by the defense suggesting a rehabilitative program for the defendant.

Unless the judge grants a motion in arrest of judgment, the judgment will be rendered by oral pronouncement by the judge. It must also be recorded, at least in summary form, in the minutes of the court. The judge must advise the defendant of his right to appeal.

Penal Code section 1202 authorizes the defendant to receive a new trial if judgment is not rendered within the time prescribed by law. The courts have interpreted this section to mean that a new trial may be granted only upon showing that the defendant was prejudiced by delay.

SENTENCING PROCESS

In the case of a felony, the offender is eligible for probation unless he fits within a section of the Penal Code which specifies that no probation shall be granted. Most of the situations for which probation is not to be granted are specified in Penal Code sections 1203.6 to 1203.09. Basically, they apply to violent felonies committed by persons with prior felony convictions, felonies committed by persons actually armed with dangerous weapons, and violent felonies committed upon aged or handicapped persons. Probation is also denied to heroin offenders under Health and Safety Code sections 11351 or 11352 when there has been a prior conviction or the quantity of heroin involved exceeded one—half of an ounce.

Penal Code section 1203 specifies that probation should be granted only in unusual circumstances in the following situations: armed during perpetration or arrest for violent felony; used or attempt to use firearm on human being; willfully inflicted great bodily injury or torture; two prior felony convictions; one prior conviction for violent felony; one prior felony conviction plus one of the following during present offense—armed, attempted to use or used deadly weapon on human being, willful great bodily injury or torture. Probation is also to be granted only in unusual cases when a public official is convicted of bribery, embezzlement of public funds, or extortion.

Probation

If a felon is eligible for probation, the judge must order a probation report. The judge may also order that the defendant be committed for a ninety day diagnostic study. The sentencing hearing can be postponed, if necessary, to obtain these reports. The written report submitted to the court will include a review of the case, and recommendations for granting or denying probation. If probation is recommended, suggested conditions or probation and restitution will be included in the report. Both the prosecution and the defense have the right to review the report before the hearing. Each side also has the right to file written statements and recommendations regarding probation and sentencing.

When a judge grants probation, he can set the term of probation up to the maximum term of imprisonment that could have been given. Where this term is less than five years, probation may extend for five full years. Jail may be made a condition of probation, as may fines and restitution. A variety of sentences to camps and farms may also be used as conditions of probation. The probation officer may be authorized by the court to require the probationer to go to work and earn money for the support of his dependents. The court may also require the defendant to submit to searches and seizures that are related to the type of crime for which he was convicted. The court retains jurisdiction to modify or revoke probation.

Calculation of Sentence

Since the repeal of the Indeterminate Sentence Act, most felonies in the California Penal Code have three sentences listed. For example, burglary in the first degree is punishable by imprisonment in state prison for two, three, or four years. In applying this type of sentence, the judge will start with the middle figure (three years for burglary in the first degree). If arguments for mitigation are persuasive, he will give the lesser sentence. He may give the greater sentence if there are aggravating circumstances in the commission of the crime. When the middle sentence is not given, the judge must state his reasons for the modification.

Penal Code sections 12022 to 12022.7 give a list of "enhancements." Enhancements are additional sentences imposed for particular conduct during the commission or attempted commission of felonies. Basically they are: one year for being armed with a firearm; one year for each convicted principal, if any one or more principal felon was armed with a firearm; one year for personally using a dangerous weapon; one year for taking, damaging or destroying property worth over $25,000; two years for taking, damaging or destroying property worth over $100,000; two years for personally using a firearm (does not apply to assault with deadly weapon); and three years for intentional infliction of significant and substantial injuries on a person other than an accomplice (does not apply to murder, manslaughter or assault with deadly weapon). Thus, a person convicted for burglary in the first degree, while armed with a firearm, would receive a four year sentence (the three year basic sentence plus the one year enhancement). The same fact may not be used for both an enhancement and as a circumstance of aggravation to get a greater sentence. The court has authority to strike the enhancements when pronouncing sentence.

Another type of enhancement is found in Penal Code section 667.5. If a conviction is for a violent felony (as specified in Penal Code Section 667.5(c)), and the defendant had at least one prior conviction for a violent felony on that list, three years are added to the current sentence for each conviction for violent felonies, unless it has been over ten years since the defendant was previously convicted or incarcerated. For felonies not designated in Penal Code section 667.5 (c), there is an additional one year term for each felony if the defendant has at least one prior felony conviction, unless it has been five years since the defendant was convicted or incarcerated. This set of enhancements is separate from those listed elsewhere in the Penal Code.

In the case of a conviction for multiple offenses, whether tried at the same trial or not, a sentencing judge has the authority to specify whether the sentences will be consecutive or concurrent. If one sentence is for life imprisonment, all other sentences merge, except for crimes committed while in prison or during escape. In other cases, the court determines which offense has the most serious punishment. This is called the principal term. It includes enhancements, and considers circumstances of mitigation or aggravation. Each additional term is called a subordinate term. Subordinate terms only include enhancements specified in Penal Code sections 667.5, 12022, 12022.5 and 12022.7. The total term is calculated by adding the principal term to one third of each subordinate term, if the terms are to run consecutively.

In addition to prison and fines specified by individual code sections, the court may impose fines where none are mentioned in the code. The maximum fine under these circumstances is $500 for misdemeanors, and $5,000 for felonies.

SUMMARY

Once a decision has been made by the defendant to go to trial, and the necessary waiting period has elapsed to obtain a courtroom, the judge will probably hold a pre-trial conference to handle details and establish procedures for the trial. If a jury trial has been selected, a group of jurors will be summoned from the jury assembly room. The attorneys will question them and may challenge them for cause, or through the use of peremptory challenges. Once twelve jurors and any alternates have been selected, they will be sworn to hear the case.

The prosecution, and perhaps the defense, will give an opening statement to the jury about the case. Witnesses will then be called. Through the testimony of witnesses and the production of items of physical evidence, the prosecution must prove each element of the crime beyond a reasonable doubt. The defense will have the opportunity to cross—examine all witnesses. After the prosecution has presented its case, the defense may call witnesses if it so desires. The defense attorney will be entitled to direct examination of defense witnesses, and the prosecution will be allowed to cross—examine. After all evidence has been presented, each side will give a closing statement to the jury.

The jurors will deliberate in secret. If a unanimous vote is obtained, they will return a verdict. If it becomes obvious that further deliberations will be useless and unanimity cannot be reached, the judge may dismiss the jury. The verdict will be read in open court if the jury returns one. Although the defendant has the right to be sentenced immediately, the case is normally continued to permit the probation department to prepare a sentencing report. The prosecution and the defense may also submit documents to assist the court in sentencing.

With the exception of a few situations listed in the penal code, probation is available to those who are convicted of either felonies or misdemeanors. The length of probation varies with the length of the maximum sentence for the crime committed. The judge has the discretion to grant probation and impose fines. He may also order confinement in the county jail for a specified period as a condition of probation.

If the defendant is sentenced to state prison, the length of the sentence will be computed in accordance with the determinant sentence law. A maximum of one third of the sentence may be deducted for the time served in compliance with the prison rules. At the end of the term, the prisoner may be released on one year parole (three years for life sentences). Parole violations can result in a six month return to prison, followed with another parole term.

DISCUSSION QUESTIONS

1. What questions would be useful on voir dire of a jury for a murder case? rape case? drunk driving case? child abuse case?
2. What questions would you ask on direct examination of an eyewitness of a murder? rape? drunk driver? child abuse?
3. What questions would you ask an eyewitness to try to show bias? untruthfulness? inability to see items he testified about? faulty memory?

4. What items of physical evidence would you produce in a murder case? rape case? drunk driving case? child abuse case? How would you establish that each item had not been altered or tampered with?

5. Based on the following sentences and enhancements, calculate the length of sentence (use both concurrent and consecutive sentences):

	Sentence
Burglary (first degree)	2, 3 or 4 years
Robbery	2, 3 or 4 years
Murder (second degree)	5, 6 or 7 years
Rape	3, 4 or 5 years
Armed during commission of felony	1 year
Used firearm in commission of felony	2 years
Intentional infliction of great bodily injury	3 years

Convictions: robbery; robbery with intentional great bodily injury; robbery and burglary; robbery and burglary with firearm used in both; robbery and rape with aggravating circumstances involved in the rape; robbery while armed and murder; robbery, burglary and murder. If full credit is earned for "good time," how much time would be spent in prison for each of the convictions?

13

Correctional
Concepts

CHAPTER OBJECTIVES

Upon reading this chapter, the student will be able to:

1. Discuss the alternatives which a convicted offender faces upon being found guilty or upon pleading guilty.

2. Recognize the percentage of offenders who actually enter the correctional process as a result of being found guilty by a judge or jury, and identify the various forms of sanctions imposed for violations of criminal offenses.

3. Discuss the creation of the Community Release Board and the specific role which it plays today.

4. Write an essay, discussing the establishment of correctional institutions in America, identifying the major systems as they were established.

5. Define minimum, medium, and maximum correctional institutions and their significance.

6. Discuss the juvenile correctional processes in the United States in general, and in California, and state the philosophy of processing juveniles in comparison to adults.

7. Identify the role and purpose of the California Youth Authority.

8. Write an essay, listing the major historical developments of the California Department of Corrections.

There are many phases to the correctional process in the State of California.   In this chapter we will be looking at the preconviction phase, jail detention, probation, corrections, and correctional institutions in California and the United States. One of the more important roles of the correctional process is that involving juveniles. We will look at the juvenile reform movement as it developed throughout the United States and California.

The history of the California Department of Corrections will be examined, as well as the new Community Release Board, which was formed as a result of California's determinate sentence laws.   The student should remember that this chapter is introductory in nature, and is not intended to be comprehensive. The correctional process plays an integral part in the principles and procedures of the justice system. It is included in this text so that the student may gain a total picture of the criminal justice system.

THE ADULT CORRECTIONAL PROCESS

We usually think of corrections primarily as imprisonment or the process after the establishment of guilt in court. The correctional process actually begins with the first police contact, and may not end until release from parole. Between these two points, various criminal justice decisions are made:

1. Whether to arrest.
2. Whether to detain.
3. What crime to charge.
4. Whether to negotiate a plea.
5. Whether to place on probation, to fine, to imprison.
6. Where to imprison.
7. How long to imprison.
8. When to parole.
9. When to terminate parole.

Police, district attorneys, judges, probation officers, jail and institutional personnel, parole boards, and parole officers are all involved in these decision-making processes. The only person who has contact with all of these criminal justice workers is the offender.

The Pre-Conviction Phase:

When a police officer has reason to believe that a person in his community has committed an act in violation of the law, he is immediately faced with the first decision: whether or not to arrest.

The arrest is the entry phase into the Correctional system. In some states, even after an arrest is officially made, the offender may be released as if he were never arrested in the first place. For example, in California (P.C. 849), a police officer may release after arrest, and the arrest shall not be deemed an arrest but a detention, under the following circumstances:

1. He is satisfied that there are insufficient grounds for making a criminal complaint against the person arrested.
2. The person arrested was arrested for intoxication only and no further proceedings are desirable.
3. The person was arrested only for being under the influence of a narcotic, drug, or restricted dangerous drug and such person is delivered to a facility or hospital for treatment and no further proceedings are desirable. [1]

If the officer decides that formal action is required, he is faced with another decision; whether to take the alleged offender into physical custody or to issue a citation or a summons to appear in court on a certain date. Those who are not cited or otherwise released are placed into physical custody; the offender is usually taken to a city or county jail to be held for a hearing, unless the offender can and does post bail.

Jail Detention

By tradition, the detention of those awaiting trial has not been the responsibility of corrections. The responsibility rests in other's hands: usually the judge's responsibility is to set bail or release on Own Recognizance; prosecutors and defense attorneys are responsible for making recommendations to the court; and while jail personnel make no detention decisions, they are responsible for keeping those who are not released prior to trial.

Although it seems more logical for corrections to assume the responsibility for pre-trial release and detention, for the most part, it is still a law enforcement responsibility.

Under what conditions are people confined or released? There are various options open to the defendant. He can post bail (money) or use the services of a bailbondsman. He can be released on a promise to appear in court (or release). If he can do neither of the above, he remains in confinement.

In summary, persons awaiting trial historically have been the responsibility of no single agency. The sheriff or superintendent of the detention facility or jail exercises physical control over them. The court controls their liberty. Neither has felt obliged to provide services. Correctional agencies consider their responsibility to be towards convicted persons only. The result is that persons awaiting trial have been ignored.

For only a few offenders does the criminal justice system concern itself with formal procedures to determine guilt. Apparently ninety percent of those convicted of felonies, and probably a larger proportion of misdemeanants, plead guilty either on their own initiative or as a result of plea negotiations.

It should be remembered that following the arrest of an alleged offender, the prosecutor's office generally has four possible alternatives in handling the case:

1. To dismiss the charges for lack of evidence, or because the offense is to minor to justify prosecution.
2. To recommend referral of the case to a diversionary program.
3. To prosecute the case on a lesser charge.
4. To prosecute to the full extent of the law.

After the defendant is found guilty or pleads guilty, he must be sentenced. This decision is the responsibility of the judge. There are many factors that influence his decision. For example, police reaction, probation reports, prosecutors' opinions, defense council's arguments, public reaction to the crime, and pressure from the defendant's family.

To assist the judge in reaching a decision, probation reports are written prior to sentence to inform the judge about pertinent facts concerning the offender, his past, and his potential for the future. The purpose is to provide the judge with information about the defendant that he would not be able to obtain in the courtroom.

The investigation is made after conviction and sometimes before conviction. California specifies that the investigation be made only after guilt is established. This report then assists the judge in sentencing. In other states, an investigation can be conducted prior to any judgment of guilt. The report would assist the judge in establishing guilt or innocence.

Some states' statutes specifically require presentence reports for particular offenders. For example, California law (Penal Code section 1203) requires that when a person is convicted of a *felony*, that the case be referred to the probation office for a report to the court regarding the circumstances surrounding the crime, prior history and record of the person, all of which be considered either in aggravation or mitigation of the punishment. The probation officer must also include his recommendations regarding the granting or denying of probation, and the conditions of probation if granted.

Court decision-making is limited by the variety of resources available. The most standard judgments are: fine, suspended sentence, restitution, confinement, or various combinations of the above, such as straight probation, probation/jail, jail and no probation, state prison, fine, probation/fine/restitution, restitution, restitution and probation.

The traditional sanction imposed for violation of the criminal law in this country was confinement.   Other sentences were considered a lenient act on the part of the court. Today, it is believed that confinement is unnecessary and inappropriate in a large number of cases. Supervision in the community—probation—has been proven to be at least as effective as confinement, and certainly less expensive. Today, probation is the most common alternative to incarceration. Confinement is retained chiefly for those offenders who cannot safely be returned to the community.   It is believed that probation, with its emphasis on assisting, and supervising the offender to adjust to the free community offers great hope for success.

Fines constitute the second most common form of sanction. The fine is as traditional a criminal sanction as imprisonment.   Fines are mostly used for offenses classified as lacking serious social harm. It is most likely to be imposed for embezzlement, fraud, larceny, battery, littering, disorderly conduct, and traffic offenses. The money received from the fine goes to the county.

Restitution.   Restitution is the payment of money to the victim of the crime. It confronts the offender with the consequences of his act, and requires that he make good the loss he has caused. In many cases restitution is a condition or requirement of probation. If the offender fails to make restitution, he can be imprisoned.

Sentencing Alternatives.   The purpose of imprisonment is the deprivation of liberty. It is usually imposed where other forms of sentences are not deemed appropriate.

In any event, it is thought that the court should impose the least drastic alternative consistent with public safety.   The court should consider each alternative, starting with the one providing the least amount of state control, but still consistent with the protection of the public and rehabilitation of the offender. Each alternative should be considered in ascending order of severity until the appropriate sanction is found.

An Associated Press story carried in the Washington *Post*, Wednesday, 3 January 1973, reported that there is a, "Small but growing number of judges throughout the country who are seeking alternatives to jail sentences for defendants convicted of a variety of crimes." The article went on to say:

Several Judges have sentenced people convicted of minor crimes to perform some kind of community service. Commissioner Marrie Matcha of Citrus Municipal Court in West Covina, Calif., said he and Judge Sam Cianchetti order about 10 to 15 percent of defendants found guilty to work in schools, hospitals, or charity programs rather than sending them to jail or fining them.

Another California jurist, Los Angeles Superior Court Judge Richard Hayden, sentenced a pickpocket to wear gloves or mittens whenever he was in a crowd. Under the sentence, Hayden said, police could arrest the pickpocket if they caught him barehanded in a crowded area.

Hayden said he hasn't heard of the man since.

Superior Court Judge Charles Z. Smith of Seattle, Wash., tried to make the punishment fit the crime.

When James M. Tidyman, 32, was found guilty of exhibiting obscene movies, Smith sentenced him to two years in jail, but suspended the sentence on the condition that the defendant contribute 100 hours of service to a charity of his choice and establish $2,000. trust fund to be used to purchase educational films for area schools. The case has been appealed.

"My approach to sentencing," Smith said, "is that prison or jail should be used only if it is necessary."

Similar crime-related sentences have been handed down in New York's Bronx Criminal Court by Judge Louis A. Cioffi, who has ordered graffiti scrawlers to perform various clean-up chores.

Judges in Florida have been among the leaders in seeking alternatives to prison.

A Miami woman found guilty of abandoning a refrigerator in which a 3 year old boy suffocated was sentenced to two years probation with the provision that her criminal record would be cleared if she found and reported at least 10 legally abandoned iceboxes.

Within a month, Earline Clark, a divorcee with two sons, had more than fulfilled the judge's order. "She had not only found and reported 10, she's found about 15 and she's still looking," reported Assistant State Attorney Terry McWilliams.

The refrigerator hunt was McWilliams' idea. "Putting someone in jail isn't really constructive," he said, "and you rarely get a chance to really see a debt repaid to society."

The Adult Correctional process then has many alternatives available in which to change the individual's behavior. The correctional process does not necessarily stop when the judgment is made and the sentence handed out.

If the indiviudal is placed on probation, the correctional process continues until the offender successfully completes probation. If the judgment was a fine and the fine was paid, the correctional process for that individual terminates.

However, for those who are sentenced to prison, the correctional process is just beginning. Depending on the nature of the crime, the offender will be confined from six months to life. Thus, for some—a very small number—the correctional process comes to an end when death occurs. The majority will be released to the community on parole. Parole is, in principle, the same as probation. The difference is that probation is a county function, in most states (including California), to handle offenders who are placed on probation, in some cases in lieu of state prison.

Parole, on the other hand, receives for supervision those individuals who are released from state prisons. The demand for parole arose from the fact that in almost all cases, except where the death penalty or life imprisonment was imposed, the prisoners had to be returned to society sooner or later. It was thought that the released prisoners needed supervision, assistance, and help for a successful reintegration into the community; parole agents were therefore assigned to fulfill these objectives.

When the individual successfully completes parole, the correctional process is ended, unless the individual commits another criminal violation and is arrested and convicted of it. He is once again introduced to the correctional process.

COMMUNITY RELEASE BOARD

The Community Release Board took the place of the Adult Authority and now has jurisdiction over both male and female inmates in the state prisons. The Board is composed of nine members who are appointed by the governor. Positions on the board are salaried, and each member is expected to devote himself on a full time basis to the work of the board.

When the prisoner is committed to state prison, his sentence must be reviewed by the board within one year. The purpose of this review is to evaluate the sentence and attempt to reach uniformity in sentencing. If it is found that the sentence is disparate it will recommend to the court that the sentence be recalled and a new sentence imposed.

The board determines the length of time a prisoner will serve by ruling on good time credits and on parole. Normally a prisoner will be entitled to a maximum of four months "good time" credit for each eight months served. Good time is earned by displaying satisfactory behavior and participating in prison programs.

The board has the authority to assist prisoners leaving prison, and may attempt to arrange employment for those released. It rules on the granting and revocation of parole. Applications for reprieve, pardon, or commutation of sentence may be referred to the board for investigation by the governor. The board may also initiate this type of investigation and forward the names of prisoners believed to merit pardon or commutation of sentence to the governor.

The Determinate Sentence Act changed the concept of parole in California. When the time served plus credit for "good time" equal the prisoner's total sentence, he may be released on parole. The board may also release the prisoner without parole in cases it determines are appropriate. If the board elects to place the prisoner on parole, the length of parole will be one year, unless a life sentence was involved. In the case of a person sentenced to life imprisonment, at least seven calendar years must be served prior to parole, but parole may not exceed three years.

One year prior to the date that the prisoner is eligible for parole, a three member panel of the board will meet with the prisoner and set the parole date. There is no automatic right to counsel at this hearing. The board has authority to set conditions it deems proper on each prisoner's parole.

If a person on parole violates the conditions of parole, he may be returned to prison. Except where the prisoner is imprisoned for a reason other than parole violation (for example, convicted of a new crime), the maximum length of confinement is six months. After the confinement is completed the prisoner may again be paroled. The length of this second parole cannot exceed the statutory parole for the offense which resulted in the initial imprisonment. The length of time served on parole prior to the parole revocation must be subtracted from the maximum term of parole in establishing the length of the second parole.

To illustrate, consider a person convicted of first degree burglary. The statutory sentence is two, three or four years. Assume there are neither enhancements nor circumstances of aggravation or mitigation. The sentence would be three years in prison. If the prisoner qualifies for maximum credit for good behavior he will be paroled in two years. The parole will be for one year. If after three months on parole he violates conditions of parole and the parole is revoked, he can be returned to prison for six months. At the end of the six months he can be placed on parole for nine more months.

CORRECTIONS AND CORRECTIONAL INSTITUTIONS

Before penal institutions were established, restitution, exile, and a variety of methods of corporal and capital punishment were used; confinement was used as a means of detention only. Those who colonized the United States brought with them the methods and laws used in their homelands to control crime. However, as early as 1682, provisions were made in Pennsylvania to build county jails to house people who had violated the law. The reason was to offer an alternative to the brutality of the British penal practices that were very much a part of colonial America.[2]   Late in the eighteenth century, the Walnut Street jail was built in Philadelphia.

In 1787, when the Constitutional Convention was active in Philadelphia, our society was actively concerned about the dignity of man and humanitarianism. During this period, the Quakers formed the Philadelphia Society for Alleviating the Miseries of Public Prisons. It was mostly through the efforts of the society that alternatives to capital and corporal punishment in Pennsylvania were seriously considered. They were also instrumental in transforming the Walnut Street jail into the first American penitentiary.

In the first three decades of the nineteenth century, the states of New York, Pennsylvania, New Jersey, Massachusetts, and Connecticut were in the process of developing and constructing large penitentiaries. Not only were the states proud of these institutions, but they foresaw an almost utopian ideal: that is, that the prison would eliminate the harsh, barbaric punishment and provide a place for repentance, reformation, and rehabilitation.[3]

The prisons were developed and planned along the lines of the various theories that explained why people commit crimes and what contributes to their becoming criminal. At the time, theorists held three factors to be the primary causes of criminal behavior: 1. a bad environment, 2. a lack of work skills, and 3. not being religious. Therefore, prison architecture and programs were designed to create an experience for the offender in which there would be no injurious influences, and where the criminal would learn the value of work. He would also have an opportunity for religious experience and to know right from wrong.

The Pennsylvania System.

Basically, two types of penal institutions were developed in the United States. The first institution developed was in Eastern State Penitentiary in 1829 at Cherry Hill, near Philadelphia. It was the most expensive public building constructed in the new world at the time, at a cost of $750,000. From the very start of the development of the prison system, the Quakers actively campaigned for solitary confinement without labor. They argued that this would bring solitary reflection as a means of achieving moral regeneration, and would prevent criminal contagion and identification of the ex-prisoner by his associates after his return to the community.

Two issues developed. The first centered on solitary confinement versus the congregate system being developed at New York's Auburn Prison. The second concerned the issue of solitary confinement without labor versus solitary confinement with labor. In 1827, a special commission of the legislature reported its opposition to solitary confinement without labor; solitary confinement *with* labor was considered to be as effective in terms of preventing communication between inmates. However, it was thought to be less expensive because inmates would work, learn an honest trade, and contribute to their own support. It is interesting to note, however, that solitary confinement *without* labor became the principle of the Eastern State Penitentiary as the prototype of the Pennsylvania system.[4] There, the offender was denied all contact with the outside world except that provided by the scriptures and visits from exemplary citizens.

The New York System.

In 1797, the Newgate Prison was opened near New York City. The major feature of the prison was the congregate lodging which Warden Thomas Eddy, a New York Quaker philanthrophist, later attributed to the prison's failure. In 1800, political appointment to the governing board supplanted the Quakers and brought mismanagement and riots. Eddy resigned in 1803. With overcrowding and disorder in the prison, it was soon to become a complete failure.

The main reason the Auburn system became popular was that the congregate confinement system at Newgate was considered a failure. The original plan when the Auburn Prison was opened in 1819 was to use the Pennsylvania idea of solitary confinement without labor. But when the prison was built, the cells were too small and close, and troubles like those at Newgate soon appeared.

Experimenting with various prison programs, a compromise plan was adopted that pursued the same three goals of the Pennsylvania system, but by a different method. Like the Pennsylvania system, it isolated the offender from society. However, the prisoners were allowed out of their cells during working hours to labor in factorylike shops. Hard labor was deemed essential to reformation of character and to the economic solvency of the prison. The contaminating effect of the congregate work situation was eliminated by a rule of silence. Inmates were prohibited from communicating in any way with other inmates or the jailers.

It is interesting to note that the warden of Auburn Prison believed that adult convicts were permanently and hopelessly incorrigible, and that the major purpose of the prison was convict labor.

Maximum Security Prisons:

From 1830 to 1900, most prisons built in the United States were maximum security prisons. Their principal features were high walls, rigid internal security, cage-like cells, sweat shops, and a bare minimum of recreation space. They were very secure. They kept the prisoners in and the public out.

Many of these prisons were well constructed, costly to build, and have lasted a long time. Together, they form the backbone of our present-day correctional system. As Table 1 shows, fifty-six of them are still in use. Many of them have been remodeled and expanded. They currently imprison 75,000 of the 110,000 felons in maximum security facilities. Today, fifty-six percent of all state prisoners in America are in structures built to serve maximum security functions.

Maximum security institutions are geared to the ultimate in supervision, control, custody and surveillance. Other considerations, such as the inmates' needs, individual or social, are allowed if they conform to

Table 13.1

State Maximum Security Prisons Still In Operation

Opening Date	Number of Prisons
Prior to 1830	6
1831 to 1870	17
1871 to 1900	33
1901 to 1930	21
1931 to 1960	15
1961 to date	21
	113 Total

Source: American Correctional Association, 1971 Directory of Correctional
Institutions and Agencies of America, Canada, and Great Britain, College Park,
Maryland, ACA, 1971.

the security requirements.   Trustworthiness on the inmates' part is not
anticipated; the opposite is assumed.

The philosophy is not limited to the older institutions.   Some of the
newest and most modern building substitute an army of guards with
closed circuit television camera and electronic sensing devices.   As the

Standards and Goals Commission's report on corrections said, "A maximum security institution represents the victory of external control over internal reform."[5]

What this philosophy means in human terms is staggering. The need for security has dictated that men live in cells, not rooms. Doors, which would afford privacy, are replaced by bars. Toilets are unscreened. Showers are taken under supervision. Contact with other prisoners or with outside visitors is severely limited.

At worst, the philosophy of control leads to inhuman living conditions. A cage does not have to be pretty or inspiring to do its job. At best, it leads to a crippling usurpation of a prisoner's responsibility for his life.

Maximum security institutions are characterized by high perimeter security, high internal security, and operating regulations that curtail movement and maximize control.

In his masterful description of penitentiaries in the United States, Tocqueville wrote in 1833 that aside from common interests, the several states: "preserve their individual independence as each of them is sovereign master to rule itself according to its own pleasure . . . By the side of one state, the penitentiaries of which might serve are a model, we find another whose prisons present the example of everything which ought to be avoided."[6]

He was right in 1833. His words are still true today.

Medium Security Correctional Institutions

According to Donald Clemmer, in his pioneer classic research on "The Prison Community,"[7] forty percent of the prisons in America have not changed. The failure to change has been attributed to prison architecture that did not stimulate change, and political corruption. However, while recognizing the truth of Clemmer's statements, it is important to point out that sixty percent of the prisons in America have made some changes.

Sutherland and Cressey have pointed out that the corrections system is experiencing a major institutional correctional trend in establishing specialized institutions.[8] In addition to the traditional maximum security institutions, medium and minimum security institutions have been developed. Special institutions for women, and youth correctional centers have been developed, along with institutions to receive and classify prisoners.

Medium Security Correctional Centers

Much of the major correctional construction in the last fifty years has been for medium security. In fact, 51 or the existing 110 medium security correctional institutions were built after 1950. Today, over 57,000 offenders, thirty percent of all state inmates, are confined in medium facilities (See Table 13.2).

The difference between minumum and maximum security prisons is that with maximum security there is a greater amount of surveillance. There is a greater degree of regimentation and less inmate freedom or movement.

Table 13.2

Security Classification of Inmate Population of State Correctional Facilities

Classification	Inmate	Total Population
Maximum	109,920	56
Medium	57,505	30
Minimum	28,485	15
Total	195,910	100

Source: ACA, 1971, Directory and Poll taken by the American Foundations Institute of Corrections which contacted the head of every state Department of Corrections.

Maximum Security Correctional Institutions

Maximum Security institutions contain the majority of the inmate population in the United States. For a time, it looked as though the United States was moving from institutional confinement to community-based corrections. In 1972, "deinstitutionalization" and "community-based corrections" had become popular terms. At the end of 1972, there were 118 fewer prisoners in state and federal prisons than in 1961 despite a two-hundred and fifty percent increase in crime.

But the trend was never as strong as it appeared. The decline in prison population had run its course by 1968. In the period from 1962 to 1968, nationally, the number of inmates decreased by fourteen percent.   But between 1973 and 1976, it increased by forty-four percent.   The prison population has increased up to the present time. This increase has caused overcrowding and a multitude of prison problems. Many states are considering a correctional institution building program.

In 1978, Governor Edmund G. Brown, Jr., from California signed bills to plan construction of new prison facilities. The prison measure appropriates $7.6 million for the preliminary planning of maximum security facilities and the razing of San Quentin and possibly Folsom prisons, the state's oldest maximum security institutions.

In California, there are five institutional classifications: maximum, close, medium A, medium B, and minimum. Maximum is the most secure form of custody—cell lock-up under supervision. Prisoners are only released from confinement in their cells to exercise, or for vocational work and academic education. Close security prisoners are not locked up all the time, but are free to enter the prison yard under general supervision. Medium A prisons allow the prisoner to work under supervision outside the prison walls, but within the fenced perimeter. Medium B security allows the prisoner to work unsupervised on the prison grounds. Minimum security allows the prisoner to work off prison grounds, unsupervised.

The Future—Community Correctional Center

A community correctional center is more of a concept than a place. To illustrate, the community correctional center concept may be structured on either a regional or network approach.

A regional approach brings several or more jurisdictions or counties together. They consolidate facilities through cooperative interjurisdictional planning, or through the operation of a new institutional facility.[9] It is more than the traditional jail, where people are locked up and forgotten. The center will provide services such as confinement for persons awaiting trial, for persons serving sentences, for short-term returnees, and confinement for persons moving to and from major state or federal institutions. The center will provide services to inmates such as psychotherapy, education and skill training. Confined individuals can also receive services from community organizations like Alcoholics Anonymous, family service organizations, legal aid, neighborhood centers, and vocational rehabilitation groups.

The overall goal of the community correctional center is to furnish physical and social environments conducive to the individual's social reintegration.

Major Institutions

The term "major institution" means a state or federally operated correctional institution for juveniles and adults. These institutions are different from detention centers, jails, or work farms, which are operated by local governments. Names used for major institutions differ from state to state. Institutions for juveniles are called schools of industry, training schools. youth development centers, state homes, or juvenile treatment centers. Institutions for adults are called prisons, correctional centers, penitentiaries, classification and reception guidance centers, state conservation centers, or state farms. There are about 200 major juvenile and 350 major adult correctional institutions in the United States.

Most of our ideas about state and federal institutions stem from the "big house" institution that has almost disappeared during the last twenty-five years. In the "big house," like Alcatraz, prisoners abided by the convict code—not informing on other prisoners, doing your own time, not talking to guards. Prison leaders taught and enforced the code. A few prisoners operated illegal activities like making "pruno"—an alcholic beverage, prison sex, where the "jockers" are the masculine partners, "punks" are the prison-made homosexuals, and "queens" are self-admitted homosexuals. Most convicts stayed close to a few prison friends, worked their job assignment, took up hobbies, read, played sports, and tried to stay out of trouble.

Today, there are still "queens," "punks," and "jockers." "Pruno" is still made. But times have changed. There is a new violence in prison in the form of race wars, stemming from organized prison gangs called the Mexican Mafia, Aryan Brotherhood, Black Guerilla Family, Nuestra Familia, and many others. Most prisoners try to avoid trouble, but it is now more difficult. They must obey informal rules of racial segregation enforced by gangs. Prisoners always run the risk of being robbed, assaulted, raped, or murdered. Convicts assault guards more frequently. Guards are more hostile toward prisoners. From the standpoint of rehabilitation and reintegration, the major adult institutions operated by the state and federal governments represent the least promising component of corrections.

Within the last five years, there has been strong support for the view that the proper business of the juvenile and criminal justice systems is *punishment.* In 1973, New York passed a law making life imprisonment mandatory for convictions of certain types of drug crimes. In 1977, California changed its sentencing laws from the indeterminate sentence to a determinate sentence system. No longer will a person be sentenced to a California prison on a 'five to life' term. Today, the judge sets the prison term in accordance with the seriousness of the offense.

Little is known about the future of these institutions. One fact is clear; if the war against crime is to be won, it will be won ultimately by correcting the conditions in our society that produce such an inordinate amount of crime. Conditions such as high unemployment, poor education, racism, poor housing, family disintegration, a breakdown of sound values, and government corruption contribute to crime. The present situation, that crime is profitable in the United States, should be changed. Correctional emphasis in the future decades must shift from the offender and concentrate on providing maximum protection to all people in society.

It should be remembered that prisons are condemned as failures because they do not rehabilitate convicts, but prisons are not intended to rehabilitate. The primary function of prisons is to protect the public; not to rehabilitate all convicts. Although it would be desirable to deter all crimes, the public must be protected from dangerous, violent individuals.

THE JUVENILE CORRECTIONAL PROCESS

Much of the focus in controlling crime has been on youth. "America's best hope for reducing crime is to reduce juvenile delinquency and youth crime." (President's Crime Commission in 1967). Why do we think this is true? Crime is a developmental process. Crime represents the maturing of adolescent delinquency. Thus, attention is focused on youth, who are more susceptible to change than adults. Behavior patterns become solidified with age. There is also concern with youth crime because it is increasing. According to juvenile court statistics, one in six male youths in the nation are referred to juvenile court. There are over one million juvenile delinquency cases (excluding traffic) handled by juvenile court each year.

Development of Juvenile Court

In 1800, with industrialism, urbanization, and the disruption of family life, juvenile delinquency became a noticeable problem. In the past, the juveniles were handled under the criminal law. Children over seven were tried as criminals. With the rise in humanitarianism, people became concerned with treatment of children.

Retribution through punishment was not seen as appropriate for juveniles. Thus, a juvenile reform movement began. There was a growing trend to build a juvenile institutions. In 1825, New York built the House of Refuge, where children were separated from adult offenders.

Juvenile legislation was enacted. In 1866, a New York statute provided for the commitment to a reformatory of any individual over twelve years who "willfully disobeys parents, guardian, or is in danger of becoming morally deprived." In 1892, New York established separate trials, dockets, and records. In 1898, Rhode Island instituted the segregation of children under sixteen years who awaited trial, keeping separate dockets and records. Also, a public and private agent were to be present at juvenile proceedings to protect the interests of the child.

The idea of juvenile court spread with amazing speed. In 1899, the Illinois legislature passed the first state-wide juvenile court act. By 1925, there were juvenile courts in every state except two. The last state to pass juvenile court law was Wyoming, in 1945. Today, there are approximately 2,700 courts to hear juvenile cases.

Who was included in juvenile court legislation? In 1899, the original juvenile court act in Illinois was quite simple; it covered only those juveniles who violated the criminal laws and municipal ordinances. By

1900, this legislation included "incorrigibles" and children who formed undesirable associations. In 1905, the definition was further extended to include those who were idle, who wandered, and who displayed bad habits. With the expansion of the definition, more delinquents were eligible for confinement in state "reformatories."

With more juveniles eligible for confinement, more and more juveniles were actually placed in juvenile halls, reformatories, camps, and ranches for "status" offenses. A study in 1971 by the Children's Bureau found that 41.6% of the 9,177 juveniles were confined for "status" crimes. [10] These are crimes that only juveniles can commit. In increasing numbers, juveniles were confined for such crimes as truancy, breaking curfew, alcohol use, smoking, running away from home, incorrigibility, and habitual profanity.

In 1973, the Illinois Unified Code of Corrections went into effect. The new code prohibited the confinement of juveniles for status offenses, since they are not criminal.

In 1977, California passed Assembly Bill 3121, drastically changing the juvenile justice system in California. A provision of the bill affected the status offender, commonly called "601 W & I offenders." The law stated that status offenders could no longer be confined in a secure facility, such as a juvenile hall or any other lock-up facility, but must be treated in a non-secure setting, such as a children's shelter or a community-based center.

There were other changes affecting the juvenile justice system in California. The juvenile law violators ("602 W & I violators") are treated more harshly. Previously, the probation officer would file 602 petitions with the juvenile court. Now, the probation officer assists the district attorney, who decides what to file. The biggest change in juvenile justice in California is the presence of the district attorney in the juvenile courtroom. The district attorney appears at every hearing, and argues what he believes the people of California want done with the juvenile. He does not necessarily speak for the probation department. The effect and importance of the district attorney in the juvenile courtroom is having an impact; more juvenile law violators are confined in juvenile hall, and to ranches or camps. Twice as many 602 petitions are being filed.

There are changes taking place in the juvenile justice system across the nation. For example, Massachusetts changed from institutional confinement to a community—based treatment approach because juveniles were not being effectively rehabilitated in institutions.

Society wanted juveniles removed and kept out of sight for its protection. Thus, "treatment" became the first step in long criminal careers for many juveniles. Juveniles who experienced isolation from the community, boredom, cold showers, beatings, individual isolation, and loneliness were expected to return to the same social conditions which contributed to their delinquency to lead law-abiding lives.

The California Juvenile Justice System

Laws relating to juveniles are found in the Welfare and Institutions Code. The code describes three classes of juveniles which fall within the jurisdiction of the juvenile court: neglected and abused children under Section 300; children exhibiting delinquent tendencies such as truancy from school, run-aways, incorrigibles, are covered in Section 601; and those juveniles who have committed any violation of a law or ordinance in Section 602.

The juvenile enters the juvenile justice system by falling within one of these three classes, and can be referred to the probation department by parents, school authorities, or by a police officer.

There are various alternatives or options available to the police officer in handling juveniles: the officer may counsel and release the juvenile at the scene; may release the juvenile to parents; may issue a citation when the juvenile is required to report to the probation department; or the officer may take the juvenile to the Juvenile Hall or Children's Shelter.

The probation officer, like the police officer, may counsel and release the juvenile. The officer may refer the juvenile to a community-treatment agency or may extend informal supervision for a period not to exceed six months. There are other options open to the probation officer; he may place the minor in custody, or tell the minor to remain at home while a petition is being filed.

The juvenile court has certain procedures to follow. In hearing a case, the court must decide whether it has jurisdiction, what the status of the minor should be, and what care and treatment is necessary to correct the problem. The court may dismiss the petition and release the minor, or may make the minor a dependent child of the court (Welfare and Institutions Code, section 300), or a ward of the court (Welfare and Institutions Code, section 601 and 602). It may place the minor on probation, in a foster home, in a private institution. The juvenile may also be released to the parents, or confined in Juvenile Hall or a ranch or camp. The court may commit more serious offenders to the California Youth Authority.

In the majority of cases, the juvenile is declared a ward of the court, and is placed on probation while remaining in the home. Probation supervision consists of working with the minor and maintaining contact with the juvenile, the juvenile's parents, and school authorities.

The California Youth Authority

According to the California Youth Authority, (CYA), its basic mission is to protect society by reducing the level of crime and delinquency among youth in California. It was created in 1941 with the basic goals of youth development, delinquency prevention, rehabilitation, treatment, and research.

The California Youth Authority has a director appointed by the governor for a four year term. The department's headquarters are in Sacramento. Institutions, parole offices, community services offices, and other special projects are located in various parts of the state. Youth Authority programs are carried out in ten institutions, six conservation

INSTITUTION AND CAMP LOCATIONS

camps, and forty parole field offices. In addition to its residential and parole programs, the department has been increasingly involved in comprehensive programs providing community services, and in youth development projects in high delinquency areas.

Youth Authority Wards

The most common reasons for commitment to the Youth Authority are for robbery and burglary. Since 1966, the average period of commitment to Youth Authority institutions has increased from 9.4 months in 1966 to 12.7 months in 1975. In 1976, the length of stay dropped to 12.0 months. Recent trends indicate that commitments will level off at about 11.0 months. The youths' average age is seventeen years.

THE HISTORY OF THE CALIFORNIA DEPARTMENT OF CORRECTIONS

When California became a state in 1850, no mention had been made of penal affairs in the constitution. Local jails handled many of the penal problems. The death penalty was meted out and enforced on the local level for a variety of offenses. Strangely enough, some of the old offenses are still on the books of our Penal Code today. In 1850, each county jail was designated as a state prison. The first legislature that convened defined various crimes, and specified the punishment and term to be served in one of the various jails. Some of these jails still exist, and are in the same condition that they were in over one hundred years ago. A few of them are being used today.

In 1851, the legislature granted private citizens the right to lease prisoners. In return for their labor, the citizens agreed to house, feed, and guard the prisoners. This arrangement did not prove to be acceptable to the state; prisoners escaped, and lessees broke their agreements. At one time armed bands of these escaped prisoners roamed the countryside. It was therefore logical, when a storm drove the old Spanish prison ship ashore on what is now San Quentin Point, for the state to decide to use the clay banks to build a prison at this point. San Quentin thus became the first prison in California. By 1858, San Quentin had already become so overcrowded that the legislature authorized construction of another prison. This statement sounds vaguely familiar today. The new prison was to be built at Folsom, from granite quarried from the ground on which the prison was to stand. The first cell block was not completed until 1880. That cell block is still in use today, although it has undergone minor renovations and remodeling. So, while San Quentin became a seething mass of human derelicts thrown together in a situation of idleness and violence in what we know today as a close security setting, Folsom became the formidable maximum security prison of the state, where the most hardened criminals were incarcerated. With the completion of Folsom, the legislature decided that they were finished with prison construction in California. They had met the penal needs of the state for all time. The 1880 legislature could hardly foresee the population explosion in future years.

In 1879, the first step was taken to improve the administrative system of the prison. The California State Constitution of 1879 created a board of five prison directors to administer the state prisons. The lieutenant governor who traditionally was the warden, was replaced by regular wardens.

**Institutions
Department of Corrections**

In 1893, the Legislature adopted parole as a release procedure, and in 1911, it authorized a state reformatory in order to segregate the younger offenders and prevent further corruption. It was also in 1911 that the first state-controlled industry program was inaugurated for prison labor. The jute mill at San Quentin was taken over by the state, and the bags which were manufactured were sold to farm groups.

In 1915, the first prison road camp was established at Liggett Valley. The work was on Route 1, which later became known as the Redwood Highway. Legislation authorized the employment of prison labor on highways, and set a "good time" allowance for prisoners. It also provided penalties for interference with prisoners.

In 1917, the indeterminate sentence became law. The California State Board of Prison Directors was authorized to set sentences within minimum and maximum periods as prescribed by law.

In 1924, the Department of Penology was formed. This new department contained six divisions: Prisons and Paroles, Criminal Identification and Investigation, Pardons and Commutations, Narcotics Enforcement, Criminology, and Women's Institutions. The last division foretold of things to come, because at this time, the women were housed in a segregated section at San Quentin.

In 1931, the Board of Prison Terms and Paroles was created. The duties of this board were the fixing of terms, granting of paroles, and restoration of civil rights. In 1932, the California Institution for Women was constructed at Tehachapi, and the women were to leave San Quentin, never to return except for cases of execution for the death penalty. Tehachapi was to remain a women's prison for twenty years, until it was severely damaged by an earthquake in 1952.

The first major breakthrough in the field of rehabilitation was made in 1941, when the California Institution for Men was built at Chino. This provided a minimum security institution with vocational training and education for younger adult members. San Quentin was adjudged the worst prison in the world. Warden Holohan had been pistol whipped by convicts in an escape attempt. While lacking some of the convictions of modern penologists, he was certainly a benevolent administrator compared to those who followed. He had succeeded in getting a bill through the legislature to change the capital punishment method from hanging to the gas chamber. Holohan had been a former United States marshal. Under his administration, some progress had been made in making San Quentin a more modern penal institution. With Holohan passing from the scene, it was decided that what San Quentin needed was a rough administrator; Court Smith, a former county sheriff, was moved down from Folsom to do the job. Smith was one of the harshest administrators San Quentin had ever seen. He reinstated the dungeon, with all of the "Chamber of Horror" effects imaginable. He painted small circles on the floor and men were made to stand for hours within the circles. If they fell out of the circles, they were beaten and otherwise severely punished. Under his rule, San Quentin became a true hellhole, but this kind of treatment bred only more unrest, until finally the governor stepped in and removed the entire board of prison directors from office. The new board immediately fired Smith and began to search for a new warden to keep the lid on the huge, overcrowded prison. They were unable to agree, but finally asked Clinton Duffy, then secretary to the board of prison directors, to take over for thirty days. Duffy, who was born and raised on prison grounds, immediately started the reforms that he had dreamed of all his life. Dungeon doors were torn from the walls and became San Quentin's first contribution to the war effort. Circles were eliminated from the floors and the entire food service was vastly improved. Duffy became the first warden to walk through the yard without a guard. At the end of thirty days, Duffy's appointment was extended to a full four years. San Quentin was well on its way to becoming a modern prison with all the concepts that this connotes.

Earl Warren, then the governor of California, saw the need for vast and extensive improvement in the penal system. In 1942, the Youth Authority was established. This was a major stride in the treatment of youthful offenders.

In 1944, by an act of the legislature, the Department of Corrections was established, and Governor Warren began to look for the most capable person he could find to operate this department. He chose Richard A. McGee, and experienced prison administrator. From this time on, the Department of Corrections in California had a direction and a goal. The 1944 Act set up a director as the chief administrator and provided for the appointment of an adult authority charged with the fixing of terms, granting of paroles, recommendations of pardons, and administration of the Bureau of Paroles. It also established a board of corrections as a coordinating group to undertake a study of the general crime problem.

The Reception-Guidance Center was established as a separate unit at San Quentin. This provided for the segregation of male prisoners prior to their transfer to other facilities of the department, where recommended treatment programs were initiated. Incidentally, the first testing program, the guidance center at San Quentin, was set up and operated by an inmate with a background in education who became an expert in this field.

It soon was apparent that California was to need more institutions to meet the needs of the exploding population. Each succeeding institution was to have a definite purpose in the overall plan of corrections. The first of these institutions was the California Vocational Institution, established at Lancaster in 1945. It was later to be renamed the Deuel Vocational Institution, in honor of Senator Deuel. This provided an institution for the incarceration and training of youth who were too inexperienced in crime to be committed to an adult prison, but who were also too mature to profit from the program in a Youth Authority training school. In 1953, this institution was moved from Lancaster to its new home in Tracy. Inmates committed to this institution are Youth Authority commitments, and younger males committed by the Director of Corrections. The median age at the Deuel Vocational Institution is 23.5 years. The institution places a heavy emphasis on vocational and academic education.

In 1946, a state prison was established at Soledad as a medium security prison. This was to be the first completely planned unit in the Department of Corrections, and was first occupied in 1951. Its purpose is to train inmates in agriculture, and to provide vocational and academic training.

California now needed a facility to house the mentally and physically ill. The medical facility opened in temporary quarters at Terminal Island in 1950. Upon completion of its new permanent facilities, it moved to Vacaville in 1955.

In 1951, the Reception-Guidance Center at Chino was opened. This was the first institution planned and built for the segregation, diagnosis, and study of court committed felons. This institution receives felons from eleven southern counties, while the northern counties received felons at Vacaville.

In 1952, an earthquake severely damaged the institution at Tehachapi. It was fortunate for the department that the construction was nearly completed for a new institution for women at Corona, California. The women were immediately evacuated from Tehachapi and moved into their new quarters some six months before the actual anticipated activation date. The California Institution for Women is still operated at Corona, California.

In 1953, the legislature created the Youth Authority Department. The legislature redesignated the responsibilities of the director of corrections and adult authority, created a separate Department of the Youth Authority, and set up a separate director for corrections and youth authority.

In 1949, the Legislature authorized an additional medium security institution for Southern California. With the increase in prison population, and the majority of the inmates falling into the medium security class, it was known that California was in dire need of another medium security institution similar to the one at Soledad. In 1953, a facility for older and chronically infirm inmates was established. It is known as the California Men's Colony. This institution housed 1,400 minimum security older and infirm inmates. The obsolete housing and changing population led to a reduction of this unit to its present level of 150 inmates in 1979. The main facility, Men's Colony East, was completed in 1961 to house 2,400 medium security inmates. One of the four 600 bed units was converted to a medical program to house 600 psychotics in remission.

In 1955, the former women's institution at Tehachapi was repaired and reactivated to house male inmates. This step was taken to provide an additional medium-minimum security institution. Known as the California Correctional Institution, it consists of a minimum security unit of 2,537 beds and a 640 bed medium security unit opened in 1967.

1959 was a milestone for the California Department of Corrections. The department created the conservation camp program. Two institutions were built. The original camp was established in 1915 as a road camp; however, the operation of the conservation centers to train men specifically for work in conservation and forestry was a new concept.

The California Correctional Institution near Susanville was originally opened in 1963 as the California Conservation Center, to serve as a hub facility administering the northern California conservation camp program. It has a design capacity of 1,224. With the diminishing number of minimum security inmates available, the camp program was cut back. In 1975, the institution was renamed and converted to provide skill center training to medium security inmates. The facility's construction reflects its original minimum security purpose.

The Sierra Conservation Center was originally designed to administer the central California conservation camp program. This was the last institution built by the department. The center was opened in 1965, and still trains inmates for placement in the fourteen outlying conservation camps still operating throughout the state. It has two 608-man units (one minimum and one medium security), each with thirty-eight 16-man dormitories. In 1961, new programs, termed increased correctional effectiveness programs (commonly referred to as the ICE Program), were created. Several programs in both institutions and parole systems stressed matching the patient with the best program for the most effective response, including intensive counseling and intensive supervision. The Therapeutic Community Program was part of this.

The California Rehabilitation Center, the civil addict program for treating and controlling narcotic addicts, was authorized by the legislature in 1961. In 1963, the department opened the Rehabilitation Center in a facility received from the federal government near Norco; it had been a former luxury hotel which opened in the 1920s, and which was converted during World War II to a naval hospital. Its capacity is for 1,963 male addicts, housed in 60-man dormitories of temporary wartime construction, and 400 female addicts housed in former nurses' quarters refurbished to house two women to a room.

Existing institutions are characterized by their large sizes. They have physical plants which are either substandard, or laid out in such a way that the ability of administrators to manage today's inmate population safely and effectively is restricted. They are generally located in non-urban areas. Further characteristics include: a concentration of male felons in northern California, although the majority of male felon commitments come from southern California; only one institution for women; and an inability to provide adequate work opportunities for all inmates.

The California Department of Corrections is responsible for the control and programming of 21,000 prisoners in institutions, and 19,000 persons on parole supervision. The Department of Corrections operates twelve major institutions, nineteen minimum security conservation camps, two community correctional centers and sixty parole offices, outpatient psychiatric clinics, and local cooperative programs. The California Department of Corrections employs 8,000 people. The two largest groups are correctional officers and parole agents.

In earlier years, the California Department of Corrections concentrated on the development of institutional programs such as education, vocational training, and counseling. In the 1960s the main emphasis was on the development of parole services, the expansion of the conservation camp program, and the establishment of the civil addict program. In the 1970s, the California Department of Corrections is planning new facilities, expanding opportunities to women and minorities, and developing Department of Corrections training academies. It is also adjusting to recent correctional legislation, and is minimizing institutional violence.

Recent California Correctional Legislature

There are two recent bills that became law in 1975 and 1977. In 1975, AB 1506 restored to all prisoners their civil rights, except those which must be held in abeyance for reasonable public protection and for the security of the institution. The bill identified certain rights which could not be denied for any reason, such as the right to marry, to initiate civil actions, or to receive personal visits.

In 1977, SB 42 took effect. The bill eliminated the indeterminate sentence represented by, "commitment to the adult authority for the term prescribable by law"—such as five years to life, and substitutes a specific release date determined by a complex formula. Thus, the determinate sentence became a reality.

California Department of Corrections' Inmates

Only about fifteen percent of all persons convicted of felonies are sent to state prison. Most of the men are sent to prison for homicide (18.2%), robbery (27.5%), burglary (13%), assault (2.8%), and drug crimes (14.4%).

The median age of male inmates is 29.2 years, and has been declining steadily in recent years. About 26% of the male inmates are less than twenty-five years of age. The women are slightly older, with a median age of 29.6, with 23% under twenty-five years of age.

Nearly half of the men in prison are native Californians. Three-fourths have lived in this state for at least ten years. A total of 55.6% are minorities—33.7% Black, 20.1% Mexican-American, and 1.8% other. Among the women felons, minorities constituted 53.4% of the total, with 34.7% Black, 16.8% Mexican-American, and 1.9% other.

The typical inmate, both male and female, possesses average intelligence, and the median educational achievement level is just under the eighth grade for males, and above eighth grade for females.

The changing characteristics of the inmate population have resulted in the department having an oversupply of minimum security facilities, and a shortage of facilities for medium security inmates. There are a number of reasons why minimum housing is not suitable for housing higher security inmates. The changes in the inmate population, which began in the mid-1960s, reflect changing community attitudes and sentencing practices, as a continually increasing proportion of the prison population is composed of those who have committed offenses against persons rather than against property. For example, in 1963, the percentage of inmates convicted of crimes against property was 35.3%, while the percentage convicted of crimes against persons was 37.1%. In 1977, the percentages were 21.5% and 58.9% respectively.

Inmate Violence and Gangs

In addition to the changing characteristics of the inmate population, California prisons are now seriously affected by the activities of prison gangs, which originated in the late 1960s and achieved prominence in the last few years. While neither gangs nor violence are new to prisons, certain aspects of the current gang activity present new problems to the prison administrator. One is the tendency of gangs to develop along ethnic lines. This means that the racial tensions which exist normally in a prison, as they do in the community, are exacerbated, and gang rivalries develop into widespread racial strife. The difficulties in identifying gang members, and in taking action to isolate them result in charges of racism, and may in fact cause certain inmates to be regarded as gang members purely on the basis of racial-ethnic background and personal association. Another characteristic is the increasing effectiveness of the organization and discipline of gangs, and the stability of the leadership. Up to now, it has been axiomatic that inmates were individualistic and were only concerned with doing their own time; they were therefore not capable of effective group action. The new gangs belie that, as the members display a discipline and willingness to carry out orders regardless of the personal consequences. This creates serious problems for prison administrators, and permits the effective exploitation of large numbers of inmates by a relatively small percentage of the population.

A recent survey of violent incidents during 1975-76, and 1976-77, reveals that male inmates committed for homicide, robbery, and assault were members of gangs in significantly greater numbers than their proportion in the prison population. This tends to support the judgment of prison administrators that the changing characteristics of the inmate population are contributing to the increase in violence in the institutions. Corollary to and further dramatizing this finding is the increase in violent incidents in the prisons. In 1970, the number of institutional incidents involving assaults by inmates with weapons was 79: in 1976, 204.

Inmates Rights

The activities of the gangs have coincided with the dramatic increase in recent years of inmate rights, and with efforts to liberalize the restrictions on inmate behavior, paralleling and reflecting the civil rights movement in American society. Through court decisions, legislative changes, and administrative actions, restrictions on visiting, mail, and access to legal services have been modified drastically. Inmates have had restored by statute the vast majority of civil rights. Their rights to constitutional liberties have been affirmed and reaffirmed, and their protection by federal courts has been vigorous. As a result of these factors, the discretion of the prison administrator has been markedly curbed.

While this basic upheaval in the balance of power between inmates and staff has certainly not created the prison gangs, they have capitalized on and exploited the opportunities these changes offered to increase the flow of contraband, to recruit new members, to facilitate communications both within and between institutions, and in general to develop financial resources and cohesion which would have been difficult, if not impossible, under conditions as they formerly existed.

The challenge this poses to prison administrators is how to deal with the problem of gangs and the violence they cause without overreacting at the expense of the legitimate rights of the majority of inmates, who respect the rules and rights of each other. Free society faces the same challenge as it attempts to respond to the problems of crime, and the depredations of the few on the many, without trampling on the civil rights of everyone and anyone.

SUMMARY

In this chapter we learned that the correctional process actually begins with the first contact with the police, and may not end until the release from parole. The police officer plays an extremely important role in the correctional process.

We saw that approximately ten percent or less of the convicted felons and misdemeanants actually are involved in the normal procedures involved with the determination of guilt. Most of these individuals will plead guilty, and are directly referred to the correctional system. We have seen what an important role the judges in the criminal justice system play as they deal with specific penalties, and recommend correctional programs for convicted offenders.

We discussed the Community Release Board, which derived its authority as the result of the new determinate sentence laws in the State of California. We saw that the Community Release Board has taken the place of the Adult Authority and now has jurisdiction over both male and female inmates in state prisons. The major responsibility of the board is to determine the length of time a prisoner will serve by ruling on good time credits while he is in prison and on parole.

In examining the development of corrections and correctional institutions in the U.S., we found that in the first three decades of the nineteenth century the states of New York, Pennsylvania, New Jersey, Massachusetts, and Connecticut were instrumental in developing and constructing formal institutions for convicted offenders. Maximum and minimum security correctional centers were defined, and we learned that the basic difference between maximum and minimum security prisons is that in a maximum security prison there is a greater amount of surveillance, a greater degree of regimentation, and less inmate freedom of movement compared to that of a minimum security prison.

The juvenile correctional process is considered to be one of the most critical phases in the overall correctional process. To rehabilitate the convicted juvenile offender is to eliminate the major cause of adult criminality. We saw that in California, juveniles enter the justice system by falling within one of three classes:
1. Neglected and abused children.
2. Children exhibiting delinquent tendencies.

3. Those juveniles who have committed any violation of state laws or ordinances.

The California youth authority was established in 1941 with the basic goals of youth development, delinquency prevention, rehabilitation, and treatment and research.

The history and development of the California Department of Corrections was examined. Folsom State prison was the first "cell block" established in California. Beginning in 1879, the legislature began to develop the Department of Corrections as it is known today. For example, in 1893 the legislature adopted parole as a release procedure, and establish a system in order to segregate the younger offenders and prevent further corruption. In 1915 the first prison road camp was established; in 1917 the indeterminate sentence became law; in 1924 the department of penology was formed; and in 1931 the Board of Prison Terms and Paroles was created.

Throughout California history, the correctional process has undergone many changes in attitudes and philosophies. Most recently, in 1977, the new determinate sentences law was established, which did away with all indeterminate sentences in the State of California.

DISCUSSION QUESTIONS

1. Discuss the alternatives which a convicted offender faces upon being found guilty, and how the actual decisions are made.

2. What are the various forms of sanctions imposed on convicted offenders, and how is the specific sanction actually imposed?

3. What responsibilities has the new Community Release Board taken from the Adult Authority of California? Discuss the role of the new board.

4. Discuss the establishment of correctional institutions in America. What are the major systems?

5. What is the purpose of minimum security institutions? Maximum security institutions? What advantages does each have? Disadvantages?

6. Why do we have a different philosophy in handling juveniles compared to adults? What is the philosophy?

7. Develop your own correctional philosophy. Discuss your model, indicating how it differs from existing concepts, and how it could be implemented in today's society.

REFERENCES

1. California Penal Code, Section 849.

2. The Great Law of Pennsylvania, 1682, by William Penn made provisions to eliminate to a large extent the stocks, pillories, branding iron, and gallows.

3. For a history of these developments, see Rothman, David, The discovery of the Institution: *Social Order and Disorder in the New Republic*, Little, Brown and Co., 1971, Chapters 3 and 4.

4. See Lewis, Orlando F., *The Development of American Prisons and Prison Customs* 1776-1845. Albany: Prison Association of New York, 1922.

5. Standards and Goals Commission, *Corrections*, p. 343.

6. Gustave de Beaumont and Alexis de Tocqueville, *On The Penitentiary System in the United States and Its Application in France*, H.R. Lantz, Ed. (Southern Illinois University Press, 1964) p. 48.

7. Clemmer, Donald, *The Prison Community*, 2d ed., New York: Holt, Rhinehart, and Winston, Inc. 1966, p. xii.

8. Sutherland, Edwin and Cressey, Donald, *Criminology*, 8th ed., Philadelphia: J.B. Lippincott Company, 1970, p. 491.

9. National Council on Crime and Delinquency, *A Regional Approach; A Plan—Maybe a Dream*, N. Y. NCCD, 1971.

10. 54.6% confined for property crime, 3.8% for offenses against persons.

Annotated Bibliography

American Bar Association. The Prosecution and the Defense Function: A Report Prepared by the Advisory Committee on the Prosecution and Defense Functions of the Project on Standards of Criminal Justice. New York: Institute of Judicial Administration, 1971. A guide for the prosecutor in modern America. Standards are set out for both the prosecutor and defense counsel.

Berkson, Larry C., Steven W. Hays and Susan J. Carbon (eds.). Managing the State Courts: Text and Readings. St. Paul, Minnesota: West Publishing; 1977. Intended as a text for future court administrators, this collection includes articles on judges, court administration, budgeting and similar subjects.

Blaustein, Albert P. and Charles O. Porter. The American Lawyer. Chicago: The University of Chicago Press, 1954. A summary of the facts, cognate material, and recommendations assembled by the Survey of the Legal Profession team.

California Jurisprudence, Third Edition. Bancroft Whitney, San Francisco. Volumes 16 to 22 of this legal encyclopedia are on criminal law. The subsection Indictment and Information gives detailed analysis of requirements for accusatory pleadings.

California Misdemeanor Procedure Benchbook, Continuing Education of the Bar, 1975. This volume sets out procedures for the trial of misdemeanors. One chapter is devoted to the complaint. Attacks on the pleadings are discussed.

Chroust, Anton. The Rise Of The Legal Profession In America. Norman: University of Oklahoma Press, 1965. An examination of the colonial experience as well as the revolution and post-revolutionary era.

Countryman, Vern and Ted Finman. The Lawyer In Modern Society. Boston: Little Brown & Company, 1966. A detailed analysis of the lawyer, his practice, profession, problems, and background.

Downie, Leonard Jr. Justice Denied: The Case For Reform of the Courts. New York: Praeger Publishers; 1971. A critical study of the American court system by a journalist.

Edwards, John. The Law Officers of the Crown. London: Sweet & Maxwell, 1964. A study of the offices of Attorney-General and Solicitor-General of England with an account of the office of the Director of Public Prosecutions of England.

Eulau, Heinz and John D. Spragne. Lawyers in Politics: A Study In Professional Convergence. Indianapolis: The Bobbs-Merrill Company, Inc., 1964. A study of lawyers as politicians, their role and behavior based on data collected in 1957 by the State Legislative Research Project.

Flaherty, David. Essays In The History of Early American Law. Chapel Hill: The University of North Carolina Press, 1969. Selected works of historians of early American law covering the seventeenth and eighteenth century.

Frank, Jerome. Courts on Trial; Myth and Reality in American Justice. New York: Athenium; 1970. A major work by a distinguished American judge on the subject of how judges make decisions and how courts work.

Fricke, Charles W. and Arthur L. Alarcon, California Criminal Procedure Legal Book Corp., Los Angeles, 1974. This is a standard text on the procedural aspects of criminal cases. Chapters are devoted to the complaint, indictment and information.

Friedman, Lawrence. A History Of American Law. New York: Simon & Schuster, 1973. A general history of the development of American law and legal institutions.

George, B. James Jr., and Ira A. Cohen, The Prosecutor's Sourcebook (2 volumes and supplements) Practising Law Institute, New York City, 1969. These volumes contain a collection of essays on a variety of topics related to the prosecution of criminal cases.

Grossman, Brian. The Prosecutor. Toronto: University of Toronto Press, 1967. The political realities of prosecution, its social implications and economic constraints.

Hayden, Richard F. C., and William B. Keene, California Superior Court Trial Judge's Benchbook, West Publishing Co., St. Paul, 1973 with 1976 supplement. This book outlines court procedures in order to assist the judge in a felony trial. Code sections and major cases are referenced.

Heyman, Phillip B. and William H. Kenety, The Murder Trial of Wilbur Jackson—A Homicide in the Family, West Publishing Co., St. Paul, 1975. By use of exhibits used in trial and exerps from the trial transcripts, the authors follow a murder case from police report to appeal.

Jackson, Donald Dale. Judges. New York: Antheneum; 1974. Based largely on interviews with judges from all levels of the system, Jackson's book has some interesting insights into the work of the American judiciary.

Knab, Karen Markle (ed.). Courts of Limited Jurisdiction: A National Survey. Washington, D.C.: National Institute of Law Enforcement, 1977. A state-by-state study of the organization of the lower courts.

Lewis, Merlin, Warren Bundy and James L Hagne. An Introduction to the Courts and Judicial Process. Englewood Cliffs, N. J.: Prentice Hall; 1978. Addresses the criminal process in great detail, along with the roles of the judge, the prosecutor and defense counsel.

Mayers, Lewis. The Machinery of Justice: An Introduction to Legal Structure and Process. Totowa, N. J.: Littlefield, Adams and Company; 1973. One of the better surveys written by a lawyer on the structure of American courts and procedure—civil, criminal, administrative and military.

McMahon, James L., et al. Court Security: A Manual of Guidelines and Procedures. Washington, D.C.: National Sheriff's Association; 1978. A comprehensive and practical guidebook, financed by L.E.A.A., examining a large part of the court enforcement mission.

Morris, Richard. Studies In The History Of American Law. New York: Octagon Books, Inc., 1964. An introduction to the early history of American law, some influences and reaction.

Phillips, Steven, No Heroes, No Villians — The Story of a Murder Trial, Vintage Books, New York, 1978. Written by the prosecutor of the case, this book follows a homicide case from time of the shooting through appeal.

Post, C. Gordon. An Introduction to the Law. Englewood Cliffs, N. J.: Spectrum (Prentice-Hall, Inc.); 1963. A paperback exploration of the historical origins of American law and legal procedure. Good beginner's book by a political scientist.

Pound, Roscoe. The Lawyer From Antiquity To Modern Times, With Particular Reference To The Development of Bar Associations In The United States. St. Paul: West Publishing Company, 1953. A study prepared for and published by the Survey of the Legal Profession under the auspices of the American Bar Association tracing the lawyer and his bar associations.

Robertson, John A. (ed.). Rough Justice: Perspectives on the Lower Criminal Courts. Boston: Little, Brown and Company; 1974. Includes articles on the evolution, sociology, politics and performance of the lower courts, as well as exploration of suggested alternatives and reforms.

Rubin, H. Ted. The Courts: Fulcrum of the Justice System. Pacific Palisades, California: Goodyear Publishing; 1976. Concentrates on roles, problems, court administration and reform.

Spaniol, Joseph F. The United States Courts: Their Jurisdiction and Work. Washington, D.C.: U. S. Government Printing Office; 1975. A citizen's guide to the federal courts, by an officer of the Administrative Office of the Courts.

Turner, David R. Court Officer. New York: Arco Books; 1970. Essentially a preparation for the New York civil service exams, this guide provides some insights to the work of court officers.

Wells, Kenneth M. and Paul B. Weston, Criminal Procedure and Trial Practice, Prentice Hall, Englewood Cliffs, 1977. This book contains a step by step review of procedures involved from filing of the case through appeal. Juvenile procedures and the rights of prisoners are also covered.

Witkin, B. E. California Criminal Procedure and California Criminal Procedure— 1978 Supplement. Bancroft Whitney, San Francisco. These two books are designed to be used together. Detailed discussions of statutes and case law are combined with references to most major works on the procedural aspects of the criminal case from filing to appeal. Pleading is covered in detail.

Index

A

ACCUSATION, 166, 167
ACCUSATORY PLEADINGS, 255
Attack on, 220
Amendment, 219
Defined, 206
Dismissals, 237
Motion to set aside, 220
Multiple defendants, 219
Multiple offense, 217
Principles of, 214
Requirements, 213
ADULT CORRECTIONAL PROCESS, 272
ALCOHOLIC BEVERAGE CONTROL, 98
Authority, 98
Enforcement duties, 99
Licenses, 99
  Off sale
  On sale
Structure, 100
ALTERNATE SENTENCE CRIMES, 119
AMERICAN BAR ASSOCIATION, 123
APPELLATE COURT
California, 140
ARRAIGNMENT, 226
Appearance of defendant, 255
Attorney present, 232
Failure to appear, 229
Felony, 231
Guaranteed rights, 228
Misdemeanors, 231

Purpose, 253
ARREST, 55
Accomplishing, 56
Defined, 52
Duty upon, 63
Duty versus requirement, 56
Felony, 62
Misdemeanor, 62
Peace officer, 57
Private citizen, 60
Summoning assistance, 53
Warrants, 64
  Abstract, 66
  Bench, 67
  Form, 64
  Service, 66
ARREST RESPONSIBILITY, 71
ARTICLES OF CONFEDERATION
Article Four, 2
Extradition, 3
ATTORNEY GENERAL
California, 102, 126
United States, 126
AUBURN PRISON, 280
AUTOPSIES, 85, 87

B

BAIL, 17, 187
After conviction, 194
Application, 189
Bondsman, 189

Categories, 187
  Bond, 189
  Cash, 188
  Equity and real property, 189
Change of amount, 190
Defined, 187
Forfeiture, 195
Nature, 192
Procedure, 192
Purpose, 187
Upon arrest, 193
BAR ASSOCIATION, 116, 119, 123
American, 123
BETTS V. BRADY, 32
BIFURCATED TRIAL, 239
BILL OF RIGHTS
Amendment I, 6, 8
  Peaceable assembly, 10
  Press, 10
  Religion, 8
  Right to petition, 10
  Speech, 9
Amendment IV, 10
  Search and Seizure, 11
  Warrants, 11
Amendment V, 12
  Double jeopardy, 12
  Grand indictment, 12
  Self incrimination, 13
Amendments, 6
English Version, 6
BLACKSTONE, 119

C

CALIFORNIA BOARD OF PRISON
    TERMS AND PAROLES, 292
CALIFORNIA CONSTITUTION, 18
Article 1, section 7, 172
Bill of Rights, 2
Executive powers, 20
History, 18
Judicial powers, 20
Legislative powers, 19
CALIFORNIA DEPARTMENT OF FISH
    AND GAME, 105
CALIFORNIA DEPARTMENT OF
    JUSTICE, 102
CALIFORNIA DEPARTMENT OF MOTOR
    VEHICLES, 101
Duties, 101
CALIFORNIA DEPARTMENT OF
    PENOLOGY, 292
CALIFORNIA DEPARTMENT OF
    CORRECTIONS, 290, 296
Juvenile justice system, 292

CALIFORNIA PUBLIC UTILITIES
    COMMISSION, 106
CALIFORNIA YOUTH AUTHORITY, 280
CANADIAN FEDERAL SYSTEM, 137
CITATION, 68
CIVIL AERONAUTICS BOARD, 108
COMMISSION OF PEACE OFFICER
    STANDARDS AND TRAINING, 104
COMMISSION ON JUDICIAL
    PERFORMANCE, 144
COMMISSION ON JUDICIAL
    QUALIFICATIONS, 143
COMMUNITY BASED CORRECTIONS,
    283
COMMUNITY CORRECTIONAL CENTER,
    284
COMMUNITY RELEASE BOARD, 277
COMPLAINTS, 207
CONDITIONAL PLEAS, 232
CONFINEMENT, 275
CONFRONTATION OF WITNESSES, 40
CONSTITUTIONAL CONVENTION, 279
CORONER
Autopsies, 85
Court, 89
Custos placitorum coronae, 82
Deaths reported to, 84, 90
Duties, 83
History, 82
Investigation, 86
Jurors, 89
Legal considerations, 83
Medical duties, 88
Police duties, 82
Qualifications, 88
CORRECTIONAL INSTITUTIONS, 278
COURT CLERKS, 146
COURT ENFORCEMENT OFFICERS, 150
Bailiff, 152
Duties, 151
California, 150
Constables, 150
United States' marshal, 150, 152
COURT OF JUDICIARY, 142
COURT OF SUPPORT PERSONNEL, 146
COURTS OF APPEAL
United States, 137
CRIMINAL COMPLAINT
Dismissal, 25
CROSS EXAMINATION, 16

D

DECEASED
Personal effects, 88
Removal, 86

DECLARATION OF INDEPENDENCE, 2
DECLARATION OF RIGHTS
Stamp Act Congress, 2
DEFENSE COUNSEL, 127
DEMURRER, 240
Lack of jurisdiction, 241
Misjoinder, 241
Procedure, 241
Uncertainty, 241
DEODANDS, 83
DETENTION FACILITY, 186
DETERMINATE SENTENCE, 268, 277
DISTRICT COURTS, 138
DISTRICT JUDGES, 142
DOMINION SUPREME COURT, 137
DUE PROCESS, 17

E

EN BANC, 139
ESCOBEDO V. ILLINOIS, 34, 127
EX POST FACTO, 4
EXTRADITION, 75
Arraignment, 76
Interstate, intrastate, 75
Procedure, 75

F

FEDERAL COMMUNICATIONS
    COMMISSION, 109
FEDERAL TRADE, 109
FINES, 17

G

GIDEON V. WAINWRIGHT, 32, 127
GORDON V. JUSTICE COURT, 140
GRAND JURY
California authority, 159, 163
Civil liability, 168
Committees, 161
Compensation, 162
Duties, 163
    County agency needs, 165
    County jails, 165
    Investigation of county and district
        affairs, 163
    Investigation of public officials, 163
    Salary investigations, 164
Federal, 158
Final report, 168
Foreman, 161
History, 158

Impanelment, 161
Qualifications, 160, 161
Rules of procedure, 162
Selection, 159
Sessions, 165
Voting, 167
Witnesses, 167

H

HAWKINS V. SUPERIOR COURT OF
    CITY AND COUNTY OF SAN
    FRANCISCO, 168, 170

I

INCARCERATION, 186
INDICTMENT, 166, 167, 213
Advantages, 169
INFORMATION, 211, 231
INNS OF COURT, 120
INQUEST, 89
INTERSTATE COMMERCE
    COMMISSION, 110

J

JAIL DETENTION, 273
JOHNSON V. ZERBST, 31
JUDGE
California, 143
Removal from office, 144
Selection, 143
    Missouri Plan, 143
State Selection, 143
JUDGMENTS, 265, 274
JUDGES
Federal, 142
Territorial, 142
United States Supreme Court, 142
JUDICIAL DECISION MAKING, 145
JUDICIARY, 129
JUDICIARY ACT OF 1789, 138
JURORS
See Trial Jurors
JURY
Challenge, 178
Instructions, 260
Panel, 176
Selection, 253
JURY TRIAL
Right to, 15, 171
Waiver, 173
JUSTICE COURT, 143

JUVENILE CORRECTIONAL PROCESS, 286
JUVENILE COURT, 286

L

LANGDALE, CHRISTOPHER, 122
LAW SCHOOLS, 119
LEGAL AID SOCIETIES, 128
LEGAL PROFESSION
Development, 119
History, 117
Roles, responsibilities, 123
Training and education, 120

M

MAGISTRATES
United States, 137
MAGNA CARTA, 158
MENTAL INCAPACITATION
Definition, 239
MIRANDA V. ARIZONA, 35, 127
Specific rules, 36
When required, 36
M'NAUGHTEN RULE, 237
MOTIONS, 264
MUNICIPAL COURT, 140

N

NATIONAL ADVISORY COMMISSION
    ON CRIMINAL JUSTICE
    STANDARDS AND GOALS, 247
NAVIGATION AND OCEAN
    DEVELOPMENT, 108
NEWGATE PRISON, 280
NOLO CONTENDERE, 211, 234

O

OWN RECOGNIZANCE, 195, 274
Requirements, 196

P

PAROLE, 277, 278
PATHOLOGY, 88
PEACE OFFICER
Arrest, 57

PENAL INSTITUTIONS, 279
New York system, 280
Pennsylvania system, 279
PEOPLE V. CALVERT, 188
PEOPLE V. DREW, 238
PEOPLE V. DORADO, 35
PEOPLE V. EUBANKS, 174
PEOPLE V. MANRIQUEZ
PEOPLE V. PECHAR, 173
PEOPLE V. RAMEY, 59
PEOPLE V. WHITE, 176
PEREMPTORY CHALLENGE, 180
PLEAS, 230
PLEA BARGAINING
Arguments in favor, 200
Defined, 200
Objections to, 202
Types, 200
PLEAS
Conditional, 232
Defined, 231
Dual, 239
Formal judgement of acquittal or
    conviction, 236
Guilty, 231, 233
    Attorney present, 231
    Effect of, 233
Nolo Contendere, 234
Not guilty, 234
Not guilty by reason of insanity, 238
Once in jeopardy, 236
Procedure for entering, 231
POLICE OFFICER
Authority, 49
Defined, 47
Jurisdictional, 48
Powers, defined, 46
Role, 44
POWELL V. ALABAMA, 30
PRE-CONVICTION, 272
PRELIMINARY HEARINGS, 170, 242
Procedures, 243
Purpose, 243
PRISONS
Maximum security, 280
Medium security, 282
San Quentin, 290, 293
PROBABLE CAUSE, 55
Variable, 55
PROBATION, 265, 267
PROSECUTORS, 125
PUBLIC ADMINISTRATOR
Jurisdiction, 93
PUBLIC TRIAL, 26
Excluding public, 27

R

REGULATORY AGENCIES, 106
Structure, 107
RESOURCE AGENCY, 105
RESTITUTION, 275
RIGHT OF ALLOCUTION, 266
RIGHT TO COUNSEL, 16, 29

S

SECURITIES AND EXCHANGE
    COMMISSION, 110
SENTENCING, 265, 267
SHERIFF-CORONER, 93
SPEEDY AND PUBLIC TRIAL, 24
STATE JUDGES, 143
Selection, 144
STOP AND QUESTION, 49
SUBPOENA, 40, 147
SUPERIOR COURT
California, 140
United States, 139

T

TRIAL
Charging the jury, 262
Closing arguments, 260
Defendants opening statements, 259
Introduction of evidence, 256, 259
Jury deliberations, 262
Procedures, 253
  Peoples opening statement, 255
TRIAL COURT, 140
TRIAL JURORS, 171
Discrimination, 173
Number, 172
Qualifications, 174
Selection, 174
  Challenge for cause, 178
  Particular, 179
  Peremptory challenge, 180
TRUE BILL, 214

U

UNIFORM FRESH PURSUIT ACT, 73
Defined, 73
UNITED STATES CONSTITUTION, 136
Amendment V. 236

Amendment VI, 7, 14, 24, 29
  Speedy and public trial, 14
Amendment VIII, 17
Amendment XIV, 17
Article I, section I, 3
Article 3, section, 2, 4
Article 6, 4
Expost facto law, 3
Framework for legal system, 4
Influence, 5
Introduction, 2
Powers of Congress, 3
Preamble, 3
UNITED STATES SUPREME COURT, 138

V

VERA FOUNDATION EXPERIMENT, 197
VERDICT, 263
VIDEOTAPE TRANSCRIPTION, 150
VOIR DIRE EXAMINATION, 177

W

WARRANT
Arrest, 64
WRIT OF PROHIBITION, 222